A Serious Pair of Shoes

of

Shoes

An African Journal

Joan Baxter

Pottersfield Press, Lawrencetown Beach, Nova Scotia, Canada

Canadian Cataloguing in Publication Data

Baxter, Joan.

      A serious pair of shoes

      ISBN 1-895900-30-1

1. Baxter, Joan.   2. Women journalists — Canada — Biography.
3. Africa — Description and travel.   4. Africa — Social conditions — 1960–
I. Title.
PN4913.B28A3 1999   070.92   C99-950249-2

Cover illustration by: Joan Baxter

Pottersfield Press gratefully acknowledges the ongoing support of the Nova Scotia Department of Tourism and Culture, Cultural Affairs Division, as well as The Canada Council for the Arts. We acknowledge the financial support of the Government of Canada through the Book Publishing Industry Development Program for our publishing activities.

Pottersfield Press.
Lawrencetown Beach
83 Leslie Road
East Lawrencetown
Nova Scotia, Canada, B3Z 1P6
To order, telephone:
1-800-NIMBUS9 (1-800-646-2879)

Printed in Canada

THE CANADA COUNCIL | LE CONSEIL DES ARTS
FOR THE ARTS | DU CANADA
SINCE 1957 | DEPUIS 1957

Contents

B = Benin
BF = Burkina Faso
Bot = Botswana
C d'I = Côte d'ivoire (Ivory Coast)
CAR = Central African Republic
EG = Equatorial Guinea
G = Guinea
GB = Guniea Bisseau
L = Liberia
S = Senegal
SL = Sierra Leone
U = Uganda
WS = Western Sahara
Z = Zimbabwe

Acknowledgements

The list of people to whom I owe thanks is longer than this book. There are some people whose names I never knew. There are others whose names are best left out, or altered (as many names of people and places have been), lest the authorities in their countries decide to track down those who dared to speak their minds — or the truth. Of course all the views and interpretations expressed in this book are entirely my own and I take full responsibility for them. I would like to single out some friends and colleagues who over the years helped school and inspire me, people who wittingly or unwittingly helped to shape our lives on the continent, and thus the words I write here. They include: Alice and her mother Epi; Andreas and Mary M; Asséto and Amade Z; Awudu and Choo T; Bernice A; Brigitte S; Carolyn D; Christine K and her family; Dali M; Dalmas; Damaris, David and Mary M; Eunice and Andrew; Gary and Terry P; Helen N and her daughter Diana; Iddrissu I; Iliasu A; Jane A and her husband; Joe and Susan; Kate A; Lawrence A; Marie-Laure M; Mumuni; Paul and Renate S; Rabiatu D and the chief of Kukuo; Rabiatu T; Roger L; Rukaya; Ted L; William U; Zenabu T.

Many thanks to Tony Simons who wrote to tell me the story of a serious pair of shoes, and to the owner of those well-travelled shoes, Peter Cooper. I'd also like to say a big thank you to Zac T and his whole team in Cameroon, particularly Marie-Laure M and Ann D, for all their help in guiding me into the forests to hear expensive voices. A word of gratitude also to all my other former colleagues at the research centre in Nairobi who taught me so much and who put

5

up with a "bloody journalist" in their midst for four years. Thanks also to Frank Plummer for allowing me to write about him and better still, to use his words in praise of his late Kenyan medical colleagues.

Very special thanks to Seidou and his Cameroonian friends, who took me under their wing and thus into fascinating African territory I might never have visited. And to Mahamane from Timbuktu, thanks for guiding me through Bamako and for helping me to glimpse the hidden and fantastic social landscape of his country. To Oumou Soumaré, thanks for all the music and musical insights. Also to Lesley Choyce for his encouragement in getting Africa into print with Pottersfield, to Julia Swan, and to Peggy Amirault for all her hard work and patience at a great distance. And big thanks to those who read, re-read or advised: Andreas Massing; Anna Gyorgy; Debby Plestid and David Baxter; Helen van Houten; Kathy Overholt; my ever-patient and faithful parents; and last but never least, Karl, Anna and Bobo for being so tolerant and patient.

Prologue

The ground is our bed and the sky is our blanket . . .
— Street boy in Yaoundé, Cameroon

Bamako, Mali

It's June, and Mother Nature has jacked up the blast furnace that she uses each year at this time to torch a good part of West Africa. So, the heat is on. But the power is off. The gods of light at the energy corporation may turn on the current for a few short hours in the wee small hours of the night. But for now it's off, and has been for fifty-four hours in my neighbourhood. It's been like this for the past two months.

All the people who rely on electricity to earn their daily bread, or at least a tiny dry crust thereof, are sitting under trees on the sides of the road, soaking up the shade and stewing in their own frustration and deepening poverty. Word has it that the situation may improve in a few months, if God brings rains to neighbouring Guinea that will then fill hydro dams in Mali. Or the crisis may be resolved in a couple of years when an enormous new hydro dam in Manantali comes into operation — if God brings the rains to fill it. Fortunately, the people of Mali have a lot of faith in God. Maybe the foreign experts and financiers who planned this country's power supply didn't notice that Mali is one of the hottest and driest countries on earth and that water here is the most precious and rare resource. Perhaps not the best resource on which to build a Sahel country's energy future.

This is what's running through my head as I sit in traffic. I've spent a good part of my morning trying to get to the National Assembly to hear the minister of energy explain this latest power shortage to parliament. The reason it's taken me two hours to get to the Assembly to hear his excuses for the energy crisis is that . . . there is no electricity. The traffic lights are dead and traffic has snarled itself to a halt. The city centre is one seething, honking, smoking, steaming mass of cars, mopeds, man-drawn or donkey-drawn carts, and humanity hoping to sell something to take in a few coins which will buy something to eat.

When I finally get to the assembly, I listen while the minister, typically, blames everyone else but Malians for the energy crisis. He says that international donors, by which he means the West, haven't come through on their pledged financing for new generating stations. Then he says the new generators that were installed four years ago have never worked because they were faulty one-of-a-kind models. For that, he points an accusing finger at the Canadian and French companies that he alleges foisted these prototype generators on Mali. Then he points out that the water levels in the hydro dams are at rock and slime bottom and perhaps it wasn't a wise idea to rely so heavily on hydropower. However, it's too late now to solve this latest energy crisis with solar or wind energy.

I know he's not telling the whole story, of course. According to just about everyone I know here, the government and its energy corporation are also culprits. They have allegedly been (a) incompetent, (b) crooked and taken large cuts from the contracts that landed faulty equipment here, (c) providing more than the fair share of electricity to privileged neighbourhoods while people in poorer neighbourhoods melt in the heat and patients in hospitals die on operating tables, (d) not getting those privileged or well-connected clients to cough up for power bills, and (e) covering up (a), (b), (c) and (d).

Since I've already braved the traffic to get to town, and since there's nothing in what the minister has said that is new or worth reporting on BBC, I decide to stay in the city centre and do some errands, stop in the market and pick up some batteries and cassettes. And maybe pop into the Lebanese supermarket, which is the only place one can find long-life milk or cheese and other luxuries from Europe, largely because only the Lebanese shops here have private generators to keep fridges running.

I navigate the car through a solid mass of vendors and beggars, through chaos that my upbringing did not prepare me for. Eventually

I find a tiny place to park in front of the Grand Mosque. It takes about ten minutes, ten heaping helpings of patience and the help of ten young men graciously turned parking assistants, for me to ease the car into a tight nook in which, back home, I wouldn't even try parking a baby carriage. Then I get out to face the music — and the heat — of the market in Bamako. I begin by greeting the gang of young men seated in front of their lottery kiosk. I politely decline their invitation to take my chances on the scratch-and-win lotto. They laugh when I say I'm not a lucky person. They probably think I'm as lucky an individual as ever walked this earth. Healthy, wealthy (relatively), and still waiting for wisdom to strike — but they don't know that.

It's just another day in Mali towards the end of a century that brought us e-mail, atomic bombs, social security numbers, debit cards, women's liberation, space walks, sliced bread, electric can openers, life by remote control. We're a little short on such signs of the times here in Bamako. Not that this is still pristine African savannah left untouched by all things modern or the destructive forces of human hands and machines and imported chemical toxins.

The twentieth century has arrived in mountains of plastic and rubbish and cast-offs from another part of the world where clothing and shoes rarely get a chance to wear out and where CFCs are no longer acceptable in refrigeration units. Here they gobble it all up as if our yesterday is just fine for their tomorrow; anyway, second-hand and third-rate is still better than nothing.

They find remarkable uses for our garbage. Old car bodies are hammered and forged into buckets, carts, wheel rims for carts. Nestlé milk cans become small kerosene lamps or, with a few scrounged scraps of Styrofoam lining, a coolbox (useful only when there's electricity to run fridges to make ice or to cool drinks beforehand). Inner tubes become containers for pulling water from deep wells, old plastic bags are twisted into rope and twine or woven into baskets.

The markets are chock-a-block full of plastic trinkets and electronic gadgets from the Far East. Tiny kiosks or roadside displays are full of consumer delights — everything from thin-skinned plastic dolls (white as snow) to tiny calculators that blink and beep until their batteries die. None of this merchandise looks much different when it's new and for sale from when it's lying in mounds of garbage, after it has broken or stopped working, usually an hour or two after purchase. Despite hand-painted advertisements to the contrary, what's for sale here is not "German quality at Chinese prices." It's the reverse.

A flushing toilet, electrical installations that light up with current, a paved road, a closed sewer, a garbage bin, glass windows, three good meals a day — all of these are great luxuries in this city. So is a decent hospital bed or a schoolroom that has more inside it than mud walls, a blackboard and some rickety benches the students have provided themselves.

I pick my way through the market, past beggars and vendors, sweating men pulling carts so heavily loaded that donkeys would balk at the task of dragging all those goods from one place to another. This is the backbone of the Malian economy and it's called the informal sector. That means no one knows how much — or little — money these people might make in a day or a week or a year and no one except they and their families even seems to care. There's a good chance that it can best be calculated in cents rather than dollars.

The physical poverty here cannot be simply measured with a figure on annual average income (officially the equivalent of $300 Cdn. a year), or reduced to words on a page. Then again, neither can the unbelievable wealth — of culture and history. This was the centre of civilization in West Africa and beyond at the same time that Europe was plunged into the Dark Ages. The world's first university, a centre of Islamic scholarship, was founded in Timbuktu six centuries ago. In 1324, the emperor of the West African kingdom of Mali, Kankan Moussa, set out for Mecca with 70,000 servants in tow in a caravan weighted down with tons of gold. When he reached Cairo, the people were wowed by the wealth he carried. The world price for gold plummeted by half, so much did Emperor Moussa carry from Timbuktu.

Today, it's different. It's mostly the Canadians, South Africans and Americans making off with Mali's gold. This is called investment and is part of globalization. It's said to be good for the Malian economy.

President Alpha Oumar Konaré, who is back from another of his many trips abroad where he is feted as a model president in a model democracy in Africa, has announced that the major focus of his second five-year term is *"la lutte contre la pauvreté."* This "fight against poverty" has been allocated 50 million CFA francs (about $150,000 Cdn.). But in the same year he upped the budget for the Office of the President to 10 billion CFA francs (about $20 million Cdn.).

And to discuss a strategy for the struggle against poverty, the UN organized a "round-table" in Geneva for Mali and donors who might pledge some money that would take the hollow sound out of the sloganeering. The Malian delegation numbered 350 dignitaries, but perhaps their airfares and considerable hotel bills were worth it in pay-offs.

A month ago, the West African Development Bank offered a huge loan to assist in this battle against poverty, adding of course to the debt, the debt being one of the big reasons the country is still so poor and getting poorer all the time.

Regular energy crises, like this one, paralyze the economy and don't exactly improve the situation.

But not everyone is poor in Mali. Far from it. Just as it is impossible to gauge the physical poverty, it is also impossible to gauge the physical wealth of the few who hold the strings of power, and thus the country's purse-strings. They are easily identified by their shining new Mercedes or Jaguars or Cadillacs, and the wealth (the part that isn't in European banks) they are putting into multistorey palatial structures that the average Canadian might associate with California dreaming and billionaire superstars.

As elsewhere in Africa, it's not that there's no money here. It's that the little money there is, is poorly distributed and rarely squeaky clean. It is seldom earned through productive hard work. Excesses are rarely curtailed by the great equalizer — taxes that should be applied across the board, even to the rich and powerful.

Most of the money supply here, as elsewhere in Africa where the middle class is almost non-existent, is in the hands of a self-chosen few who appear not to care two hoots, or less, for the plight of the other 99 per cent. This is one of the paradoxes I cannot fathom or even begin to explain in Africa, with its strong sense of right and wrong and social obligation. Those who are stinking rich can be that way without any evidence of a social conscience and all too often their riches come from money "chopped" from the state.

There is old money here, found in the most elite or "noble" families and dating back hundreds of years to the days of Mali's great empires and social strata, which are still going strong today, with the nobles on top, then the castes and the former slaves at rock bottom.

A small new elite has risen out of the ruins of the twenty-three years of dictatorship that preceded the country's transition to democracy in 1992. The *nouveau riche* in this new Mali, which the outside world describes as democratic, are widely known as the "millionaires of democracy." They have taken advantage of the new laxity and liberalized economy and increased money flow into the country to enrich themselves. They cruise by in their luxury cars, freshly washed and sparkling in the blazing sun, tinted windows closed, air conditioners whirring. That way, perhaps they can ignore the outstretched arms of the less fortunate, the vast majority, the hundreds of thousands of people who clog the city centre with need.

Every few metres I am accosted by beggars. There are the legless, armless, handless, eyeless, and all permutations and combinations of the above. There are garibouts, pupils from the Koran schools, with their ubiquitous red tins that once held Italian tomato paste and are now held out for tossed coins or bits of food. There are tiny tots who are — or who are merely masquerading as — twins. Some of these twins are on hire by unscrupulous adults, the pimps of the begging world, who abuse the traditional right to beg that is afforded mothers with twins by putting together small armies of big-eyed toddlers to pull in money for them.

To give or not to give?

This is a constant philosophical debate among expatriates and Malians themselves. One school of thought says those who give to beggars merely perpetuate and exaggerate what is a demeaning, unfruitful and an "unsustainable" human endeavour. They complain that imams are corrupting Islamic tradition that permits a certain amount of begging by the handicapped (a category that here includes mothers with twins) and the garibouts. I've also heard Malians hotly denounce the imams who send the boys from the Koran schools out to beg, saying the imams merely take the money from the garibouts to "enrich themselves." Others say there is no point in assuaging a beggar's daily needs when no one is taking care of their long-term needs. Their reasoning is probably sound.

The other school of thought isn't really about thinking and reasoning; it's about feeling the overwhelming pressure of the need here. This view is prevalent among some of my devout Muslim friends, for whom giving alms to the handicapped or to the less fortunate is commended by the Holy Koran. It is also prevalent among the children I ferry through town from time to time. I think my own children adopted it spontaneously the hot evening we landed in Bamako for the first time, already two years ago now. As we strolled out of the airport towards a waiting car, they were swallowed up by beggars — some propelling themselves along the ground using their hands in lieu of legs, others leaning on hand-made crutches to keep themselves upright on a single remaining leg. My daughter looked up at me, her mouth wide open and her forehead a washboard of worry. "Doesn't anybody here have two legs, Mommy?" And then she asked for some coins to hand out, her reasoning being this: "Because I've been so lucky in this life, I might not be lucky next time and I might come back poor or without legs, so I better be kind now while I am one of the lucky people."

For whatever reasons, for right or for wrong, this is the approach that I've also adopted. Handicapped people — be they tiny children without legs or ancient women without eyes or young men whose hands have been eaten away by leprosy — always get some coins. And on Fridays, the Muslim holy day, I also give to those garibouts who roam the city in small gangs. I also give to street children, not just because they are there and in need but because I recall from my days in Nairobi how nasty they can turn. The angry street children in Kenya no longer ask; they attack and help themselves. Perhaps naïvely, I believe that if passers-by show these more innocent children in Bamako a hint of compassion and human kindness, maybe they can help defer this progression from polite begging to aggravated assault.

Mostly, though, I don't think long-term any more.

A young man is approaching me quickly, and at first I fear it's my nemesis, the beggar who haunts my days and sometimes even my nights. He patrols the streets of the city like a phantom, popping up everywhere I go, as if he had wings that could get him from one place to another a lot faster than I can in my car. Whatever else is wrong with him, the most obvious problem is his eyes, which appear to be falling out of his head like one of those gargoyles on a French cathedral. To protect his bulging eyes from the sun, he shades them with the stumps that have formed where his hands used to be, before leprosy caused them to disappear.

For almost two years this man seems to have been attached to my trail by an invisible chain. Perhaps he can just sense my presence and fear of him with an extra-sensory capacity he possesses that has yet to be defined. Or perhaps he just does a lot of traipsing, so it just seems he's on every corner of town at the same time. No sooner do I remember that I haven't seen him in a while, than there he is, ambushing me at the red light (if there's power), or at the next traffic jam (if there isn't). He has a nasty habit of appearing at eye level, tapping on my car window with his stump and grunting while his eyes roll out of his head and mine involuntarily find something else —

anything else — to look at. I always give him money, mostly because I want him to move away from me as fast as possible. On occasion I've even run red lights in my need to escape him.

And I really, really do not want him to accost me now, when I'm on foot. So I shade my own eyes and walk fast.

"Madam, you give me money. I'm hungry."

I turn around quickly. It's not the man with the bulging eyes at all. It's a boy in his teens, in rags, holding out his hand and standing there defiantly. "You give me money. I want to eat."

It's not Friday and there's nothing wrong with this kid that isn't wrong with most kids in town — that is, he's dressed in tattered clothes, but dressed all the same. He has flip-flops on his feet and he's got two arms, two legs, two hands, two feet and his eyes are even in straight.

I shake my head and smile lightly. "No," I say.

He catches me up and then blocks my path, looking aggressive now. "You are in Mali here. You give me money."

My tone also hardens. I really don't like his attitude. And this time I use a bit of my limited vocabulary in Bamanankan. In his own language, I say, "*N te foyi di i ma.*" No, I'm not giving you anything.

I do a quick two-step, trying to side-step him, put some distance between us.

He jogs along beside me. "You are in my country, you give me money."

I don't answer and my head is down, my arms pumping. I'm sweating furiously, probably because that's exactly what I am — furious.

"This is my country here," he says. "This is Mali here. This is not Europe. You should go home to Europe. We don't want you here. You go back to your village."

I stop then, prepared to lecture him on his manners (or lack of them) and the fact that in Malian society, a young person never ever speaks to an adult, his elder, a woman older than his own mother, the way he is speaking to me. Either that, or I'm ready to swat him. I'm angry and hurt enough to do both.

He's running ahead of me, taunting me and shouting that I should go home to my own village. Mali is an independent country and they don't want Europeans here any more.

I feel hurt, confused and angry as hell. I want to scream lots of things at him, about how many years I've been living in Africa and what I've sacrificed (*feel* I've sacrificed) over seventeen years on the continent. I want to tell him I'm not a tourist out for two weeks of sightseeing, souvenir shopping and photo snapping. I am self-righteous and indignant, anxious to hammer a few truths into this mouthy little brat.

But I don't make a sound, not out loud although I can hear the whimpering of a spoiled puppy somewhere in the back of my head. I know I don't have the right to say any of those things. He's said what I'm always expecting Africans to be thinking. What Africans have every right to say. Few ever do, although I do get earfuls all the time about how Africans are treated in Europe and North America — starting with nasty searches and interrogations on arrival at international airports, even when they are carrying valid visas and there for valid reasons. They can be subjected to stupid and hurtful racist comments muttered through grimaces when they happen upon the wrong shopkeeper or person on the street or police officer.

When I hear these tales told by African friends, I want to crawl under the nearest table to hide my own shame on behalf of a world that has left Africa off the map. During President Clinton's visit to Africa in 1998, the first ever by an American president, he made a memorable comment that the biggest crime ever committed against Africa by the world was its ignorance of the continent. On that one, he was absolutely right.

Even after all this time of living in Africa, I still feel I've come nowhere near understanding what makes the continent work, and it does work in its own indomitable way. Africa has kept its heart and a soul — a spirit — that is difficult to miss but impossible to describe. It defies all reason and all statistics and plays havoc with the five senses.

I came to Africa for what was meant to be a short visit, to get married to a German man working in a small town in Niger. That short "visit" has turned into a very long one, which has included not just that marriage and two children but also another five countries — Cameroon, Burkina Faso, Ghana, Kenya, and now Mali.

In the many years of working as a reporter, a consultant or just being a curious stranger, I swear I've asked a million questions, listened to at least a million answers. I still can't come up with any words that would come near expressing or explaining my affection for Africa. But with Africa as my muse, I spend most of my time trying to unravel and then capture in words something of the magic, complexity, turmoil, contradictions and charms of each city or town in which we've wound up living on the continent.

Ghana

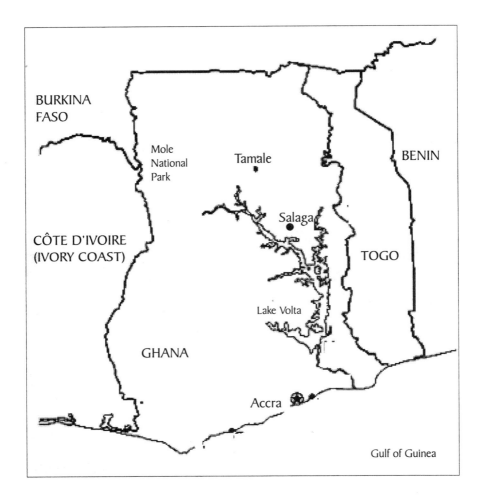

BURKINA FASO

Mole National Park

Tamale

BENIN

CÔTE D'IVOIRE (IVORY COAST)

Salaga

TOGO

Lake Volta

GHANA

Accra

Gulf of Guinea

Chapter 1

It could have been worse

Ghana, 1989

It was the end of a long, bumpy and blistering day when we hauled into Tamale. We'd been ten hours on the road — what was left of it — heading due south from Ouagadougou, capital of Burkina Faso, across the border into Ghana and then a couple of hundred more kilometres over a road that had seen better days, perhaps thirty or forty years earlier. In 1989 it was a rutted mud track that spewed dust and made me ache all over — for a ribbon of Trans-Canada Highway.

Karl stopped the pickup in front of our new home. An infant son was tucked under my right arm, a two-year-old daughter tugged at the left. She stood there staring about her. As far as I could see, there was nothing in any direction except flat savannah stretching off into a horizon of scattered and scraggy trees that squirmed in the waves of heat bouncing off the hard-baked surface of the parched earth. It made my daughter mute, and it didn't exactly turn me into a fountain of cheerful chatter either.

We'd been out of Africa for eight months, long enough that Tamale's well-camouflaged charms weren't going to leap right out and strike me in the face. All those months in the rich world had played havoc with my eyes and senses. I looked around me at Africa and found myself wishing for the very things that I tended to complain about in Canada — obsessive hygiene, rigid rules (written and obeyed), shopping malls surrounded by more pavement than an entire African nation might boast.

Over the years I've always carried on to anyone who would listen that if there was one thing I didn't miss in Africa it was those massive, energy-guzzling, overheated (in winter), overcooled (in summer) shopping malls with all the consumer excesses that I believed — rightly or wrongly — were killing the planet.

And yet . . . there are moments. And there were certainly moments back there in my early days in Tamale. I did a lot of thinking about home. I hummed Rita MacNeil's Nova Scotian ballads, turning them into dirges. Hard as I tried not to, I kept thinking of what we had just left behind, yet again. Three tantalizing images always sprang to mind. One involved a pristine Nova Scotian meadow in full bloom with Queen Anne's lace and black-eyed susans rippling in a summer breeze. This was ridiculous because it was still grey and cold March over there. Another daytime fancy involved those overgrown and overfed dairy cows which, combined with the luxury of a regular supply of electricity, made it possible to step right up to the fridge for a glass of frothy, *cold* milk. The third little dream involved a leisurely bit of window-shopping in a massive shopping mall.

There is nothing like a stroll through one of those malls to lull a body into believing that all is well, the universe unfolding as it should. Just a few weeks earlier I had been just another Canadian consumer, armed with credit cards, sauntering through the mall to do a bit of casual shopping. In that context, with the hypnotizing buzz of Muzak and busy shoppers all around me, it was impossible to imagine that at that very second thousands of hungry and malnourished children were dying somewhere of diseases that could be cured, of famine that could be stopped if a little of the energy and money that went into military development around the world were put instead into human survival and welfare. Sipping Colombian coffee in a food village in one of those shopping centres, it was impossible to imagine people dying in wars generated and fuelled by arms from richer countries. Munching through a whole-grain muffin while ogling diamond-studded watches gleaming in the window of a spotlit jewellery store, it was inconceivable that somewhere blood was being shed or limbs hacked off in wars financed by international interests trying to get at deposits of diamonds, gold, oil, timber, copper, cobalt — whatever resources they needed at the time. All the same resources used to produce those consumer items filling all those shelves and making my mouth water for more.

But now we were far from that land of plenty. There was no war here (not yet) and no famine either, although it couldn't be said that obesity was a problem. Still, what we saw in those first days in northern Ghana silenced both my daughter and me.

We had left Burkina Faso in mid-1988. We arrived in Tamale in March 1989. When we'd left Ouagadougou, our daughter had been developing a healthy little working vocabulary in French. Then, in the space of just a few months, we'd spent time in Germany, crossed over to Canada, gone back to Germany and then flown back to Ouagadougou, en route to Ghana. Anna had given it her all, making a valiant effort to pick up new words on each continent and try them out even as she struggled with the linguistic puzzle of that trip. In the end, she was speaking a smattering of French, German and English and could not understand why no one at all understood her. On our arrival in Tamale where English and twenty-five other languages were spoken, she decided to give it all a rest. She stopped talking the evening we arrived, retreating for the next three months into those grunts and noises that seemed to be universally understood by adults. So much for all those theories I'd developed about more languages being better. It was only one of the first small disappointments and big worries that filled that first year in Tamale. A first year in any place is an initiation period that either makes or breaks the newcomer.

It wasn't just memories of what and whom we'd left behind in Canada that plagued me. Before that we'd been three years in Ouagadougou, a capital with real city amenities such as electricity, running water, well-stocked grocery stores, good communications — if you could afford them. We could. I'd been spoiled. Tamale was, I saw, going to be a whole new gunnysack of surprises.

On the very first day, Mary, a Ghanaian friend I'd met in Ouagadougou, took me on a tour of Tamale to help me get my bearings. I settled in for a long drive, wanting to get the lay of the roads and landmarks so that I wouldn't get lost the first time I headed out alone. She showed me the market, the post office, the old United Trading Company store where one could buy some basic packaged foodstuffs (Maggi cubes, imported margarine, vinegar, tinned tomato paste, cocoa, tea, coffee). It reminded me of something one might have found in Canada's Arctic — a hundred years ago. Mary pointed out a couple of small "chopbars," or roadside eateries, the bush taxi station, told me something of how pito (a delicious local brew made of sorghum) was made, and showed me a few of the better pito bars. We cruised past the hospital, an imposing structure that Mary said looked a lot better on the outside than it did inside. It had no water and no generator for those prolonged periods when Tamale was powerless. After that she turned the car around and said we were heading home.

I'd read that the town, as much as it looked like an overgrown village, was actually a fairly large place. Not in area, but boasting a population of almost a quarter of a million. I was still looking for something big and urban, perhaps one of those ubiquitous bank buildings which even in Africa's poorest capitals are opulent monuments occupying entire blocks. Surely there was something like that in Tamale, capital of Ghana's largest region, even if it was the poorest part of the country. I said I was in no hurry, that we still had time to make a sweep of downtown.

Mary laughed. "But that was downtown," she said. "That was the main street. You know, where UTC and the Point Seven bar were. Look, this is Tamale here. Not Ouaga. Not Frankfurt. Tamale."

"I can see that," I said.

We had been allocated a decaying little prefab bungalow, trailer-park vintage. Word had it that these had been imported and plopped onto a large compound by a Montreal company, contracted to provide housing for Ghanaians, Canadians and other staff of the big rural development project that had got off the ground — or at least been started — in the early 1980s. There were lots of vague stories about how many millions of dollars the company had been paid to supply that housing. There were many more conflicting stories about how many — or few — of the terms the company had fulfilled before it declared bankruptcy, but not before it had collected in full for the project from the Canadian agency that funded the rural development project to the tune of $40 million.

But these were just rumours that went round and round over tables full of beer on Tamale nights. For the devotee of hard facts, Tamale wasn't the best place to be. We were far away from the investigative *Fifth Estate* journalism in Canada. The nearest telephone was seven kilometres away in the town post office and there was an understandable reticence on the part of the team of Canadian consultants to divulge actual names and addresses lest they lose their jobs and end their careers in development. It was impossible to investigate or prove much of anything if it wasn't a strictly local scandal, and even then I would learn it wasn't going to be easy.

But who was I to complain? My husband pointed out repeatedly that at least we had a place to stay, even if it was a prefabricated bungalow imported from Canada. That spared us from having to hole up in a room in one of the local hotels, where running water was a mere pipe dream, electricity a vain hope in the dark. We moved in. To borrow from that special language of development theory, these flimsy little homes were neither "adapted" nor "appropriate technology" for Ghana's sweltering Northern Region. Actually, I doubt prefab bungalows like that were adapted or appropriate for any place on the planet. Presumably, though, they were cheap and easy to put up. Pressboard was the most substantial building material I identified in the whole unit. In a strong windstorm, and we had plenty of those, the eaves and shingles just blew away like so many more fluffs of kapok when the pods exploded on the majestic silk cotton trees that towered over the compound.

Canadian development experts, who knew a lot more than I did about how things worked back home, spoke derisively about the houses and the company that manufactured them. They alleged that this firm had previously done well with government contracts for the housing market in the Arctic. This was the kind of housing, they said, that had been put up to house Canada's First Peoples in the far north. I imagined the pressboard and cardboard insulation, next to those thin aluminium shingles, must have been useless against the bitter Arctic winds. In Tamale, they were not better as insulation against the heat. Unlike thick mud or concrete brick walls that kept the interior of a house relatively cool during the heat of the day when the sun was a blazing inferno, the low ceilings and the thin walls allowed the heat to build up inside from the minute that dawn broke. By mid-afternoon it was impossible to sit inside without feeling faint and there were no cold showers or snowbanks handy to leap into, which would at least have made it a true sauna. Strangely enough, that bit of papery insulation seemed to keep the airless heat in quite effectively through the night.

It wasn't just the heat. The humidity in Tamale before, during and after the rainy season (June through September) spawned population explosions of insects — termites, ants, cockroaches. And all of those loved to feed on pressboard. The walls were simply caving in, disintegrating. And those low ceilings were ludicrous in a Ghanaian kitchen. Most of our Ghanaian neighbours who wanted to consume local favourites such as *fufu,* boiled yam that is then pounded using a pestle (big as three or four baseball bats moulded into one) in a huge mortar, moved their cooking facilities out to the locally made brick "boys' quarters" (staff housing) behind the bungalows. That way, they could pound to their hearts' content without damaging the ceilings. But the great gaping holes in the ceiling tiles in a few of the houses showed that not everyone had been that considerate of their prefab home, and that some women at least had just gone ahead and made room for the rise and fall of those enormous pestles. They had merely adapted those Canadian houses to their needs.

Actually the worst damage to the houses had not been done by any human hands. On our first night there, I climbed into the bathtub and turned on the shower, not yet realizing that water running from a faucet or showerhead was a great luxury in Tamale. But it wasn't the layers of dirt on my skin that came cascading off under the trickle of water — it was the entire wall and its resident population of termites, along with the black crud they had used to construct their colony, digested and excreted pressboard probably. The termites looked just as put out as I was, as we both scrambled to get out of that pink Canadian bathtub.

Karl listened with only one ear when I started listing what was wrong with that Canadian prefab bungalow. Coming from Germany as he did, where they like to build homes that can last a thousand years, or even two, I think he felt that house was my just reward for coming from a country that specialized in homes light and flimsy enough to be carted around on the back of a trailer truck. Not the example he thought Africa should be following.

He also reminded me constantly that the whole situation would look a lot brighter (literally) on the day that Tamale was hooked up to the national hydro gridline. Everyone in town, or at least the small minority that could afford electrical installations and a light bulb in their homes, was waiting for that day when Tamale would start receiving power from the Akosombo Dam, a quarter of a century after that massive dam on the Volta River had been built.

Meanwhile, the town would have to make do as it had done for decades, with the sporadic and severely limited amounts of electricity produced by the tired old ship's motor that doubled as the generating plant to provide "town power" in Tamale. That diesel workhorse had been running valiantly, on and off, since well before Ghana was born as an independent nation in 1957. Shortly after we arrived, it was out of order for three months while ingenious repairmen found a way to remedy the damage done by a bolt of lightning. They did so, fabricating their own spare parts, in that unbeatable way that Africans have of dealing with the mostly second-hand and third-rate technology that washes up on their shores.

Town power had been back on for a few weeks when the dam just across the road and uphill from the power plant — a dam the same age and in the same sorry shape as the generator — finally collapsed, flooding the generator house and a good part of town. Thirty children were washed away in the torrent of water that swept through town; five were never found. Nigeria and other benefactors immediately sent in planeloads of blankets and other relief supplies for the victims. Next day, many of those relief goods, which had to pass "top down" through the hands of the regional Powers That Were, could be found for sale in the market. Next to the big tragedy of lost lives, the permanent loss of town power — the diesel generator was irreparable this time — seemed like a mere inconvenience.

There was to be no more electricity for Tamale after that until the gridline linking us with the south was finished. That was slated for the end of 1989. We were in the month of July. We made do in the intervening months with a couple of solar panels on the roof that fed a battery that provided us with two lights during the night. Canada came up with about $70,000 for a generator that was installed on the development project's compound, but fuel seemed to be in short supply. The problem was traced to the watchman, whose job it was to take care of the generator and the fuel supply. Perhaps they had been careless in specifying exactly how they meant those words "take care," neglecting to specify that it didn't include selling off the fuel in town. To be fair to him, he did have fourteen children to feed — I know because after his eldest son started working for us and then stealing from us, I went to talk to his father and see what he knew of the affairs of his thieving son. "Madam, it dis way," he said to me, wringing his hands. "When you got fourteen children, you got to expect one or two rotten eggs."

A few months after we arrived in Tamale, we all began to suffer from infectious sores. I had one on my left arm, which felt like a volcano erupting under my wrist. I had swaddled it in miles of gauze but it still seeped through. After days of agony, I finally approached a Ghanaian doctor friend who lived on the compound. He took a glance, said it had gone septic and then asked me gently if I had never heard of antibiotics.

I had. I'd heard a lot about them. I'd heard some AIDS researchers suggesting that the HIV scourge was the natural outcome of the overuse and abuse of antibiotics in the '60s and the '70s, which still continues today. I'd always been reluctant to overdo the antibiotics, thinking in my lay and perverted way that it was good to let infections take hold a little. I pictured the immune system like a muscle that needed a good workout from time to time to build its strength — like biceps building bulk and force on a weight machine in a health club.

Besides, the evidence was in on the abuse of antibiotics everywhere in the world, and especially in places I'd lived in Africa, where you could buy any drug you wanted over the counter, if you had the money. The pharmacists were helpful and willing to listen as you listed your symptoms, before putting together a special cocktail of tablets just for you. These they would dish out individually from original packages or bottles, handing them over to you in little paper packets they fashioned from old newspapers or bits of brown paper lying around their shop. Labels and instructions were apparently considered superfluous, maybe because only a minority of adults in Tamale could read.

Many drugs, particularly those originating in Nigeria, were said to be complete fakes, placebos made of useless — but harmless — powders and syrups. This, on the surface, seemed like a terrible crime against the people who bought and consumed them. On the other hand and in the long run, they were possibly less harmful than the improper (sometimes dangerous) combinations and doses of "real" medicines coming from genuine pharmaceutical companies — a hash of pills that people popped like sweets in Tamale. Many of these "real" medicines were outdated and out of favour in the developed world.

One day a friend asked me if I would pick her up some medicine from the pharmacist, since I was heading into town anyway. I said I would and asked her for the prescription. She said I wouldn't need that and she rattled off what she wanted as I took notes. One tablet chloramphenicol, one tablet tetracycline, one tablet metronidazole, more commonly known as flagyl, a medicine that had once made Karl, tough as he was, collapse when he took it to treat intestinal amoebas. I looked at that potent little list, amazed that she knew these names by heart and could pronounce them; I couldn't. I looked up at her. "Zara, what on earth have you got?"

She massaged her stomach. "A touch of the diarrhea," she said. "Since yesterday night."

"But," I said. "But . . . is this what the doctor says you should take for a touch of diarrhea?"

"This is good medicine. I take the same thing always," she said.

"Just that, a single tablet of each of those things?"

She nodded.

I asked her to wait a minute while I fumbled about trying to locate in the mess of my bookshelves my medical Bible, which was actually a guide put out for primary health workers in Africa. I flipped through it. She couldn't read or write so I began to read it to her. "Look, Zara, it says here that chloramphenicol should be used only for typhoid and for very serious diarrhea. There is some danger in using it even when it is needed for these serious cases. Furthermore, you are supposed to take three capsules four times a day for several days."

She was studying me but not saying anything. I turned some pages.

"And here," I said. "Metronidazole is for use only in cases of amoebic diarrhea or dysentery. For it to be effective, you would need to take three tablets a day for five to ten days, depending on the nature of the pills. Furthermore, it is dangerous and can cause liver damage, even liver cancer."

She was tapping her fingers on the table. I looked up from the book. "You see, it's a waste of money and dangerous to your health to take just these three tablets like this." I could read those words in the book, but I couldn't read the look on her face.

"I'm sorry I don't have the money to pay you right now," she said, not meeting my eyes. "But if it is a problem these three pills, I will come tomorrow and give you the money."

"It's not the money," I said. "I don't mind paying for the medicine. It's just that the medicines you want to take are dangerous, and just one tablet of each won't do you any good. In fact, taking one tablet is not good. It makes the medicines lose their effectiveness because the bacteria that cause the illness develop immunity to . . . "

She stood up abruptly. "I'm sorry to trouble you," she said.

"It's no trouble," I said. "That's not the problem. I can buy you any pills you want, but honestly I . . . "

"Fine, you get them for me. I go and come. This afternoon fine?"

I closed the book with a snap. Nodded. Told her I'd get what she wanted and bring it to her. I was willing to break every pharmaceutical rule in the book if it meant saving a friendship.

The Ghanaian doctor had said our infections were likely caused by staphylococcus and told me to try to track down a new antibiotic that had just come out on the Ghanaian market because it was only the very new (and expensive) antibiotics that were still effective against such infections. He said that few people could afford to visit modern doctors and then pay for a full prescription of anything. Instead they visited traditional healers or diagnosed themselves and went and got a handful of mismatched pills that they swallowed. He said people tended to come to the hospital only when they were at death's door, which meant many died there, which in turn led people to have still less confidence in Western medicine.

The one thing people did seem to trust about modern medicine, ironically, was the injection. Over the years that Western medicine had moved into Africa and rapidly been distorted by the realities here, people had come to believe that without an injection, they had not been treated by a health official. And doctors themselves, aware that most people would never fill an entire prescription and take a full dose of oral medicines, also tended towards injections because that way, at least, they could be sure the patient had had a full dose. Trouble was that even in the early '90s in Tamale, the cost and shortage of new syringes often meant that people being treated for one minor ailment might be contracting another — deadly — one when that needle went in. These included hepatitis B, AIDS and any other disease that could be transmitted through blood contact.

Not that the nurses weren't aware of the problem — they had had some basic training on the dangers of infected syringes. When a meningitis scare hit in the first dry season we were there, a group of parents organized a small immunization day for all of our children. We purchased a large bottle of vaccine, enough for some fifty children, and solicited the help of two public health nurses to administer it. I took along several syringes of my own, thinking there might be a shortage, but the nurses told me indignantly they had enough and they were professionals who knew all about the dangers of AIDS. Red-faced, I moved aside and concentrated on calming some of the children who were screaming blue murder about the injection to come. My son dragged me forward when it was his turn. I watched the nurse conscientiously fit a new needle onto the syringe and, before I could stop her, plunge it into his arm — injecting into my son's arm the vaccine mixed with a little blood that had been drawn when she extracted the needle from the previous child.

This time it was my turn to scream blue murder. I tried to explain to her the syringe had to be changed as well as the needle, but she steadfastly refused to comply. She said they had been taught to change the needle and that was good enough for her. I should move aside and leave the professionals to their business. A year later, when we went to Germany and underwent full medical examinations, my son's blood tests revealed antibodies, showing that he'd been exposed to hepatitis B. It could have been worse; it could have been HIV.

I kept my distance from that public health nurse after that. But I trusted implicitly our Ghanaian physician. Following his orders, I got the new and expensive antibiotic he recommended (the full dose) and started to treat that painful abscess on my arm. And that evening, doped up on painkillers, shrouded in enough gauze for burial in an Egyptian tomb, I headed off behind Karl to a small party.

It was hosted by an elderly German couple who tended to drink vast quantities of hard spirits each evening at their living room bar, and complain in the mornings about "migraine" headaches. They pined for the colonial days in Africa when they had been treated with respect owing "Die Wiessen" (the Whites), and exacted praise from the rest of the expatriate community for their determination to cling to their German standards and to the newly formed far-right Republikaner party in Germany. And they moaned about how the German government owed them a cheque for a million Deutschemarks for all the good works they had done in Asia and Africa over thirty years in development work.

We were still new enough in town and I was lonely enough to have taken her seriously when she warned me, the first time we met, that I had to take great care how I behaved in Tamale. Not because it was a small town and local people would be watching my every move, but because it was a small town and she — who considered herself matron of that community — would be watching my every move.

"You're either in or out," she had said the first time we showed up at one of their almost weekly invitations. "And if you do not exercise great caution," she said, wagging her finger at me, "you will be OUT!" This was followed by more lessons in party etiquette. She offered me her succinct definition of a "good party" — one in which the only black skin to be seen was on the people doing the serving.

After that initiation, I had gone along to such cocktail parties reluctantly, complaining to Karl's back the whole way. But he felt at that point, so early on in our induction into Tamale, that it would be unwise for us to snub the couple. They were prominent figures in the Tamale Rotary Club and terribly influential with Big Men in town. He said it wouldn't kill me to go and I told him it didn't matter if it did; I was about to die anyway from that infection on my arm. Angry red streaks had already started to snake their way up my arm and down towards my heart, as the poisoned blood mapped out its paths through my veins.

I found myself perched in front of Madam's famous living room bar, head in hand, beside an amiable German Catholic Brother who taught in a technical school for boys. He'd been teaching there since the early '60s, when, he said, Tamale had been a veritable pearl. Running water, regular electricity in amounts to go around to all those who wanted it, shops full of wonderful delicacies (cheese, for example) that could be kept in refrigerators that were running. Madam said that she and her husband didn't bother trying to find what they needed in Tamale or even in Ghana; they had their consumer essentials — laundry detergent, canned sausage, whiskey — imported from Germany. She then went on about how, even in times of extreme shortage, a water tanker would be at the door to fill their many tanks. They needed many water tanks because she and he liked to have their full baths every evening. That said, she turned away to entertain other guests.

I moaned to the Catholic Brother about the shortage of water and how it was not helping us lick the infections that were an epidemic in our house. I told him how my children's faces were covered in these sores and held up my arm to emphasize the point, just in case he had missed it. He made sympathetic noises, sipped his beer, shifted on the stool in front of the bar that took up an entire wall in a spacious living room.

"It's been fourteen days," I said, petulant and indignant. "Fourteen days there's been not a single drop of water from our taps. We don't have a water tank and so right now I'm getting people to bring water and put it in buckets outside. It's not possible. How can people live without water?"

He seemed to be contemplating this. Or at least that's what I assumed he was doing as he gazed into space. Another good possibility was that he had forgotten I was there. Perhaps I was tiring him out, sounding like a spoiled and demanding foreigner (guilty on both counts) who didn't belong in a place that required more fortitude than I could lay claim to.

"Fourteen days," I whined. "Two whole weeks. How long can they make one of these water cuts last? How long has the water been off at your end of town?"

He looked perplexed. Squinted. Hemmed and hawed a couple of minutes, as though I had tossed him a tricky math problem. Apparently I had.

"Let me think. Hmm. I guess we haven't had any water, for, let's see . . . seventeen years," he announced finally. "Yes, I think we had water for a few weeks in 1972. I may be wrong though. It might have been back in the '60s. For a few years we tried to get Ghana Water and Sewerage to repair the main line that came past the school. After a while we gave up and put up our own water tanks that we have filled."

That silenced me. I sat there for a little longer, nursing my inflamed and painful arm until I could convince Karl it was time to go home. There I could coddle my woes in the privacy — and heat — of our own little termite-infested house without being reminded that relatively speaking I had nothing to complain about.

Chapter 2

Drowning lesson

The water problem for us was a mere inconvenience. We had bought a water tank that we could afford to fill from passing tanker trucks. For most people in Tamale and the whole Northern Region of Ghana, the water problem brought real suffering. Even death.

When it was running, water in Tamale's tired old water system came from the Volta River several kilometres outside of town. Electricity was required to keep the pump running and, more importantly, so was the goodwill of GWSC, the Ghana Water and Sewerage Corporation or more popularly, the Gods of Water Scarcity Corporation. Water, being the most essential of many scarce commodities in town, was the best way for the unscrupulous to make some quick and dirty money. People spoke of the "water mafia." They said it was run by well-placed and well-heeled people with the money to purchase water tanker trucks. They also said that the mafia was either composed of or working hand in hand with Big Men in the water corporation and regional administration. When these men decided it was time for a quick injection of money into their private accounts, they simply turned off the taps. That fleet of either privately owned or state-owned trucks then filled up wherever was easiest (at silted, filthy ponds or the Volta River) and trundled through town, selling water by the bucketful at exorbitant prices to the crowds that gathered behind them.

Here was a state corporation that apparently orchestrated shortages of the most essential commodity of all, allowing its employees or friends thereof to raise the prices and pocket the profits. This was certainly evidence of entrepreneurial spirit, a novel approach to privatization that I doubted even the World Bank or imaginative economists on Wall Street could have come up with.

As I say, we were privileged. We always had five hundred gallons of water just outside our door in that new water tank. That solved our own water problem — and created a new one. The neighbours, from kilometres away, came to beg for water. Occasionally, when the women and children at the gate overwhelmed me, I would lose the thin veneer of self-control.

"But, why me?" I would say plaintively. "Why don't you go march on GWSC? All of you. You know. In unity is strength. Rattle your empty water cans in front of the regional administration. Why do you come to me to sort out your problems when it's the local Big Men causing them?"

Most of the women just kept smiling serenely at me, still optimistically clutching their plastic jugs or buckets in outstretched hands. A few turned away and headed off, putting their empty buckets on their heads as they went. But one woman stood her ground and spoke up. "We did so," she said. "Back two years it was. We march to the regional administration and we say to dem stop dese water cuts. Stop dis chopping from us. Dat be what we do say to dem."

"What did they say?"

"No ting. No ting at all. Dey run from dat place. Take dey cars and run. So we break all de place. We break it proper. All de window. Then police dey come. Dey shoot us and arrest us. To this day, we never see some friend again. Bad time-oh. Now we do stay quiet."

"But staying quiet isn't helping anything either," I said.

She stood straighter, tilted back her head a little and levelled me with a steady gaze full of patience, one I imagined a child would merit — a child who has trouble learning how things work and how life must be lived.

"Madam," she said. "Dis one be fo' God. When God give too much, we want mo' and mo'. So sometime, God He do take some ting back, make remember us to be grateful fo' blessings we do have. Dat how it be."

Nobody was moving away. I shrugged, then gave them all water. I decided not to worry about tomorrow. I hoped God was watching.

If Ghana Water and Sewerage were really behind the chronic water problems in Tamale, I suppose that in some ways God could be deemed responsible for the general lack of water in the Northern

Region. There was an inherent problem with the water table, which was extremely deep and hard to reach. Over the four years we were in Tamale, a steady stream of experts — from hydrologists to geologists to diviners — passed through the region trying to site wells that would provide good drinking water for years, not the salty brine that seemed to surface in boreholes after a few months of use. A candid development expert told me that what the projects were doing, drilling boreholes and putting in pumps that worked for only a few months before the water dried up or turned salty or the hand-pumps failed, could be construed as criminal negligence, even involuntary manslaughter. He pointed out people were accustomed to dirty water, that thick brown liquid they were used to collecting from tiny streams or puddles left over from the rainy season. He'd talked to rural people who were suspicious of the clean borehole water the first time they saw it emerging from the faucets. They complained that it couldn't be good water because it had "no colour" and "no taste."

He said they were right to be worried because they had "a certain tolerance" to the high bacteria count they consumed every day. This tolerance disappeared rapidly, he said, as soon as someone converted to sparkling clean water. If, after a few months they had to go back to their former water sources, he said there was evidence in the development and medical literature that they would fall seriously ill.

In Tamale, however, the problem was just to keep that river water running from the faucets, a problem that was very much in human hands. And apart from the questionable tactics of GWSC in keeping the water flowing, there were other factors that further complicated the matter — at the user end.

When Tamale was eventually hooked up to the national power grid and regular electricity kept the pumps going that brought water from the Volta River to town, many communal faucets that had been dry for many years began to spout the precious fluid. The neighbouring village of Kamville found itself suddenly on the receiving end of clear running water — and water bills. This was something the men in the village were supposed to take care of. The women fetched the water, did the household chores, farmed, raised children, often tried to earn a little money to educate the children or put something away for the future by selling produce in the market. But it was the men who were supposed to handle household finances and pay the water bills. When they failed to do so, GWSC made very legitimate water cuts, until the outstanding bills had been settled. If the men didn't settle them, this meant the women were back to long pre-dawn treks, often up to ten kilometres to the nearest functioning well and ten kilometres back, until such time as the men came up with the payment.

I asked a friend from the village why the women, who were obviously annoyed by the irresponsibility of the men in the community, didn't just go on a sort of strike. "They could just refuse to fetch water until the men went and paid the bills," I said, using that same old simplistic if–then reasoning that just wouldn't go away and leave me alone, even after all those years.

He laughed.

"Well, why not?" I said. "President Rawlings is always on about women's rights. Mrs. Rawlings heads up that 31st December Women's Movement that is supposed to be empowering women. There's political will at the top. Why couldn't the women just stop fetching water to force their husbands to settle the outstanding bills and get the water flowing again from the communal faucets in the village?"

He was still chuckling when he replied. He made it short and simple enough that even the hot-headed foreign woman could understand. He said, "The men have not one wife. They have several. The women call each other rivals. It means that they have to compete all the time for their husband's divided attentions. There's always a prettiest one, a younger one, one who is more compliant and submissive than the others. You know. If two wives refused to carry water for the man, the third one will do so to gain his favours. The other two will just lose out."

It was a divide-and-rule aspect to polygamy that I hadn't considered before. And it certainly made it difficult for women — as a group — to take a united stand on even basic life-and-death issues that so affected them, starting with water.

Even with steady power supplies, there were water cuts that had nothing to do with unpaid bills. These persistent cuts — whether deliberate or just a sign of incompetence — continued to cause inconceivable (to me, not to them) hardship in town, and mostly among the women and girls, whose job it was to get water into the home.

They rarely had the money to pay for water sold from the backs of those tanker trucks (some of which were supposed to be out on road construction projects in town). Instead, the female population had to head off before dawn each day, those fifty-litre water cans on their heads, in search of a functioning well in a village somewhere or a miserable little puddle left over from the rains, where the water was suitable for livestock only.

Those who weren't up to such a trek or who needed a bucket of water in a hurry could always head to a place known as "Nkrumah Valley," the only available source of standing water in town now that the dam had broken. This was the name given to the cavernous basement of a huge and unfinished building on the outskirts of town, in what was known optimistically as the "industrial area." Started in the 1960s under Ghana's first president, Kwame Nkrumah, whose visionary dreams had rapidly outstripped the nation's money supply, the huge three-floor concrete edifice had been intended as a place to store staple grains after harvest and throughout the long annual drought. The idea was to buy up staple grains after harvest in September when prices for the millet, sorghum and maize were low. These essential foods could then be sold back to the local people when hunger struck near the end of the dry season and into the cropping period, before the next harvest replenished village supplies. By keeping the grains in state hands, the theory was that the prices could be kept stable and reasonable.

This was, if there is anything to the theory that the state has the people's interests in mind, a very good idea. It would have prevented ruthless merchants from profiting wildly from their own people's hunger, as they often did in West Africa during periods of food shortage, or even by *creating* periods of food shortage. They did this by buying up the harvest, hoarding it, and then when hunger hit, selling it back to the people at outrageous prices none could afford, or shipping it across borders to people who could. That is undoubtedly what Nkrumah's government had been trying to thwart when it began building that enormous grain warehouse in Tamale back in the '60s. Alas, for whatever reason, the money had run out or been "chopped" by those state officials charged with the building. The grain facility had never been completed.

The imposing concrete superstructure stood, discoloured by years of dust and rain, in a weedy field just on the outskirts of town. For some, it was a poignant memorial to those early dreams of a fair and equitable country, a conspicuous reminder of how things had gone awry in Ghana. For others whose quest for survival precluded an interest in symbolism, it was a convenient source of water, however stagnant, which collected in and filled the basement during each rainy season. You just walked — carefully — down the slime-covered concrete steps into the "basement" and there it was: Nkrumah Valley. Big as an underground parking lot under a city centre bank tower in a richer country; a huge lake, black and still in the gloom.

In a pinch, and there was no shortage of pinches in Tamale, girls went there and lined up to take their turn negotiating their way down those slippery steps to dip their buckets into that deep and menacing subterranean lake. It was tricky work and each year, some-one fell in and drowned. This happened again in 1992, during what looked like another of those intentional water cuts.

I tracked down the family home of the fifteen-year-old girl who had lost her life fetching water in that eerie black lake in Nkrumah Valley. They invited me inside their two-room home, bade me sit on the worn maroon couch. They quickly collected coins and sent some-one to buy the visitor a Coke. Then they waited in polite silence for the questions from the stranger in their midst. I began by asking for details of how it had happened. Her father said she had lost her foot-ing, fallen in and sunk right away, before her friends could grab for her hands. Then I asked them if the loss of their daughter hadn't made them angry. They looked perplexed, and shook their heads. They said they were very sad and deep in mourning.

"But," I persisted, "such an accident was so unnecessary. If the water had been running, she wouldn't have had to go to Nkrumah Valley to fetch it and she would still be alive today."

There was suddenly an oppressive silence around me. More and more people were cramming into the small room; there were now dozens of people, relatives, friends and neighbours listening to my questions. They were squeezed up against those deep blue walls in that tiny room, blotting out the light coming in through neat lacy curtains on the two small windows. I had no idea why everyone looked so baffled by my question, by my logic.

I decided I must have said it wrong. I tried again. "If GWSC didn't cut off water like this, she would have got it from the faucet out there on the roadside," I said. "So isn't it their fault? Aren't you angry with them?" I still had not learned to curtail my misplaced need to seek justice here on earth by finding a direction for blame, or for asking questions that far exceeded the limits of good manners here.

Eventually it was the girl's father who spoke, while he studied his clasped hands. "Madam, all death be dis ting, act of God. It is not fo' we small people to feel dis ting, anger. God take my daughter. He know why. We know no ting of that."

I can't pretend I understood how he was able to be so forgiving of those who terrorized Tamale by turning off the taps as they wished and when they wished. To me it smacked of a crime against humanity, a chargeable offence that ought to be punished in a court of law. The lack of decent water caused not only those deaths by drowning in Nkrumah Valley but also uncountable deaths brought on by water-borne diseases and diarrhea, which increased exponentially each time the populace had to resort to swamps or fetid ponds for their water. To the people of Tamale, that was just how it was. The Big Men who did such things would get their comeuppance.

God would deal with them.

Of course this threw me into another mental tailspin. I couldn't reconcile this generous acceptance of acts of God, caused in fact by unscrupulous and unaccountable Big Men, with the reaction in town to petty thieves who broke into homes or picked pockets in town.

One Monday morning we awoke to learn that a portion of the population of Tamale had gone out on a raid during the night. People told me that they were fed up with the theft of their precious few possessions, fed up with the police who, they said, would arrest the young men only to release them the next day. The police did this, of course, only after taking a percentage of the booty. That morning, in ditches around town, the police picked up eight burned corpses of men that the "town justice system" had identified as the guilty parties, hunted down and lynched, then burned. This was the infamous "necklace" punishment that was said to have originated in either South Africa or Nigeria. It meant pinioning the victim inside a tire, tossing fuel on it, and then a lit match. It's almost ubiquitous in West Africa, this people's justice. In Mali, they refer to it as "Article three hundred and twenty-eight," because a litre of petrol costs three hundred CFA francs and a packet of matches twenty-eight. It has to do with people's lack of faith, not in God and the eternal, but in their own security forces to take care of their interests and security.

I asked people about this, trying hard to grasp the apparent contradiction. On one hand, there seemed to be almost limitless tolerance when it came to "crime" committed by state employees, theft of public money or abuse of power by government people to extort still more money out of the population. On the other hand, that night of village justice in Tamale showed, starkly, that the people had very short fuses when it came to petty crime — very real and straightforward theft by one person of another.

I came up with lots of theories that I tried out on Ghanaian friends, some journalists who, like me, wanted to dig where others preferred to bury sensitive issues. They suggested that the people of Ghana had always felt themselves so far removed from the modern state and the powerful men who ran it, that they never really considered public property as their own. In days long gone by, traditional rulers had governed and to retain their positions they had to be just, wise and equitable in their rule. In return, their people offered them total obedience, compliance and tithes. These days, traditional rulers were still there, but many had been corrupted by money and speculation in the lands they controlled. Chiefs weren't always what they were supposed to be and the modern state had never been all it should have been and people were confused. They felt betrayed by the very Big Men who were supposed to be protecting them from all sorts of social and economic ills — while they did exactly the opposite. But those Big Men were untouchable. They rubbed shoulders with even Bigger Men from abroad, from the very donor countries who propped them up. That was too big for any one small person to change. And so, when it came to how the country was run and who ran it, back then when multiparty democracy was still just a promise on a distant horizon in Ghana, the people chose to let God deal with the Big Men and their Big Crimes.

But there was nothing stopping them from dealing mercilessly with the petty thieves. Theft was an immediate and unforgivable crime. It touched directly on the victims who had so little they could afford to lose. The average family could be ruined if a thief entered one night and made off with prize possessions, worth years of hard toil in the fields and sacrifice, or pathetic bundles of Ghanaian Cedis that represented their life savings — the only insurance people had. The loss of those possessions or savings could mean that the next time a child fell ill, death would be inevitable because there would be no means to pay a doctor or to buy medicine. Or there would be no means to pay school fees and the children might have to be withdrawn from school. Theft, for most people who were its victims, was truly a matter of life and death.

For me, with my indignant outbursts about the brutality of town justice and lofty statements about innocent until proven guilty, the theft of our credit cards and travellers' cheques that same year meant only a lot of phone calls to cancel the cards and cheques. That didn't mean it wasn't annoying, that it didn't make me furious. But it didn't really affect us, that loss of a few hundred dollars. Not the way it would, say, average Ghanaians for whom a few hundred dollars was a large fortune and also a matter of life or death.

Chapter 3

In search of BBC

Set against the strong reticence I sensed around me to challenge the way things were, to challenge the Almighty, my approach to life had started to look downright hilarious — even to me. There I was, getting up each morning, rolling up my sleeves with every intention of taking on the weight of fate, yet again, armed with long mental lists of things I had to accomplish that day as I battled to . . . to . . . do what? Get ahead? What was ahead? What were we missing?

I realized it had become easier to list what we had already than it was to come up with lists of things we might feel we needed or wanted. We had: our health; a roof over our heads; the water tank; electricity (the gridline from the Akosombo Dam was in place) and the luxuries it ran (television, radio, stereo, computer); no fears of starvation or of finding ourselves without money for medicines or doctors when we got sick. I even had a range of freelance jobs I loved — reporting for BBC, writing letters to Peter Gzowski at CBC's *Morningside*, editing, translating, and doing some consulting on energy programs in the region. Still, an internal voice nagged at me to push harder. Perhaps I was seeking understanding of things I was not meant to understand. I really don't know.

I began to worry that I'd lost my way, even if I hadn't lost all that tiresome "drive" and "ambition" to get to some destination that had suddenly become elusive. Part of me envied many African friends and acquaintances who were able to make do with fewer of all the amenities that I had and seemed so much better versed in the art of accepting and even enjoying the human condition.

In this context, all those amenities of the modern world were actually nothing less than luxuries. They were also inconvenient more often than they could be said to be "conveniences" — each time the electricity went off, for instance. Electrical goods caused more headaches because they so rarely worked well, either because high humidity combined with blown dust instantly corroded or jammed electrical switches or simply because they were shoddy bits of junk that were not meant to last in the first place.

Even as I searched constantly for that peaceful place of mind that a simpler life might lead me to, I was busy making lists of places I needed to go and things I needed to find.

So it was that in early 1991, drawing once again on that troublesome urge to go where whim led and common sense had not intended me to go, I headed out on a self-appointed reporting assignment for BBC. My goal was to track down a certain village hidden somewhere along the banks of the Volta River. The reason? In an obscure document, I had read there was a village called BBC. It was said to be located just up the river from a fishing village called Bethlehem and just downstream from a place called Rome. The point of my river journey was to get to BBC and find out from the chief, on tape of course, why the villages had such, well, fascinating names.

I headed before dawn to Buipe, a bustling rural market village set on the muddy banks of the Volta River during the dry season and half submerged by it after the rains. There I asked around and found Wilson Yakubu who knew Jonas who led us on a round of negotiations that gobbled up two hours and spanned six languages: Ewe, Twi, Ada, Gonja, pidgin English and a smattering of formal English, the last being the only one I understood.

Then Jonas led us to Dartey, the proud owner of something they called a "flying boat," with the name of "No Play." This was what I needed, they assured me. It was roomy, made of loosely joined wooden planks. The floor looked solid enough to keep out more water than it let in. It had a twenty-five horsepower Yamaha motor that by their definition was "new." It would make that boat "fly past" those slow-moving, hand-paddled dugouts, or pirogues. It was also a boat that could swamp those low-floating, slow-going pirogues, as I would notice a few times once we were on our way down the river.

First though, I wanted to take care of my own safety in that flying boat. Obviously I wasn't going to find life jackets for sale in the market, where smoked fish was the main item on both buyers' and sellers' minds. However, I was insistent that Jonas equip the boat with enough fuel for the journey, enough for a journey right down the Volta River and into the Volta Lake to the Akosombo Dam if need be. And I figured need might well be — not Wilson, not Dartey and not even boatman Jonas seemed sure of just how far we would have to travel before we found BBC.

They had agreed among themselves that "it wasn't far." But such reassurances are typical in Africa where people almost never hesitate to graciously offer directions when asked for them, even if those directions may turn out to have little to do with real distances and real time. "Not far" may mean a day's trek and "just around the bend" may be a distance of a hundred kilometres, or more, and involve an awful lot of bends. Rural people who have never seen a map, or bothered themselves with matters of scale, or seen a functioning speedometer have a distinctive and often idiosyncratic take on the meaning of "near" and "far." Anything they can walk to is near, even if it is two or three days away on foot. Any village they have been to may be deemed "near," even if the place in question is around many treacherous and arduous loops — be they over rugged terrain or down a long river. It's all a question of perspective. It's unlikely they'll tell a stranger that any destination in their own country is "far" when the person asking the question is a stranger who has jetted in from somewhere really distant — Canada, for example.

Jonas was arguing that because BBC "wasn't far," one jerry can would do us for the journey. I argued back that it would be foolhardy to set off without oodles of fuel. I pulled out wads of money that I was hoping the BBC (the one in London) would reimburse one day. With this, I rented three more fuel cans that I insisted be filled, despite all objections from Jonas. This all took a good deal of time.

It was mid-morning when Jonas and I clambered into the boat and prepared to pull away from the chaos of the market and the aromatic displays of fish and vegetables laid out on the mud banks for sale or, failing that, for roasting in the hot sun. As the motor kicked into action, nine men leapt into the boat, having decided "by heart, jes like dat" to come along for the ride. I guess they had not woken up with long mental lists of things they had to do that day, or for however many days it would take us to find BBC and then make it back upstream to Buipe. I settled onto the thin wooden slat that was to be my seat for the journey ahead, trying not to notice the water pouring in through the gaps between the boards as we roared out into midstream. The extra passengers began to bail, taking turns with the two cracked plastic cups, which doubled as drinking glasses. Jonas moved through the boat, stuffing clumps of fluffy white silk cotton — kapok — into the leaks to slow them a bit.

Except for the nine passengers perched on the gunwales making the boat rock and roll, we were not heavily loaded. We had all those fuel canisters I had insisted we bring along "just in case." Apart from those, the only luggage on board was mine. There was a large metal trunk (watertight, I hoped), a backpack I was wearing to keep it out of the water that was sloshing about underfoot, and then another large canvas bag in which I had packed a folding camping bed, sleeping bag and mosquito net. Not the African Queen at all — just an ordinary Canadian heading down a river. Planning ahead, precluding pitfalls by foreseeing all possible contingencies.

Jonas had brought only a single metal drinking cup and those two plastic ones that were in use by the bailers on board. The other men came without even shirts on their backs for a journey that might last any number of hours or days. They were clad only in shorts, wearing plastic thongs or nothing at all on their feet. The water underfoot was getting deeper. The term "flying" really didn't apply to that boat.

I decided to try to Stop Worrying and to concentrate instead on the tranquil beauty on the shores on either side of us. Birds were circling the grassy riverbanks. Cattle grazed on leftover maize and millet stalks and gazed at us with blank, uncurious eyes. I pulled my camera out of its watertight bag, wanting to make a celluloid record of my journey. I had taken one photograph when the shutter seized up, wouldn't budge again. I spent the next fifteen minutes removing and studying the tiny alkaline battery and wondering if there were any way to resuscitate it. This led me to realize I had no idea what it was that made it work in the first place, although I was sure we'd covered that in grade school — in another life that was very long ago and far removed from the here and now. I regretted my own ignorance about the technology on which I depended so heavily. I put the battery back in, fiddled with the mirror inside the camera, gave up, put it all back inside its watertight bag with a sigh.

Now what to do? It was hot. The sweat was dripping off my nose. I knew that somewhere in my trunk I would find a hat and sunscreen. I figured that would be a good way to fill some time, retrieving those things from the jumbled contents of that metal case. I reached into my trunk of treasures and found the hat and the yellow plastic bottle of sunscreen, factor thirty-six — whatever that meant. But this was no time for me to ditch all my blind faith in manufacturers and labels on plastic bottles. I diligently smeared my face and neck and arms with sunscreen.

Next I checked my backpack to see that I had not forgotten my tape recorder, extra AA batteries, microphone, headphones. After that I dug into my treasure chest to confirm I'd remembered the first-aid kit, and then went through its contents to make sure it was complete. My inventory went like this: antibiotic creme, chloroquine tablets lest I succumb to a sudden attack of malaria, pills with acetaminophen and codeine in case a migraine descended in the heat, insect repellent to counter the inevitable swarms of mosquitoes on the river, bandages, syringes (part of the AIDS kit we had been instructed to carry with us at all times, not that I knew how to use them).

I tucked my medical kit back into the trunk and rifled some more through the contents, feeling reassured by the presence of all those things from my own distant world, which always felt safe because it was propped up by consumer goods. I checked to see I had my notebook, pencils and pens. Then my overnight kit: drinking cup, portable water filter, water purification tablets, soap, towel, shampoo, travel toothpaste and brush. Local people, most of whom had beautiful teeth, used chewing sticks they harvested on their ways past certain trees for everyday care of their teeth and gums. But I found them too bitter and I'd been raised as a Colgate kid with regular dentist visits and had suffered regular fillings despite the regular brushing.

I also had two mystery novels, lest we get stranded and I find myself with a few hours with nothing to do to amuse myself and my troublesome brain, with its fear of boredom. I hadn't forgotten a thing. And I had a portable cot, of course. In case we had to spend the night. You never know.

Nothing could happen for which I wouldn't *be prepared*. Wasn't that something honourable that had been drilled into us from an early age? It was. And I still adhered to it as though it were the eleventh commandment. I glanced up. Ten pairs of eyes were on me. Ten smiles. Said Jonas, "What all dat be fo'? What you do wit dat?" He pointed to the portable water filter lying right on top.

"That's for making the water clean. To drink," I said. The men were scooping river water up with their hands or those red plastic cups and slurping at it, making me thirsty. I reached for my own thermal water bottle. Not only was I not going to drink that river water, I wouldn't even put my hand in it. It was said to be infested with bilharzia flukes that would infest blood vessels and cause a condition called schistosomiasis, which over time could destroy the kidneys. Although, as I met their smiles, I had to admit none of these men who had probably been drinking this water and wading in it for years looked to be in anything but the prime of a good healthy life — and good spirits too. They were all listening with bemusement as Jonas continued to quiz me.

"And dat ting?" he said, pointing at the plastic bottle of sun block.

"That's so I don't get sunburned. You know, white skin gets burned by the sun."

This evoked a lot of discussion, lots of grunts of sympathy for me with my skin that couldn't take a bit of sun without burning. More inappropriate technology for the tropics.

"And what dis?" said another man, pointing to a bag full of party balloons I had stuck in at the last minute, along with some cola nuts and a bottle of gin, customary gifts for any village chief. I thought the balloons might be a good ice-breaker with the kids in the village — if we ever got there. I blew one up to show them, but the wind quickly blew it from my hands and I turned around to watch the silly red balloon sailing away, back up the river.

The questions continued. I continued to explain, the best I could, what each item in my metal case would be used for, and what emergency might befall us that would make it indispensable. The men were laughing. Bantering back and forth in their own languages, slapping each other on the back.

Jonas finally joined in the merriment.

"What's so funny?" I said, realizing — and not for the first or the last time in Africa — I had become the butt of a great big joke that would probably become the stuff of fabled foreigners' foolishness for future generations.

"You whites," said Jonas, still laughing. "You white men . . . "

I waited while he worked on getting the words out through his laughter.

"It be true, you see, the white man tink he so smart he can be able to outsmart God Himself!" And he hit his knee and laughed till tears dripped from his eyes.

I closed up the trunk and didn't open it again, not even when we got to BBC. There we found an idyllic fishing village in repose in the afternoon heat, a few mud huts nestled among trees and termite nests that grew out of the ground like sandcastles. The silence, after the roar of the motor on the flying boat, was almost claustrophobic. No road led to this village so there were no sounds of the twentieth century. Nor was there any plastic litter in sight, which was a sure sign in more "developed" parts of Africa that times were changing. The compounds were swept clean. Fishing nets had been laid out to dry in the sun. There was only the muted sound of human voices seeping through the wall of afternoon heat to disturb the peace, or rather to serenade it. Women and girls were sprawled in the shade, tressing each other's hair. The men, who were between morning and evening fishing excursions, were gathered under thatch roofs to talk and to mend their nets. The chief, a lean and soft-spoken man of about sixty, received his gifts with decorum and dignity and welcomed all eleven of us. He bade us sit with him and asked us the nature of our mission — with Jonas doing the translations.

When the chief learned that we had come all this way to discover the reason behind the name of the village, he launched into a brief history of his people. They came from the south, the Volta Region, and they were of the Ewe ethnic group. When the Akosombo Dam was built some thirty years earlier, their fishing village along the Volta River had been flooded by the huge new lake that had formed behind the dam. So they got in their pirogues and paddled north, upstream, until they found the river again and here they had settled. As for the name, well, each headman had chosen a name for his new community. His father had liked the name BBC, so that's the name he had chosen for his new settlement. His father was now dead but the village name had stuck.

The chief then folded his arms and leaned back against the mud bricks of his dwelling, not obviously eager to say any more. I had the impression he was obeying the edicts of African tradition and humouring the bizarre whims of this stranger who had interrupted what should have been a quiet and peaceful day in a lifetime of quiet and peaceful days, far from any madding crowds — and journalists.

But I'd promised a story to BBC, the one in London. I'd risked my life in a leaking boat to get here. I continued to pry.

"But do you know what the BBC is?" I said.

"This is BBC," he replied, indicating the neat collection of huts around us.

"But there's another BBC," I insisted. "I'm recording this interview right now for the BBC. The British Broadcasting Corporation. You know, radio."

"I don't have one now," he said. "We had one here, but it spoiled."

"But you have heard the BBC?" I said, eagerly.

He nodded. "Oh yes," he said, emphatically.

I could see he had no idea what I was on about.

Jonas was nudging me, murmuring in my ear not to forget the balloons I had brought. I fished them out, looked around at all the children who were moseying in to see what I was up to now. Jonas grabbed a balloon from me and started to blow. Then he handed it to the chief for his inspection before passing it on to one of the chief's small daughters, who was draped over her father's bare knees and eyeing me with what looked like a mixture of curiosity and fear.

The chief wanted to know what it was for, what use it had. Jonas explained the balloons were for the children, something for them to play with. The chief nodded and Jonas and his friends began to blow them up and hand them out. Within seconds, the silent calm of the afternoon was broken with the sharp sounds of exploding balloons. Several of the children began to cry in fear and to run, hands over their ears, towards the women who had been watching with calm disinterest from the shade of their small huts. Within minutes, the formerly cleanly swept mud patch in front of the chief's hut was littered with coloured bits of rubber, those withered and sad remains of that Party Pack of balloons from Zellers. The kids were all crying into their mothers' naked breasts.

Some party.

The sun was starting to sink over the tops of the scrubby trees on the horizon, and I was already getting nervous about travelling up the river in darkness. I asked Jonas to thank the chief for his hospitality and we made our rounds of the tiny community, saying goodbye to the men and women. The children peered fearfully at us (me) from behind their mothers' backs. I wondered who was happier that we were leaving — the villagers or myself.

Dusk was falling and the red sun dipping into the bank of low clouds on the horizon was far more splendid than any balloon a human hand might create. I was happy to be back on the river, roaring upstream, heading in the direction of home. At least I hoped we were. Suddenly it was very dark on that river, impossible to see where we were.

We'd been moving along nicely for about a half an hour when the motor cut out. We drifted in silence for a few minutes before I asked Jonas what was wrong. He said he didn't know. It was much too dark to make out any details on the motor, even to see the motor. I wondered if it had fallen right off. I reached into my backpack, felt for one of my flashlights and handed it to him. He took it quietly and began fiddling with the Yamaha. None of the others looked in the least perturbed by the possibility that we might just drift down-stream for a day or two, or that we had no paddle in the boat, and that if the current took us too far we'd wind up in the turbines of the Akosombo Dam. They were bantering and chuckling and apparently enjoying themselves just as they should have been, given that they'd come along for the ride.

I sat there fretting for a good while, wondering if we would eventually float ashore so that I could mount my mosquito net and my camping bed and make myself comfortable for the night. I could hear voices on the river and then the beam from the flashlight illumi-nated a pirogue, loaded to the gunwales with women and children and baskets of market produce, and paddled by two men, coming to-wards us. The men exchanged greetings and then the pirogue was gone, moving at a good tilt ahead downriver, propelled by those pad-dles and the river current. In the darkness and the still heat of the night, I was no longer sure which direction was forwards and back-wards. I wasn't even sure we weren't turning around and around in an eddy.

I was about to launch into a lecture about the perils of leaving everything in the hands of God, especially when one was depending on human-made technology — like motors — when Jonas worked his miracle and fired the engine into action. And just like that, we were heading full-tilt upriver, going hard against the flow, towards home. It took a good strong motor, in working order, to beat the weight of that current. I hoped it would keep working; in fact I did more than that — I looked skywards at the magnificent spread of stars and prayed it would. Then I sat back and tried to relax and have faith in that Yamaha motor and in the gods that govern such things, wondering what I had learned this time. I suspected I had probably learned something, but whatever it was, I wasn't quite ready to study it — not until I was home and surrounded by the artificial security of the comforts that money could buy.

Chapter 4

Sweet mother

It was a grey morning in Tamale. It was also oppressively hot, but that hardly need be said; it was almost always oppressively hot. I was tooting through town in our green VW van. Not driving very fast — that was impossible on that old road with the remnant pavement and shoulders eroded into deep chasms on either side. Slow motion was appropriate in Tamale. I never failed to drive through the neighbourhood of Sakasaka without admiring the ancient and monumental baobab tree on the roadside, its hollow interior filled with fetish charms tossed in there over the past couple of hundred years to nourish the tree's powerful spirit.

Its days were numbered. World Bank money and a British construction firm were about to drive a new "double-carriageway" boulevard right through town and the baobab would have to come down. But it would take the British road construction company another four years, until 1995, to find a bulldozer operator brazen and disrespectful enough of the tree's spirit to perform the task of uprooting that magnificent baobab that awed me each time I passed.

Just before I reached the main mosque, I had to slow for a herd of cattle crossing the road, then stop because the lead bull had decided to take a look-see right in the middle of the road. I braked, waiting for him to finish staring me down. I was listening to hi-life music on the car stereo, always a great balm for anything that ails the spirit. Particularly the magical tune "Sika ya mogyo" (Money is blood), by Ghanaian Pat Thomas, who was at that time living and recording in Toronto.

The cattle finally began to move and I slowly wound my way around them by veering into the deep mud rut of the shoulder. Well into our second year in Tamale, I was inexplicably as happy as a proverbial Nova Scotia clam on a warm summer day on a Northumberland Strait beach, waiting for the tide to come in or go out, no matter which. I hummed along with Pat Thomas as I moved slowly along the main road towards town centre. I already had one of those long mental lists made, this one detailing all the things I had to do in town. I was going to stop at the second-hand clothing market to see what new "Dead White Man's" clothing had come in that morning. Thursday was the day the bales of frippery arrived in Tamale and it was best to get there early as they were being unpacked along the roadside to get the best of the cast-offs before they were snatched up. The children could use some new T-shirts — theirs were permanently stained red by the laterite soil they rollicked in every day, worn thin from exuberant washing and scrubbing.

After that, I planned to make my monthly stop by the Central Music Depot to see what new LPs had come in. The man who ran the record shop, a blue kiosk right in the melee of the bush taxi station, had thirteen tape decks set up to do the quick dubbing of anything new on the market. By buying those pirated cassettes I knew I was breaking international copyright laws and robbing Ghanaian and other African musicians of their royalties, but at that point there was no other way to get music in Tamale. The local music kiosks were the only ones that got copies of new LPs and these they then copied (dozens at a time on separate decks) onto cheap cassettes and sold.

A couple of years later the new Ghanaian copyright law would come into effect to try to reduce large-scale pirating in public places by ensuring a better supply of original cassettes sealed with a special sticker to close the cassette case. Nimble-fingered and enterprising young men in Tamale would get around this by leaving the seal intact and simply opening original cassettes from the back. These they would then dub for the black market, which provided Ghanaians with more affordable access to their favourite music. But the copyright law, those seals and the readily available original cassettes did at least put a damper on the most flagrant piracy.

So far, though, that law had not yet been enacted and in the meantime, the only way to get new Ghanaian music — any music — was illegally. In Tamale, as elsewhere I'd been in Africa, I could buy on the black market cassettes by Dolly Parton, Michael Jackson, Marvin Gaye, or whatever was topping world charts at the moment in collections of Pop Hits, Country Hits, Slow Hits, Love Hits. But I figured those artists weren't going to miss their royalties nearly as much as the African musicians. Anyway, I didn't indulge in the pirated Western music on those poor-quality cassettes.

I rationalized a lot, told myself I was buying the black market Ghanaian music because that was all I could find in Tamale. Typically, it was generally easier to find original African cassettes or records (and later CDs) in Europe and North America, where most artists were recording, than it was in Africa itself.

My mind was leaping all over the place, as it always did when I drove through town. I was just slowing to allow a huge group of men in full prayer regalia, magnificent flowing boubous, to cross the street in front of the mosque, when the child darted out in front of me.

Right smack in front of me.

By the time I hit the brake, I had hit him. There's no point trying to describe how I felt; even now I can hardly force myself to mention the thump I heard and felt as my bumper struck that child.

I can't recall clearly what happened next. I wept and shrieked, put my head on the steering wheel, anticipating what horror I would see. I was trembling so badly I couldn't get a grip on the door handle so I could get out of the car. I was positive I had killed him, or her. The child. I had seen only a streak of yellow and brown of the ubiquitous school uniform before he or she disappeared under the van. I was hysterical, asking if I had killed a child as the crowd gathered on the roadside moved in on me. I expected to be beaten to death. A foreign woman in her big lumbering vehicle, uninvited in their midst, murdering their children. I prepared myself for the worst. Covered my face in my hands. I wanted to die anyway. But I wanted them to be quick about it. Beat me senseless quickly, before they slowly beat me to death.

Four months earlier, a fellow Canadian who headed a development project in the region had been speeding out of Tamale in his Land Cruiser, the very early morning after the very late farewell party that had been put on for him on his last night in town. We all knew that he — I'll call him Bob — had been drinking very heavily at the party. We all knew that he always drove much too fast for those treacherous roads, which generally had more pedestrian and livestock traffic than they did vehicles with engines. That morning at dawn, he struck an old man on a bicycle near a village just a dozen kilometres out of town. The old man died almost instantly. The villagers advanced on Bob, ready to inflict village justice. Bob fled in his Land Cruiser back to Tamale, where Ghanaian counterparts advised him to get out of the country fast and leave some money with them to at least help pacify — if not begin to compensate — the man's family and village for his death. He had done just that.

I sat there waiting for the worst. I had my face covered with my hands and felt hands groping at my shoulders.

There was chaos around me. Everyone was shouting.

"Mama Bobo!" They seemed to know me. Or rather, they seemed to know my son, who had come to be known in town as Bobo. Apparently, since I had a son I could now claim my identity as a woman.

"Mama Bobo, he's not dead. Look!"

I looked.

Several men and women had pulled a small boy, five or six years old, to his feet. They now had him propped up among them to show me he was still alive. He had a gash on the back of his head that was bleeding a little. His knees and elbows were scraped from the tumble in the gravel on the side of the road. He was silent. Not even crying. That terrified me. I thought he might be unconscious with his eyes open.

I muttered incessantly about getting him to the hospital and fumbled with the key, trying to unlock the back door so the helpful onlookers, one of whom seemed to be a father or brother or uncle, could lie him down on the back seat. My hands shook too much and the father/brother/uncle told me "Don't be worry" while he unlocked the door for me, loaded in his son/sibling/nephew and pushed in a whole extended family as well.

"Now Mama Bobo," he said. "Stop dis worry. Dat boy he fine."

"I'm sorry," I said. "I don't think I can drive. I'm too shaky."

He smiled. "Dat no problem. I do drive fine fine." As if I were the victim of the accident, he bundled me into the passenger seat, then proudly took his place behind the wheel.

"Dat boy he no good," he said as he put the key in the ignition. "Troublesome boy. Dat three time he do run like dat and car come like dat hit him. Bad boy." He was shaking his head in dismay about this troublesome child as he turned the key.

"That's ridiculous," I said through sniffles. "He's just a child. It's not his fault. I was the one . . . "

He had neglected to press the clutch and the car leapt forward, scattering the crowd. Behind me I could hear the rest of the passengers scolding the boy — who was still mute and bleeding from behind his ear — for being a menace to the cars on the road.

The VW stalled. The man tried to start it up again, but it kept leaping forward even as it kept stalling. Behind us, a whole line of cars had stopped. People were shouting and honking their horns.

"Are you sure you know how to drive?" I said.

"Yes, yes," he said. "No problem."

But there was a problem. He seemed to have flooded the engine. Still shaking but fearful that the boy would expire before we ever got near the hospital, I diplomatically convinced him I was fine to drive now and he graciously gave up what was obviously a cherished place behind the wheel. The engine finally coughed into action and off we went to the hospital.

We carried the boy into the emergency ward, which comprised a grim concrete floor with a few blood-spattered mattresses flung about on it. In the big open area that passed for a waiting room, there were already a couple of hundred people sitting quietly waiting their turns to see one of the nurses or doctors on duty. Somewhere. Wherever. I made a lot of indignant noise until a doctor emerged from his office to see what was happening. He had a look at the boy's head and told me there was nothing serious, and a couple of stitches would have him right in no time. But he couldn't do that without a razor blade to shave the hair around the wound, some surgical gloves, some disinfectant, and a needle with catgut. The supplies were not available in the hospital and I would have to drive to town to get them from a pharmacy.

One pharmacy turned into three before I had everything the doctor ordered. An hour later I was back and the doctor quickly and effectively put in the two neat stitches. That "troublesome boy" still hadn't made a sound. I asked the doctor if he didn't think the child was in shock, or worse, had brain damage or a bad concussion. He laughed.

"No, it's not that," he said. "The boy is afraid that if he makes any noise after causing the accident they'll really give him something to cry about."

"But it wasn't his fault," I said. "He certainly didn't cause it. I hit . . ."

"It was. He ran across the road."

"Yes, but maybe he's never been taught not to. Road safety isn't something they teach in his school."

He agreed. And then he went on to say he was bracing himself for the day that spanking new "double-carriageway" road was pushed through Tamale, and the numbers of accident victims that would bring him. He said that such a road was neither necessary nor appropriate in a town like Tamale. He shook his head in dismay, saying no one listened to doctors anyway and his only role would be to keep quiet and to make sure he was there to mop up the blood that would flow on a super-highway through an overgrown village.

I deposited the boy and his family at their small tin-roofed house of clapboard, which was located down a rutted path close to the main road and the scene of the accident. The mood in the house was hard for me to define — under other circumstances I would have sworn they were celebrating. I was welcomed inside as though I had done something wonderful and even the boy himself began to chatter and smile at me when I bought him a Fanta. I said I would come back and see him the next day, and check on his progress after that. And if they liked, they could also come over to visit us. It seemed that another child in the family attended the same Kiddies' Crèche as my son, and couldn't shout my son's name often — or loudly — enough.

They didn't come to our house, but I did return several times to see them and to take the boy a small Lego set as a gift from the famous Bobo. Then one day the father took me aside and suggested I really shouldn't overindulge his son, for fear the boy mistook this as a reward for crossing the road without looking. He actually feared that if I didn't stop making such a thing of it all, he wouldn't put it past his son to deliberately try to run out in front of cars.

I said I thought this was unlikely and that the boy had suffered a lot of pain with the stitches and so on. He levelled me with one of those looks he might have given his bothersome son and said, "Look, dis boy be troublesome-o. Now you no do spoil him more."

In fact, I've never understood how it is that African friends produce such polite and well-mannered children. On one hand, I found people incredibly indulgent with children, particularly children who were not theirs. The women who worked in my house and babysat my two quickly intervened and defended the children the minute I raised my voice with them.

"No, Madam, she's just a child," they would say, coming between my daughter and me.

"Please, Madam, don't be angry. He's just a small boy," they would say, scooping my son up into their arms protectively and possessively. I learned that if I were going to try to discipline either child even with stern words, I would have to do it when I was alone with them.

And yet, and yet . . . there were many other times in Africa I had had to turn away from ugly and violent scenes in which parents or adults in the streets were using sticks or whips to beat children. This I did not and still do not understand. I recall clearly in Ghana the speech of a child welfare officer at a conference on child abuse. The woman said parents should exercise caution and restraint when disciplining their children. Her exact words were: "burning with a hot iron, beating with a metal stick or hitting hard over the head with a hard object should by all means be avoided."

Some Ghanaian friends spoke with regret and pain about the punishments they suffered as children. One woman told me how, when her parents wished to teach her a lesson, they inserted hot pepper up her vagina and she recalled, with tears in her eyes, going off into the woods to howl out her pain for hours. She said this did a lot to make her fear her parents' (and uncles' and aunties' and grandparents') wrath, and she then just took her naughty behaviour outside the house where it was less likely to be punished.

One Cameroonian friend told me if I wanted to have children who didn't speak back to me, who obeyed my summons to come and greet visitors with their hands outstretched, I would have to raise them "the African way."

"And what is that?" I asked.

"Ha, the way I was raised."

"And how was that?"

"Beating. Plenty of beating."

"But how can that be when Africans all seem to love children so much? When children are gifts of God?" I asked.

"Of course we love them. We want them to grow up knowing right from wrong, as God would have it. And for this reason, we have to educate them with the stick."

"And how do you educate your children?"

He smiled. "The same way I was raised." And with a flick of his wrist and a snapping sound of his tongue, he indicated that the rod would not be spared. "Raising children, it's no joke."

"Then why do you always tell me not to get angry at my own children? Tell me I shouldn't even raise my voice?"

"An adult shouldn't get angry with a child. When I beat my children I am not angry. I do it for them."

"Then you think I'm soft on discipline, I should beat my children?"

"No, not yours," he said, enigmatically.

"I don't understand," I said. "You say you'll beat your children but I should never ever touch mine or even get angry with them?"

"Your children are being raised for a different life. My children will be African and they will have to survive in Africa. They have to be educated the way they need to be."

That we were finally settled in and even happy in Tamale had come as a sort of revelation about a year after our arrival. The occasion was a Christmas show put on by the toddlers at the local crèche. Zena, the woman who ran the crèche, had put on a much-loved piece of Cameroonian music, a song called "Sweet Mother" and the children had begun to dance while they stirred pretend soup in giant aluminium cauldrons and sang along: "Sweet mother, I no go forget you . . . "

Zena and the three other women who worked in the day-care centre stood behind the row of small kids, dancing, laughing and clapping their hands. This was the stuff that raises lumps in the throat, maudlin tumours of parental pride, which can be toxic to just about everyone whose child isn't up there on stage. The little girl in green standing next to my son kept edging closer to him. She wanted to take his hand. He was trying to back away from her advances. If he moved much further to the right, he would tumble right off the concrete veranda that fronted the house cum kindergarten. Zena suddenly hoisted him up in her arms and held him against her as she danced across the stage.

The women who worked in that kindergarten were part of a substantial group of strong and independent single women in Tamale who impressed me deeply with their fortitude, humour and determination to raise their children on their own. Despite the fact that none of them even hinted (not to me anyway) at wanting to marry again, they had begun to call my two-year-old son their "husband." They even bickered about which of them had first grabs on him as husband, until they usually wound up dissolving into giggles. I wasn't sure about this at all, until someone kindly took me aside and explained that it was a playful way for people in the region to forge relations and bonds where there were no blood ties. But I wondered if it might also not be a gentle way of poking fun at the "old" ways that marriages had been and often still were made — arranged by parents sometimes without consulting the future bride. And sometimes, as was the case among the Konkomba people in the region, future marriages might be arranged by the groom's family when a future bride was still in her mother's womb. In that case, if the bride-to-be didn't turn out to be female, then the husband-in-waiting just had to keep waiting for the next one and hope it would be a she, or else ask for the bride price back and cast his lot elsewhere.

But these traditions were breaking down. Young women throughout West Africa, particularly students in urban settings, told me they would submit themselves to almost any torture before they would take a husband whom they didn't love. One young Malian singer, Oumou Soumaré, recorded a lovely ballad that rapidly became a hit, almost an anthem for young women in her country. In the song, she spoke to an imaginary father, defiantly telling him he could beat her with a big stick or put a pistol to her head, but she would never marry a man of his choice, a man chosen for his wealth. "Money can finish," went her refrain, "but love will never die. I will marry only the man I love."

This attitude of the youth didn't sit well with the elders, who firmly believed that a young woman s hould marry not the man she loved but learn to love the man she married. And that would be a husband chosen by the parents, who chose with the family's interests at heart, and not the individual daughter's. Indulging young people's fancies and desires was not a big part of traditional upbringing. Nor was romance. Marriage was a practical business that involved matching equals as partners, strong women who could bear and raise strong and healthy children, strong men who could hoe any number of yam mounds in a day, and not illusionary criteria such as "romantic love."

So I was told. Rebellious young people could make parents physically ill when they defied tradition.

But when they were very small, it seemed children could do no wrong at all. Before he was even able to walk, our son (his teachers' husband-to-be) had become part of that Kiddies' Crèche, which had just opened in a garage up the road. At that point, he was the only non-African child and he was being seriously spoiled by all the women who worked there. This was a part of the world where healthy children were revered as God's gifts, no matter what colour their skin. The crèche had been opened by a Ghanaian woman, Mrs.

T, just in time to accommodate our son. And while she solved the problem of early childhood education for Bobo, her husband helped keep us alive. Dr. T was a physician who would come to our house and treat us at any time of day or night — doctoring the children through serious bouts of malaria and croup and stitching up my son's forehead by candlelight on his first birthday when he collided with a chair. For a long time Dr. T refused to take payment until finally I managed to convince him that we had an insurance policy that would reimburse us and that we would like to at least get a little of our money's worth out of that expensive scheme. He relented, but still refused payment from Ghanaian patients, as he had a salary from the government for his work on the rural development project in the region.

The Kiddies' Crèche was named after Dr. T's adoptive father, an American journalist who had come to Ghana in 1957 and taken out citizenship. The day-care opened its doors just a few months after we arrived and, in a small way, that was a revolutionary moment in town. Formal education in the region had never been exemplary. During colonial times, the entire region had been handled as a "protectorate" by the British who used a system of indirect rule through the four paramount chiefs of four separate ethnic groups, to govern (keep in line) the twenty or more other ethnic groups that lived there.

The British had, for whatever good or nefarious reasons, wanted to force education on the children of the chiefs. The chiefs had resisted, for whatever reasons. Probably an inherent and perhaps justified fear that the British were aiming to turn their children against the old ways, transform them into model British gentlemen and ladies with British values and tastes, including a distaste for anything that was African or traditional. Nevertheless, the chiefs in the Northern Region who were handling the indirect rule for the British wanted to comply to some extent with Westminster's wishes. As a result, many princes and princesses (sons and daughters of village, district or even paramount chiefs) had been formally educated and so the official administration in the country was heavily peopled with members of these royal families.

Formal education in the Northern Region was still by far the poorest in the country. Steeped in tradition and oral history, the mostly Muslim population had been reticent to push their children into either secular state schools or Christian ones put up and run by missionaries. Elderly people spoke disparagingly of the youth of today, repeating an adage that went something like this: "The mother carries the child on her back all those years and the child looks over the mother's shoulder to see how she hoes and weeds and cultivates. You send that child to school and the next thing you know, the child has leapt right over her shoulder and is telling her how things should be done. There's no respect for age and wisdom any more."

This reluctance to allow the young people to "leap off their mothers' backs" and onto the teacher's platform meant that the people of the region had not pushed for more schools in the early days of independence when there had been ample money and political will to build them. By the late '80s, however, the situation had flip-flopped. Northerners had decided they were not getting their fair share of that national cake, which they saw being gobbled up by the better-educated populace in the south. They were now desperate to send their children to school because they had come to believe that education was the only way out of perpetual poverty in rural areas. One well-educated son in a good position either in the capital or abroad could keep enough money flowing back to the family in the village to keep them alive and functioning in what were very hard times.

So there were many good reasons why those who could afford it sent their children to private schools in the south, where there was good, formal education, which could lead to a career in the industrialized world — often abroad.

With the crèche, Mrs. T was introducing something completely new to the region — early childhood education. Most children who entered public schools in town at the age of six or seven spent the first year or two trying to make sense of what the teachers were saying to them. They generally landed in school speaking no English, the official language in the former British colony. Once in school, they were forbidden to speak their own language(s). Those who did were punished viciously or "caned" (beaten with a stick) without mercy by the "masters," as the teachers were still called. It was all too reminiscent of the long-gone Dickens era in Britain, still alive and well and inflicting pain on children by the thousands in Ghana near the end of the twentieth century.

Caning wasn't the only archaic aspect of formal education in the region. Colonial methods and attitudes still prevailed in the schools. Subject matter was largely European; local traditions and values and history were ignored or dismissed as unimportant. If there were any textbooks they were just like the ones I had grown up with thirty years earlier — those dreadful readers about Susan and Tom and their dog, Spot. I often wondered if it wasn't those readers foisted on kids in the '50s and '60s that helped to turn off an entire generation from reading and books. When I saw some of those readers in Ghana, I wondered if they weren't the very copies of the books I had yawned over as a child back in Canada, which had been donated over the years to the developing world.

Nor was there any emphasis in schoolrooms on children's creativity. And any teachers who might have wished to encourage their pupils' creative impulses had no art or music materials anyway.

Dr. and Mrs. T and the staff at the crèche focused on creativity, making sure the tiny tots and toddlers were drilled not in the alphabet and number work but in creative playing and performing. They then had to set about educating the parents of the children in the crèche. Some of them were complaining that their children were coming home "dirty."

Each time the parents gathered for a crèche meeting, I heard the same litany of complaints. Their children weren't learning anything. They were being spoiled and the discipline was not rigorous enough. They didn't see why they should pay "good money" to have their children playing with blocks and plastic shapes and crayons. Children, even toddlers, should learn right off to sit quietly in their chairs reciting number facts and the alphabet. The parents believed that if they forked over the money, usually at great sacrifice to themselves, to send their children to pre-school, it was a huge investment in their children's futures. And they expected immediate pay-offs, which they defined as a child who could write, read and perform sums with numbers.

The staff of the crèche were extremely patient and accommodating. They knew that re-educating the parents was just as important but far more difficult than giving those children a good pre-school education. Even at the Christmas show performed by all those tiny children, Dr. T had to take time to answer the same old questions about what kind of education the crèche was offering. He delivered a gentle lecture on how play developed conceptual abilities and manual dexterity and other skills they would need, along with their knowledge of English, for the tough and competitive British O- and A-level education they would be facing once they went into grade school.

While our son was at the crèche perfecting his natural talents for getting dirty and having fun, our daughter was attending a Catholic school, which admitted pre-school children for morning classes and espoused none of the progressive attitudes of the crèche. Each day she headed off to school with her pink plastic lunchbox, wearing her beloved brown and yellow uniform, just like all the older Ghanaian girls in the neighbourhood who had taken her under their wings in the first year. She was just three, young enough that she didn't notice that sitting on a small bench for four hours every morning listening to the Sister reciting facts and figures was not the most stimulating way to learn anything. So far, she hadn't been caned and she seemed to enjoy the school because it meant she got to be with her friends. I used to pick up about ten of the neighbourhood children at the school every day at noon and drive them home in the van. I heard their stories. One of the girls had been caned repeatedly by the Sister because the socks she was wearing were not white, as specified in the school's book of rules. She had told her mother she needed white socks but her mother said she didn't have the money for them right now. Another girl had been caned for slipping into her own language on school grounds. And of course anyone who came late and was not there to sweep up the dusty compound also earned themselves a few lashes.

Attitudes could not and did not change overnight, but there were now long lists of people trying to get their children into the crèche, and that meant pressure on Mrs. T to expand the school to include primary grades. Eventually, she would do just that and parents in town would also join forces and get two small private schools off the ground — with a bit of help from donations by people far away, namely United Church women in River John, Nova Scotia, and Woozles bookstore in Halifax.

But mostly, Ghanaians were doing it on their own, trying to erase some of the negative legacies of the colonial era and to introduce a few of the positive aspects of the "modern" world, which they adapted to fit local needs and conditions — for the children of Tamale and even a few fortunate foreign kids who happened to land in their town.

Chapter 5

Letters for Karen

In June 1990, I wrote a letter to *Morningside* about Karen Leslie, a Canadian woman who was living in Tamale. It went like this:

The orphanage in Tamale is, quite literally, at the end of the road. You follow a series of rutted paths out of town, until they suddenly end unceremoniously in front of a collection of skeletal buildings. Leftovers from colonial times. As the car motor dies, the sound of children's voices can be heard coming from one of the buildings.

They're singing. "The people on the bus go bump, bump, bump, all through the time." Karen Leslie gets out of my car, chattering away to herself, about all the things she has forgotten to bring. It doesn't look to me that she has forgotten anything but the kitchen sink. She scoops up a heavy bundle of newspapers, outdated issues of *The Globe And Mail,* and a tub of home-made paste for the children. Over her shoulder is a red sports bag full of crayons, books and children's scissors she bought in Eatons when she was home on vacation last month. A thermos of drinking water dangles from one hand, because there is no water in the orphanage, except what the children fetch themselves in buckets from suspicious sources. In the other hand she clutches a bouquet of flowers from her own garden. "Something colourful for the children to look at," she says.

I can imagine Karen, dressed in the same summery blue skirt and white blouse, heading off just as cheerfully to a day-care centre in

Canada. Back home in Peterborough, Ontario, Karen is a teacher of day-care workers, a lecturer in early childhood education, a mother and a grandmother. She came to Africa only a year ago for the first time. Her husband thought it would be an interesting experience to work for Ghana's national electricity company for a couple of years, a kind of exchange program with his Canadian employers. It took Karen two months to find herself two jobs: one here at the orphanage, another at a newly opened day-care centre, the first of its kind in northern Ghana.

Unlike the dozens and dozens of foreign development workers who are in town in the name of bilateral aid, nice salaries, healthy fringe benefits and yes, sometimes, development, Karen does her jobs voluntarily. No one pays her a penny, or supplies her with materials or transportation. As I follow her into the orphanage I can't help but think about so many of the other expatriate wives I've met in Africa, who can idle away years moaning about their slovenly "houseboys" and the lack of good washing powder and mostly about their own boredom. Karen's days are filled with other things. There are teddy bears to sew, stories to type out, games to prepare, and training programs for the kindergarten workers.

She approaches the orphanage "kindergarten" as though this were nothing new to her at all. There are no doors or windows, and the corrugated tin roof has been mangled over the years by tremendous windstorms. It glints in the sun like a piece of angry sculpture in downtown North America. Florence, the teacher who spends her mornings with the sixty children in the orphanage kindergarten, asks the children if they are glad to see Mrs. Leslie, who has been away in Canada.

They rise and shout, "Yes."

"I'm glad to see you too," Karen says, then giggles and starts digging into her red sports bag. She hands me an old Dominion Seed Catalogue and a pair of scissors and asks me to start cutting out pictures of flowers for the children to paste onto old news stories in Canada's national newspaper, which is torn into sheets, one per child.

While they're waiting for their paper, the children continue their song. "The wheels on the bus go round and round. Round and round." Karen stops handing out crayons long enough to dip once more into her red bag of tricks, and produces triumphantly a picture of a bus to show the children what they are singing about. Few of them speak English, so the words to the songs they are taught don't mean much to them. They squint at the photograph as it is passed from one pair of eager hands to another.

The older children are left with Florence, who commands them to be silent while they're working on their individual pieces of art. Karen leads the younger ones outside, talking away to them as though they understood her. One toddler who can barely walk clings to her skirt for support. Florence shouts at a small girl, whose legs are shaped like flippers, to get a move on. She drags herself along the ground using her hands, following Karen who is leading the children in search of stones, which she then piles up and wets down with her drinking water, to make them shine.

"You've got to be inventive," she says, laughing. "You can do a lot with very little. But I've never worked with nothing before!"

An hour later, after leading the children through elephant walks and some songs about bumblebees and seeds growing, she leaves the day-care where the children are still pasting and colouring. We head off to visit the babies in the other section of the orphanage, a long squat building that resembles a prison more than anything else.

The women who tend the infants ask Karen all about her visit to Canada. They proudly show her the newest addition to the family of infants in the orphanage. Adam is a three-week-old baby boy, whose mother died in childbirth. Fathers often bring babies to the orphanage if they are the progeny of deceased mothers. Something to do with good and bad omens and spirits that no one here likes to tangle with.

There are six other babies lying unmoving on a blanket on the floor. One of them, bone thin, looks to me as though he's dying. Karen exclaims that he has improved. She kneels beside him on the floor, playing little piggies on his tiny fingers and whispers, "Seybou, I was worried about you all the time I was away." She lets him play with the bracelets on her arm, and murmurs, to herself, that she's got to bring some more tin can rattles for them. Something, anything for stimulation. She's gentle with her advice to the orphanage workers, merely suggesting that they spend more time playing with the babies, helping them to sit up, checking the supplies of milk powder. She's so natural, that it looks as though she's been working under these conditions for years. To me, the conditions look hopeless. Karen, undaunted, is already thinking up ways to get a grant, or even a few donations from her friends back home.

The rest of the expatriate development contingent in this region doesn't even know who Karen is or if they do, they don't take much interest in her work. Development experts live in a fairly closed world of meetings and reports and clubhouse soirées. They speak a special language, the jargon of the development expert: phrases like "top-down" or "bottom-up approach" or "participatory development" that is "sustainable." Such words fill volumes and volumes of studies the Canadians, Germans, Danish and Dutch have carried out here in the past decade — in theory, to develop the Northern Region. Millions of Canadian tax dollars go into Ghana every year for massive projects that all too often produce little except more vehicles and reports and confusion at all levels.

All the while Karen Leslie goes merrily about her business, doing something that cannot be measured in monetary terms — giving her time and energy and expertise to one hundred small children, helping them to discover the unlimited capacities of their minds.

After that letter was aired, there was a stream of replies from listeners, which were forwarded to Karen and me in Tamale. Canadians wanted to know how they could help, what they could send to the children in the orphanage. Entire communities in Canada had mustered forces and put together box after box of children's toys and teaching aids and sent them to Ghana. Karen was overwhelmed and spent the next year struggling to get these donations out of customs in Accra, without paying huge sums as "duty" on donated toys and books and games sent by *Morningside* listeners to benefit the children of northern Ghana.

It was more than a little gratifying to see that reaction among Canadians and to hear them express their desire to help and their questions asking how best they could. Many had lost faith in official government development assistance and wrote to ask us advice on which charities or non-governmental organizations were the best to support. They wanted to give, but they wanted to give in a way that would help and not hurt.

In the letter I had been deliberately vague. I had not said, for example, that one Canadian project in Tamale now had a fleet with more than one hundred vehicles, which the Ghanaian director felt obliged to hide when there was a visit from the Canadian foreign minister. I figured I'd been pretty gentle and very discreet in avoiding mentioning any development agencies or projects by name. For one thing, I didn't want to arm any reactionary elements back home who were critical of development assistance, but for entirely the wrong reasons — presenting it as if it were altruism (it was anything but that) which Canada could not afford. And secondly, many of the people working on those projects were our friends, both Canadian and Ghanaian.

The problem, as I saw it, was not that Canada gave money to Africa as development assistance. It was that Canadians were given too little information about how those development funds were spent and who actually benefited. Some of that money seemed to come with economic strings attached — in exchange for mining or logging concessions in a country or hefty contracts for Canadian companies in construction or equipment or telecommunications. I learned from candid Canadian diplomats that the development assistance could be almost like a trade deal — Canada would put, say, $15 million into a country and in exchange would expect that country to back, say, a Canadian bid for a seat on the UN Security Council, or to sign Canadian-led treaties.

But in my mind, the biggest problem was that so much of the money that was budgeted for "development assistance" actually didn't even come to Africa — it went to cover overheads and consult-ant contracts in Canada. I had not wanted to get into that tangled and complex discussion in that letter to Peter Gzowski. So I wrote primarily about Karen, and set her accomplishments against the sometimes dubious ones in northern Ghana that had gobbled up so many development dollars, a good percentage of which had never left Canada.

A few months later a high-level delegation arrived from Ottawa. By high-level I mean the men who handled the Canadian develop-ment projects in northern Ghana from their offices in Hull. To mark their visit, there was a soirée at the "clubhouse" on the compound. The clubhouse was one of those prefab Canadian bungalows, which had been set aside as a place for project staff and their families to gather in the evenings. It was also used for small receptions when delegations flew in from Accra, or foreign capitals.

When the German contingent was invited to such soirées, I usu-ally wound up tagging along to play the role of the interested (but not too interested) wife of a development expert, as my husband was officially called. The Germans also had a term for us, the tag-alongs: we were called *mitausreisende Ehefrauen*. That translated: *wives who travel abroad with*. Employers generally expected tag-along spouses to take a casual — hobby-like — interest in the place and the work that had landed them in an out-of-the-way setting in Africa. The theory was that this way the family would remain "stable." The development expert would perform better. If my take on it was right, this meant that the female spouse was supposed to amuse herself in suitable ways — getting involved with local women's groups, perhaps joining the Inner Wheel of the Rotary Club, having tea regularly and ensuring that the house ran smoothly and so on. Beyond that, there seemed to be some suspicion of any wife who took too much interest in the work that was ongoing, especially if she was a journalist or a writer. After all, the experts had lengthy and windy project documents and briefings and insider information that no outsider could ever be expected to understand.

At the reception to honour the visiting Canadian delegation, someone took me by the hand and introduced me to one of the men who was behind that rural development project with all the cars, and another project that was just getting launched to improve water supplies to the north of the country.

He looked down on me from his superior height. "I know your name," he said.

"You do?" I replied, smiling.

"Yes, I do. You think we don't hear *Morningside* in Hull?"

"Oh, that's good," I said brightly. "I really miss it over here, it's..."

"Let me make one thing clear to you right now," he said. "I don't ever want to hear my f . . . ing name on the Canadian f . . . ing Broadcasting Corporation. You got that?" For emphasis he jabbed his index finger towards my nose and then my stomach. "Never."

I was completely taken aback and my stomach was turning knots just as it had when I was five and summoned to the front of the class because I'd forgotten to do my homework. I stood there feeling small and that gave him the opening he needed to tell me more about what he thought of my letter about Karen Leslie and my allusions to the "real" development projects in the area. He meant the ones run by the experts.

"But I didn't write about those," I said. "I specifically did not name names. I could have been a lot more explicit."

"You were explicit enough."

"I was not, but even if I were, don't you think Canadians have a right to know how their money is being spent? In the name of development?"

"This stuff is far too complex for Canadians back home to understand. That's what you fail to understand. So I had better not hear my f . . . ing name . . . "

I decided it was an isolated incident — that bit of bullying from a man who seemed to exhibit all the symptoms of something I call the Development Expert Disease. These include arrogance and hubris to which a few ordinary human beings can succumb after a few years of jetting about to exotic destinations and sumptuous hotels to discuss devastating poverty. Fortunately, it is still a rare disease that hits only those with a certain inclination for self-aggrandizement in the first place. I decided not to fret about it or about him.

But then a new Canadian family arrived in 1992, fresh from their three-day orientation training at the agency headquarters in Hull. The incoming family had been told back in Ottawa not to talk to me and to avoid divulging any information whatsoever about their work or about the agency. We became good friends and of course exchanged all the stories we wanted to, wondering why some individuals at Canada's development agency were behaving as though they worked for a secret service organization.

One woman consultant working on one of the projects told me she had had to sign a contract vowing never to publish anything at all that referred to her work on the project or on the project itself. The only conclusion we could find was that they had a lot to hide from the public. That seemed a great shame. I figured that the more the public knew about the difficulties of development work and the tricky business of "development," and the more they heard about real Canadian accomplishments (and there were lots, even if that big project in Tamale wasn't one of them), the more willingly they would agree to increased Canadian involvement abroad.

Shortly after the encounter with that imposing man who didn't want his name on the CBC, a monitoring and evaluation commission arrived in Tamale to have a look at the impact of the ten-year-old development project in the Northern Region. The head of the mission was a former government employee at the agency, now turned consultant, who was candid and apparently heedless of any advice he may have received not to speak with me.

After a few days in Tamale, he told me that there was one quick and easy solution for that particular rural development project that had only a few functioning boreholes and the multitude of cars to show for all the millions spent.

"Really?" I said. "A solution?"

"Yes," he said. "A simple atomic bomb ought to do it."

At the end of his monitoring and evaluation mission, he dropped by again.

"So," I said. "Surely it wasn't so terrible? Do you still think the solution is an atomic bomb?"

"No, no, no," he said, laughing. "I was wrong. An atomic bomb isn't the solution at all, not for this project."

I waited for him to continue, wondering what he had seen that had changed his mind.

He eyed me with a grin. "Not one atomic bomb," he said. "I think it would require two. Two might just be enough to do the job."

I asked him if he was going to write that down in his report to the agency on the effectiveness and impact of their development project, which engaged three separate consulting companies, representing — not coincidentally — three separate regions of Canada and affiliated (unofficially of course) with the three main political parties of the time.

He laughed. Shook his head again. "You think I want to be unemployed?"

As far as I could tell, it worked something like this. In the mood of increasing disenchantment with what is known euphemistically at home as "aid" (the official term is bilateral development assistance or cooperation — money given by one government directly to another for development), the government agencies had decided they had to run much tighter ships if they were going to survive. For this reason, they came up with the "M&E" business to monitor and evaluate the outcome of each development project. This cost a lot of money, maybe even as much as "implementing" the project itself, but it was meant to ensure that money that was spent was well spent.

Unfortunately, in the unaccountable world of foreign affairs, this sometimes meant that consultants who lived off the avails of M&E were not very likely to admit that any particular project was a complete failure, not to the mother agency that ran the show. If they did, the project might be shut down and they would be right out of a contract. The back-scratching world of international development left me scratching my head.

Call me naïve. Many did, rightfully. Call me a utopian dreamer. Many do, with good reason. But it still seemed to me that Canadians deserved to know more about what happened to their development dollars when those dollars left Canada, *if* they left Canada. One former employee at Canada's development agency told me that about 80 per cent of those development dollars never do leave Canada. He also said that within the agency, there is a feeling this is what Canadians want. Neither he nor I believe that.

The media could do it, provide the public with information — good and critical — about what Canada is doing abroad. By 1999, Canada had only one correspondent resident in Africa, in Abidjan, the capital of Côte d'Ivoire (Ivory Coast), who filed primarily for the French Radio Canada and not for anglophone Canada at all. For many news or features editors in Canada, the continent seemed to be more or less off the map. For those who did have the interest, there was usually little money to bring stories from obscure places that some producers or editors — mistakenly I believe — thought were not of interest to Canadians. I was often told that Canadians wouldn't be interested in a story from this or that African country because "Canadians don't know anything about that part of the world." And if I replied, which I usually didn't, I would say, "Well, how can they know anything about it when you refuse to cover it?"

I heard recently, at another chance encounter at another evening soirée among Canadians in Mali, that the project in northern Ghana, like all those massive integrated rural development projects in Africa, had gone out of style and been closed down.

Shortly after that, I got wind of the truly tragic news that Karen Leslie had died suddenly one night in her sleep, of an aneurysm, after spending a day with her husband gardening around their home in Huntsville, Ontario. I think about her still, as she was those hot mornings in the orphanage, laughing and chattering away with those dispossessed children for whom a pair of scissors was a magical thing. I think about the tiny girl with club feet, dragging herself along on her hips and tugging at Karen's blue skirt, everyone laughing in delight as Karen told them stories and brought them paper and glue and crayons they used to discover their own hidden creative gifts. She is deeply mourned still in Tamale by all those teachers and children who worked with her. Her legacy lives on in the small schools that are flourishing and expanding in that northern Ghanaian town.

She is greatly missed.

Chapter 6

Trespassers won't be prosecuted

The village was Sankpala, thirty kilometres south of Tamale. There were three of us making our way towards the chief's palace of mud bricks and thatch — two Ghanaian consultants and myself. Both Ben and Zara seemed to feel obliged to greet everyone we met along the way. Actually they were indeed obliged; Ben had already told me more than once that if you neglected to pause and greet someone you passed, it was a "social crime," an indication that you regarded that person as already dead.

This greeting business didn't come naturally to me; I'd grown up believing that a grunt or a slight nod of the head was sufficient acknowledgement of those I knew well. Strangers passing on the street in most of Canada weren't in the habit of greeting each other at all. In fact, people who smiled and spoke to passers-by might be viewed with suspicion, believed to be after something or just regarded as dangerous lunatics on the loose.

Our progress through Sankpala was painfully slow; at least it seemed that way to me. We had to pause, shake hands and exchange pleasantries with all the adults on our path. I tried to ignore the ever-growing mob of children following us, who chirruped repetitive greetings at our backs. Occasionally Zara would turn around and cluck disapprovingly at them, tell them to go away and leave us alone. Their numbers only grew. So did the racket.

The village was a labyrinth of narrow paths lined by mud walls, which seemed to collect and intensify the heat from the blazing sun and to re-emit it in waves that were roasting me alive. As usual, I was impatient and edgy. I fretted aloud about the time it was going to take us to go and greet the village chief, when all I wanted to do was to get on with the survey we were doing on fuelwood and energy needs in the region.

Zara laughed and told me to stop behaving like a "white man." Ben merely smiled and pointed to a message scribbled in chalk on the plaster of one house wall we were passing. It read: "No hurry in life, so my brother, take your time."

I put my head down and kept on trudging. They were right, of course. If we didn't obey protocol and greet the chief, we would be trespassers in the village. And the villagers would feel no compunction whatsoever to provide us with a shred of accurate information, although they would probably still be polite and gracious even as they fed us a load of half-truths or fictional figures. No one would turn us away at the compound — the way I surely would a bunch of consultants that showed up at my door in Canada, nosing into my private life and asking me about my cooking habits. Trespassers are almost never prosecuted in West Africa, at least not if it's peacetime and they're not from an enemy tribe. However, if we took the time to see the chief, explained to him our mission and respected tradition by offering him a handful of cola nuts, we could be sure of a sincere welcome and honest replies to our questions.

The chief's palace was a cracked circular structure topped with a perky thatch roof. The only thing that set it apart from the huts in the village was that it was larger and plastered with faded posters advertising this or that vaccination or family planning campaign. The mob of children dispersed quickly, chased away by a young man wielding a horsewhip. Following the example of Ben and Zara, I removed my shoes and padded into the palace barefoot.

After the brilliant glare outside, I was at first blinded by the obscurity inside the chief's palace. Zara escorted me to the wooden bench in the centre of the room and bade me sit while we waited for the chief to acknowledge us and give his linguist the go-ahead to start the long, convoluted process of "greeting."

The chief sat on his throne, a raised platform of mud covered with skins from lions and other species no longer to be found in the region. He was directly across from us, but just beyond the reach of the rays of sunlight that filtered in through two separate open doorways, so it took me some minutes to make out the details of his appearance. He wore the habitual blue and white smock of locally grown and woven cottons, and despite the age that showed up in the wrinkles on his face and hands and in the white of his goatee, his eyes were youthful, alert and very bright, even in the gloom. He gazed impassively at us as he sat there, leaning against the rear wall of the palace.

Behind us, a tethered stallion snorted down our necks and stamped his hooves, apparently the only impatient living thing in the palace — apart from me.

The chief remained silent for a good long while, long enough that I began to fidget, fretting that his silent gaze was one of disapproval. Beside him squatted his linguist, an elder who looked like he might have already spent a century or even more on this earth. As a rule, chiefs were not addressed directly nor did they speak directly to visitors. Each chief had a linguist whose job it was to transmit and if need be, to translate the messages that visitors brought. And in that polyglot Northern Region of Ghana, messages could come in any one of two dozen languages — in any of a couple of hundred languages if visitors came other regions in the country.

I forgot my studied patience and finally whispered to Ben, asking him what on earth the chief was waiting for.

He held up his hand and whispered back, "Just wait small."

I waited "small." The whole business was making me nervous, probably because I was such a novice when it came to village protocol and how one was supposed to behave in the palace of a chief. A few days earlier, we'd greeted a paramount chief, the supreme traditional ruler of the Nanumba ethnic group, and I'd done just about everything wrong. I'd trod right on the carved fetishes implanted in the doorway, which were meant to be avoided by human feet and believed to obstruct the entry of evil spirits or human beings with evil intent. After that I'd sat on the bench gazing at the chief when I was supposed to be kneeling and studying the floor, then stood up when I was supposed to be sitting on that bench. I'd spoken when I was supposed to have been silent and been silent when I was supposed to have clapped praise for what the chief had just said.

I suspect I'd also failed to hide my amazement when two of the chief's younger wives (he had a few dozen), one with a completely shaven head because of her recent marriage to the chief, had approached their husband on hands and knees, forbidden by traditional etiquette to raise their heads and meet his eyes.

This time, I told myself, I was going to do it correctly. Unfortunately, in Sankpala there was a new set of rules to obey. This was a Dagomba village rather than a Nanumba one, and this was merely a village chief and not the paramount chief of an entire ethnic group. So I would need to watch Zara and copy her every move. Ben came originally from the south of the country, so he wasn't yet fully versed in the finer details of Dagomba protocol. But Zara was a Gonja, born and raised in the Northern Region. She seemed to know just how to behave everywhere we went on our survey, not to mention that she also spoke a dozen languages fluently.

I was still waiting "small" when the linguist and Zara began to converse in Dagbani, the language of the Dagomba people. At the best of times, that is when people were speaking Dagbani very slowly to thick-headed foreigners like me, I might be able to make out basic words like "hello" or "how are you?". When Zara and the linguist were speaking normally, I had no hope of understanding a single word. The talk continued, and Ben scuttled forward in a crouch to deliver the cola nuts and a bottle of gin into the hands of the linguist, who then deposited these in two separate calabashes resting beside the chief.

The chief spoke, apparently thanking us for this generosity. The linguist listened and then spoke and there was a good deal of clapping and then more discussion between Zara and the linguist in Dagbani, and between Zara and Ben in his native Twi tongue. Then the whole complicated linguistic puzzle repeated itself. I stifled a yawn.

It was deliciously cool inside the thick walls of that mud palace, and I contemplated the unpretentious advantages of local building materials and architecture. The mixture of clay, cow dung and straw used to form the bricks in traditional homes may not have sounded particularly grand, or even appealing, but it certainly made for good insulation against the heat of the day. The plaster that coated the walls was made from pure clay, which was then polished to a hard brown shine using residues from sheanuts, oil-rich nuts produced by a tree indigenous to the region.

A Malian architect once told me that, unlike concrete, mud floors allowed the soils underneath these houses to "breathe." She said when one of these houses was no longer needed because the villagers had decided to move to a new location or because the owners had died, the structure simply sank slowly back into the very earth of which it was made, adding to the organic matter in the soil on which it had stood.

It struck me that the introduction of more "permanent" construction materials from abroad might not really be construed as positive development. They often contained lots of noxious chemicals and other substances that might not biodegrade in a millennium; pesticides such as DDT were sometimes mixed with cement when "modern" bricks were made. I certainly would have preferred a house of mud bricks like this palace (without the horse perhaps) to the prefab bungalows in the development camp where I lived.

Belatedly I noticed that everyone in the palace had gone silent and I glanced up to see that the chief's amused eyes were on me. "He's inviting you to speak," whispered Ben. "You must now tell him our mission."

"You tell him," I muttered. "Or better still, Zara should tell him in Dagbani. He'll never understand it if I say it all in English."

"He speaks English," Zara whispered.

"Then why are we going through all the rigmar . . . "

She silenced me with a look.

I didn't know how to begin or even if I should bother trying to explain anything to the chief.

We were there to do a survey about firewood consumption. People in rural areas cooked with firewood over open fires, the cooking pots perched precariously on three-stone fireplaces in their compounds. Many villagers, desperate for some kind of income that didn't depend entirely on good rains for successful harvests, also brought in a little cash by cutting trees and burning them to produce charcoal. This was the preferred energy source for cooking in urban areas such as Tamale.

We were using a questionnaire that aimed to find out how much firewood people used each day to cook, how long it took the women and girls to collect it, and whether they might be interested in learning how to fashion for themselves "improved cookstoves" of clay, cow dung and rice straw — the same materials used in their houses. The results of the survey were to be used to design and carry out an improved cookstove program. Behind all of this were lots of studies that showed deforestation was degrading the countryside and contributing to poverty. Too many valuable (economically important) trees were being cut down for firewood and for making charcoal. Cooking over open fires with firewood was wasteful and charcoal was even more wasteful than open fires because eighty per cent of the wood energy was lost when the charcoal was made. Improved cookstoves could reduce firewood consumption in villages by 50 per cent and also reduce the urban dependence on charcoal, thus easing pressure on the woodlands, as well as on women and girls who collected the wood. Improved, energy-efficient stoves could, in theory, solve a whack of problems all at once.

I decided there was no need to go into all of that highfaluting logic with the chief. I made it short and as simple as I could, thinking (mistakenly) that it probably wasn't of much interest to him. I said we needed some information on trees and firewood, so that we would be better able to help his people. My presumptuous and condescending attitude makes me cringe even now, years after the fact.

After I had finished saying my bit, the chief fixed us with a stern look, his eyes pinpoints of light that made me think he had me figured and also that he probably knew a lot more about the subject that I did. He would though. This was his land and this was his world and these were his problems. And it was a grave mistake to assume (as I was assuming then) that traditional rulers, chiefs and kings in Africa were uneducated, in the Western sense of that word. All were versed in every detail of their own history and land. And many were university graduates and professionals before they became chiefs and assumed the "skins" (which is what chiefs sat on in northern Ghana) or the "stools" (which was the chief's or king's throne in southern Ghana). A month later I would read about a young computer programmer who had just taken up the stool in a town in southern Ghana, having left a top position with an information technology firm in the UK to become chief in his village.

The linguist was often just a formality, part of the trappings that came with the chieftaincy, because many of the chiefs spoke several languages themselves. And as Zara had said, the chief in Sankpala did indeed speak English. In fact, he was now speaking it directly to us, leaving the linguist out of the circle altogether.

"This is interesting," he said. "I remember when I was a small boy and people began this making of charcoal to sell it. They said this was the modern way to cook: the white people cooked with charcoal in burners and not over open fires. My grandfather said this charcoal business would kill us. He said that we should never cut a living tree for firewood, and never turn wood into charcoal. He said this was wasteful. He said that we should be careful when we cleared the land for crops and always leave trees in our fields. That is how we always did it. He said that the young people with their foreign ideas would cut down all the trees and then we would be hungry. The rains would stop. The crops would wither and die."

He paused, then made a sweeping gesture that embraced much more than the humble interior of his palace. "That day has come. You see the trees are almost gone. The rains don't come as they used to. The soils are poor. And we are hungry. But go ahead and ask my people. Let them tell you this themselves. This is your mission, is it not?"

Yes, that was our mission.

He was smiling when he gave us permission to leave, and bestowed blessings on us and on our work. With his blessing we did ask his people. We went from one compound to another, each a hive of human enterprise and endeavour. People were threshing millet, chopping firewood, making charcoal, pounding grains in mortars, grilling sheanuts. Sheanuts came from one of those invaluable tree species we were, in theory, trying to help save. The oil from the sheanut tree, which grows only in West Africa, is found in everything from President's Choice shampoos to Body Shop sunscreens and is also commonly used by European pharmaceutical companies as an emollient in medical ointments. It's a wonderful cooking oil, akin to olive oil in nutrient and health value. It's also used to protect hair from cracking and skin from blistering during the long dry season when the desert wind, the harmattan, sweeps down from the Sahara and blankets all of West Africa in dust.

People in West Africa have nurtured sheanut trees for centuries because it is as important to their survival as is, say, their millet crop. They also consume the oil as a medicine, to ease stomach problems and ulcers. And as if that were not enough, they then use the dark paste left after oil is extracted to burnish their pottery and to polish their clay walls and floors.

Sheanut oil was just one of the many tree products people were busy processing in their compounds when our team of three trooped in and started asking rapid-fire questions.

They were accommodating, not just in Sankpala but in every village we entered. They tried to answer everything we asked, even when the questions were intrusive and in some cases downright ludicrous. I recall the reaction in one village when we were still testing the questionnaire to see if it would solicit the information we needed. We had asked the first woman we met how many people she cooked for: fewer than five, fewer than ten, fewer than twenty, and so on, right up to fifty, which was quite normal in a large extended family. Her compound was large; there were eight small separate huts arranged within the walled circle; each of the circular huts housed one of the wives and her offspring, while the square ones were for the husband, teenage sons or members of the extended family that for one reason or another lived there.

The woman didn't reply. I asked Zara to repeat the question. She did. "How many people do you cook for every day? How many men, women and children come to eat the evening meal that you cook? Is it fewer than five, fewer than ten . . . ?"

The woman hesitated a little more then cupped her hands around her mouth and began to shout in Dagbani. I asked Zara what she was saying, and to whom she was saying it.

"She's calling the whole family together," Zara replied. "She has to count and see how many family members eat here."

"You mean she doesn't know?"

Zara went into one of those giggling fits that made it so much fun to work with her on that survey that took us from one side of the Northern Region to another, over a period of two months. When she'd wiped away her tears, she said, "Of course she doesn't. Nobody counts the mouths they feed. They just cook for everyone who lives in the compound. They couldn't even tell you how many people are in the family without counting them, which you've asked her to do. That's why she's calling everyone together now, so she can count."

"But that's ridiculous. I don't want her to do that. If this is such a silly question, why didn't you tell me so?"

She shrugged and offered me an inscrutable smile, which served as a polite way of saying that she, at least, wasn't in the business of questioning the logic — lunatic as it might be — of visiting strangers in her country. She was merely doing as she was told.

We dropped that question from our form and eventually streamlined the questionnaire until we could sample a handful of people in each village, visit the chief, and finish up in one community by midday, to squeeze in a second before dusk. It became clear, even before we'd analyzed the data, that firewood was a critical problem for women and girls, who might have to spend every second day walking up to eight hours to collect enough firewood to satisfy the household needs. The taboo on cutting live sheanut trees and other species that produced commercially important products was breaking down. Fortunately for the woodlands — and unfortunately for the women — they had only hand-hewn axes with which to chop the wood and so they still found it easier to hack off bits of dead or dying trees than they did to chop down live ones.

We had almost finished the survey when we found ourselves one afternoon in the compound of an elderly woman, who was obligingly replying to our whole long list of questions. When we had finished we thanked her and prepared to take our leave, but she wasn't quite done with us. Translated by Zara, this is what that old woman had to say to us through her toothless smile.

"You people with your education and foreign ways, we don't understand you," she began. "When I was a young girl, you came here and you told us to cut down the trees we always left growing in our millet and sorghum fields. You told us to cut them down and plant maize. Only maize. You told us not to plant it with beans or around the trees the way we always planted our millet and sorghum. You said we should grow it by itself. You told us to buy tractors and to use modern farming methods. So we did. We bought fertilizer. We cut down our trees, even the economic trees we needed for protecting our soil and for sheanut butter and our foods. We bought your maize seed. We did everything you said. Our tractors broke down and we couldn't get fuel. You sent the tractors but not the means to run them or repair them. Next thing, you people came here and told us never mind the tractors; tractors were not good. You said we should go back to using bullocks to plough our fields because it was better than tractors after all. Then we couldn't buy fertilizer any more because it became too costly. So our harvests just get poorer and poorer. We don't have our own seed any more and we cannot afford to buy the seed you sell us. You come again and tell us we should use manure and trees to fertilize our fields. But we don't have any of the trees left that used to feed us and make the soil rich because you told us to cut them down. And so we can't find fuelwood. We spend our days walking, walking, walking to get some small firewood and water. Now you strangers come again and tell us we should plant plenty of trees, not cut them down."

She paused, finally, eyed us each carefully. Then she ran her tongue over her lips and said, "Why don't you make up your minds? We are tired of this. Why do you bring your mistakes here?"

We had no answer for her. What she was describing was the advent of the much-touted Green Revolution, which was meant to modernize agriculture and improve harvests in the tropics. Apparently, it hadn't worked very well in northern Ghana. In lieu of a reply to her question, we asked her if she would like to participate in a few days of training in how to make her own improved cookstove to save herself firewood.

She shook her head and said she'd rather wait and see this time — she'd prefer that younger women tried it and if the cookstoves they made were good, then one of the younger women could come and teach her how to make one. That way, she could decide for herself whether this was a good idea, or just another mistake disguised as help from abroad.

A few months later, Ben, Zara and I headed out again, this time to hold those training courses on how to make improved cookstoves. Zara was the expert in this, as she seemed to be in just about everything — languages, human relations and women's issues. Officially, she was called the "animator" and Ben was the technical expert with experience in stove design.

This meant I was away from home for extended periods of time, as each training course lasted several days and we were moving from one village to another. One of the last villages we worked in was Kukuo, home to a famous dewitching shrine. For this reason it was also home to a disproportionately large number of elderly women, who had been sent there to be "dewitched" and then stayed on because the chief and the district assemblywoman welcomed them and helped care for them. Although they'd been dewitched by the fetish priest at the shrine in Kukuo, it was unlikely that any of these old women who had been accused of witchcraft would be welcomed back in their own villages.

We were into our third day in Kukuo and the women were up to their shoulders in clay and mud as they struggled to form their own cookstoves. I was keeping a low profile in the shade of the monumental baobab tree in the small plaza in front of the chief's palace. That small patch of ground had been turned into a makeshift workshop for the women of the village, while the chief looked on.

Zara and Ben were helping the women, and Rabiatu Damba, the village representative in the district assembly, was berating the younger women who had dropped out of the course. They were still showing up each morning but kept themselves off to one side, applying beauty spots to each other's faces using luminescent shades of nail polish. After the first day they had lost interest and stopped participating, telling Rabiatu that as they were all the newest and youngest wives of their husbands, they didn't need such cooking technology to earn their spouses' favours. They had their youth and beauty to keep their husbands interested, whereas their older co-wives — or rivals — needed to make special efforts and possess special skills to keep their husbands attracted. Rabiatu, an outspoken advocate of women's rights, was having none of that and lecturing them on the importance of conserving fuelwood. I was doubtful that her lecture was serving much purpose.

I had often wondered if we weren't just adding to the heavy workload the women already had, by introducing this "adapted technology" to their lives. To make the stoves, the women had to collect large amounts of clay and cow dung from around their villages, find the rice straw and stock it after harvest each year and then spend a good part of the dry season fashioning stoves of all sizes for the various cooking pots they used each day. I wondered how many of them would actually "adopt" this technology once we had gone and the novelty had died. Would they find it paid off, that it really saved them time and energy? I consoled myself that the women seemed very merry as they worked and seemed to be having fun, comparing their efforts and laughing a lot.

I was musing over the time and technology gaps separating the developed world from those rural communities in northern Ghana. My grandmother had cooked over a woodstove; my mother had cooked over an electric stove and I now cooked with gas — and with a microwave oven. And yet here we were trying to convince overworked and underfed rural women in Ghana how to make their own stoves of mud and dung so that they would save some firewood — *if* the stoves they built were done well, *if* they were used correctly and *if* all the literature on such stoves was accurate. Let's just say I was wondering if I was wasting their time and energy and if I wasn't part of yet another mistake disguised as development assistance.

I woke from my depressing reverie when a vehicle approached and then pulled to a stop beside the chief's palace. Cars were not part of the landscape in that small village so far off any paved road and at the very end of a sorely eroded path better suited to four-footed livestock than to anything with wheels. Everyone stopped what they were doing to see who it was that had braved that rutted path in a vehicle.

I was probably more surprised than anyone when Karl leapt out, followed by our daughter, four years old at the time. What came next transpired so fast that I wasn't sure I wasn't imagining things, or perhaps succumbing to illusions caused by the magical powers that were said to be at work in that village with the powerful dewitching shrine. Instantly, it seemed that all three thousand people who dwelled in Kukuo were present and all those young women, the disinterested young wives who had refused to participate, were scooping up handfuls of clay and preparing to join in the stove-making. Hundreds of children had appeared from nowhere and had surrounded the Volkswagen and Karl, who by now had Anna up on his shoulders to keep her from being trampled or handled to death. There was wild shouting and a furore that made me cover my ears.

Anna was crying and trying to hide behind her little hands. Rabiatu and the chief were on their feet and shouting for calm and decorum. I turned to Ben and Zara and suggested that perhaps we should have thought of this strategy earlier — if we wanted to entice the women out of their homes to join in the training course, all we needed was to bring my daughter along, as she could obviously be a main attraction.

Zara laughed and managed somehow to get all the new participants going on their cookstoves and to convince the others to get back to work, so "the white man could see their good work." That made me want to cover my face with my hands the way my daughter was doing.

Ben just stood there smiling at the bedlam my daughter's presence had caused among the children of the village. "Really," I said, "I'm used to being followed everywhere I go and I understand the children's curiosity in the villages, but this is a bit much, isn't it?"

Ben continued to smile.

I said, "You'd think no one here had never seen a white kid before."

"They haven't," said Ben. "That's what they're so excited about. They're saying they thought the white man was born big, you know, that they weren't human beings at all who were born small and then grew up. This is the first time they've seen a white child and they're suddenly coming to the realization that white people are human beings, just like them."

It was the chief who saved the situation, by parting the mob of children like Moses did the Red Sea. He led Karl with Anna back through the crowd and into his palace — so that he could greet them correctly and vice versa. Rabiatu beckoned to me to join them inside.

The chief in Kukuo was a warm and open man, and I'd come to feel at ease inside his small palace. He was exceptional in his informality and interest in development and change, unusual where chiefs tended to be the custodians of tradition. He also ruled a village that many a man wouldn't set foot in, a village that was full of women said to be "witches."

Anna must have sensed his benevolence quickly because she stopped crying the minute we were inside. Karl whispered to me that he was there only briefly, checking on a health centre that was going up in the district, and that Anna had begged to come and see where I was working. Anna, however, had already forgotten us and was heading towards the chief, who was beckoning her.

He took her hand and shook it and smiled. She took a step backwards and opened her hand to see what he had placed there. She came skipping back to us, waving a note worth one hundred Cedis that "the man" had given her. And after the chief had chewed the fat for a while with Karl, and Anna had thanked the chief profusely for that unexpected gift he could so ill afford to give, they took their leave and calm returned to Kukuo. We resumed the cookstove training, and after that, attendance was no longer a problem. Even the young wives joined in with gusto.

Six months after the cookstove training finished, we made follow-up visits to all the villages to see how the women had fared with the new technology, to see whether the program had been a success or had any "impact."

Many women had built new stoves. Many used their own ingenuity to improve on the design, or at least to make it more suitable to their needs. Many had done nothing at all with their new skills. And some said they had tried to make new stoves but they had broken. There was no sign of the snowball effect we had hoped would happen when women shared their knowledge with their peers and co-wives. It seemed that those who had worked hard to master the technique were loathe to share it with their "rivals," or co-wives. However, many were teaching their daughters how to do the work. And perhaps most surprising — and most encouraging — was that we found five men who had taken up making cookstoves. Tradition didn't allow them to work with clay and cooking was strictly women's work, but they had begun to try making improved energy-efficient stoves out of scrap metal.

So was the program a big success or a dismal failure? I mulled that over for weeks and decided that it wasn't either. It was something in between. I reassured myself that at least it hadn't caused any harm; it hadn't consumed vast amounts of money or exaggerated social inequities or put the participants into debt, which is more than can be said of some of the bigger mistakes that have been made in the name of development.

As for impact, well, I'd say the biggest impact was probably on me — and on my daughter, who to this day safeguards that soiled and wrinkled note with an official value of one hundred Cedis (about five cents) that the chief gave her. That and the memories of the welcome and wisdom the villagers showed us are worth a small mountain of gold to me.

Chapter 7

Give and mostly take

"Before this ting, structure adjustment, we had lots of money and no many ting to buy. Now deh be plenty to buy, ever ting be deh, but no money to buy." — A young man in Tamale, 1991

One of the small miracles we'd witnessed while we were in Sankpala for the stove training was the posting of speed limits on the national highway that bisected the village. On the day we arrived, so did a vanload of policemen. They were armed with brand new signs declaring a speed limit of fifty kilometres an hour, and radar guns to trap any motorists who exceeded that maximum. To my knowledge this was a first. People travelled on the main highway as fast as their vehicles could move, or would move without vibrating to pieces on the rough patches. Police might flag motorists down to collect money from them for any one of many — often fictional — infractions, but speeding had never been one of them.

Well, it was now. The policemen told us that the World Bank had donated radar guns and road signs for enforcing speed limits. At first, when I saw the policemen set themselves up there in Sankpala, I thought that the World Bank had done something right. Here was a tangible innovation that surely couldn't do any harm and might do something to end the slaughter caused by reckless speeds on Ghanaian roads — at least on the paved ones where reckless speeds were possible.

On the third day, Ben and I were sitting in the car on the side of the road, waiting for Zara to finish visiting with "her women" in the village, so that we could return to Tamale at the end of a long and hot day of training. Just about every single vehicle, with the notable exception of a few Mercedes and BMWs driven by Very Big Men who were obviously above the law, was getting caught in that speed trap.

I had been watching with some amusement the drama of this new rigour on Ghana's roads. Each time a car approached, a policeman would leap out from the bushes to ambush those demons of speed with his radar gun. He would take a stance in the middle of the road like the hero of an old western film, keeping the radar gun pointed right at the drivers as though it were a loaded and lethal weapon. Then of course the drivers would have to pull over, get out of their vehicles and follow the policeman back into the bushes, where Ghana's finest had set up their roadside office in the shade of a sheanut tree.

To Mumuni, our driver, I commented on this effective new way to ensure sane speeds and commended the police for their enthusiasm with their new gadget.

He laughed so hard I thought he would choke.

"You don't see how they do?" he asked me finally.

"I see quite well how they do," I retorted. "They wait until the motorist has entered the fifty-kilometre zone and then they monitor the speed and they stop those who are speeding. That's how it's done all over the world. Our policemen in Canada have been using radar for years."

"I don't think the police in your country use them like our Ghana police-oh," he said. "You don't see? In the morning the policemen aim the radar at the first car that is over-speeding. Say he is going ninety-five kilometres per hour. This number shows up on the gun in red and so the driver can't deny his speed and he has to pay. They don't give him a real ticket that he pays in Tamale town to the police, because then they wouldn't get all the money. They make him pay them here. And once they've stopped someone for over-speeding, they just leave the radar set at that ninety-five kilometres per hour for the whole day. Even if you are moving at thirty, they stop you and say that you were travelling ninety-five kilometres per hour. You haven't seen that most of these cars he stops are not over-speeding at all? This new radar thing, it just give them another way to chop from us."

I didn't fully believe him until a couple of months later, one bright and sunny morning when we were driving through Sankpala on that main road, heading south to the coast. We had slowed to twenty-five kilometres an hour and were moving through the speed zone at a snail's pace when two policemen leapt out of the bush on the roadside, blocking our path. One of them was pointing the radar gun at us. The kids shrieked, Karl cursed and I laughed. The digital red numbers showing up in the small barrel of that radar device read ninety-five kilometres per hour. Karl stopped the car and was arguing belligerently even before he'd got out.

I waited a bit before I followed him into the bush, where the exchange had grown very heated indeed. For once, I was happy it was my usually calm and patient husband losing his cool. For perhaps the first time in more than a decade, I was going to get to play the mediator's role between Karl and the authorities, rather than the reverse.

I approached them slowly, smiling, and reminded them that they'd met me here some time back, when I'd congratulated them for their "diligence" in enforcing the speed limit. They dropped the gun, shook my hand heartily and said even though my husband was rude and should actually go to court for his insolence, they would let us go because I was their "friend."

I couldn't blame the World Bank for the devious way their gift had been put to work. But those radar guns served as a pretty good example of how good ideas can make an extraordinary little detour before they land on the ground, especially when the good ideas were conceived in lofty places far from the reality of where they would be applied.

So it was too with structural adjustment, or many aspects of that recipe for reform that was supposed to bring economic rigour and development to Africa. In the early '90s, the World Bank considered Ghana one of its best "pupils" in Africa. For almost a decade, Ghana had obediently adhered to structural adjustment programs, or SAPs as they are commonly known.

Structural adjustment is the broad term for a whole set of sweeping changes demanded by the Bretton Woods agencies — the World Bank and the International Monetary Fund. Any country that respected all the tough fiscal restraint policies of structural adjustment and paid the interest on their debt would then qualify for more loans from the international lending agencies.

Ghana, as one of the first countries to adopt this recipe for economic reform, was also the country that the World Bank and the world's industrialized economic giants that ran it, held up as a shining example of the success of their reform packages. At least they did in the early 1990s, before the lustre began to fade as it became apparent (to some at least) that the glowing report card given the country's economic reforms didn't mean that actual living conditions had improved, and the economic growth that had been running around five per cent a year started to drop again.

As some critics explained to me, World Bank advisers had pegged Ghana's economic recovery mostly to earnings from cocoa, along with two export commodities — gold and timber. Over the years, as other cocoa-producing countries in West Africa followed similar advice from the experts at Bretton Woods, production increased and cocoa prices fell. Ghana's remaining forests, the ones that had not come down for cocoa plantations or other cash crops such as pineapple and oil palm, were rapidly disappearing. Remaining tropical forest was heading off to Asia as logs, to meet an ever-growing need for export earnings to service the growing debt. And the debt was growing because of all those loans granted as part of structural adjustment. Tautological? Critics of these World Bank and IMF economic development plans certainly thought so, especially humanitarian and development experts who worked on the ground.

Some of the reforms worked well. I was especially impressed by the liberalization of currency exchange, which all but eliminated the black market in currencies. These reforms made sense of official exchange rates. They also made life one heck of a lot easier for anyone trying to do honest business or for people wanting to change money. I'd never mastered the art of making the black money market work to my advantage with fast-talking, sticky-fingered money-changers on street corners. I preferred to change money in a bank, where I could more or less follow what was happening and be sure that I wasn't about to be cheated or arrested.

Privatization also seemed like a good idea, at least in theory. Many state corporations in Africa were still a terrible drain on the economy or else they were plundering grounds for the men who ran them, who were more often than not closely connected to the men at the very top who appointed them. Over the years and across countries, African friends had taken perverse glee in pointing out to me the luxury vehicles and palatial homes that belonged to directors of state corporations. Their take on this unhappy state of affairs was that these were perk posts for friends or relatives of the very top men in the government, handed out every few years like a rotating banquet table — so that everyone with connections would have his turn to "chop big." The most sought-after posts were the most lucrative, heading state energy, telecommunications, mining, or manufacturing corporations.

Alas, tendering being what it was — or wasn't — in most of Africa, when the time came to privatize, those same men tended to be the ones with the connections and the funds to buy up shares of the state company that had been their private fiefdom for years anyway. They knew the ropes and they knew how to twist and pull them to their advantage when state corporations were being sold off. So did foreign companies that for years had profited big-time from development funds and loans pumped in to prop up or modernize state energy or telecommunications companies in Africa, particularly a few Canadian companies with close links to Ottawa.

This was not the only reason that many Africans viewed the sudden rush to privatize with some scepticism. Profitable or even potentially profitable state corporations — gold mines or tourist lodges in a prime location such as a national park — would be sold off easily and not always to the highest bidder but to the most powerful or best-connected one, either from that country or from one of the so-called "donor" countries demanding privatization.

Other state enterprises, decayed and ill-conceived factories that hadn't once produced a bag of cement or limestone for example, could sit there unsold forever, as part of the foreign debt in many cases. The problem was not privatization, per se, it was the way in which it was being done.

The World Bank and IMF also said they were cracking down on corruption in Africa. This would have been music to my ears had it been obvious that they were going to crack down on foreign companies that bribed their way through Africa, and impose real sanctions on all those involved. But African opposition figures, who didn't have to watch their tongues for fear of offending donors that propped up a ruling government, were adamant that this concern for corruption was just more self-interest. In their jaded view, the donors' real purpose in tackling corruption was to ensure that African governments had the funds to service their debts. I didn't argue; I just took notes and wondered where the truth lay.

Structural adjustment also demanded massive reforms in the civil service, which in most countries was vastly inflated and inefficient. Once again, it wasn't clear that the cuts were going to improve the situation, not when I watched how the cutting was done in the Ministry of Agriculture in the Northern Region. First of all, it was the Big Men in the ministry who were entrusted with this task. Right off, that meant they would be immune from the guillotine because no one in his right mind was going to lop off his own head. Instead, those Big Men removed lots of the people who actually did the work — technical officers, gardeners, janitors — all the small positions held by people who cost almost nothing and had no power to argue.

The civil servants who survived the cuts were often the same ones who for years had helped themselves freely to government-owned harvesters and vehicles and seed supplies to run their private rice or maize plantations. So they stayed on and continued to squander public funds, whatever was left of them. The people who were sacked — "redeployed" was the euphemism preferred by the World Bank — were the little guys on salaries that wouldn't pay for even a hill of beans.

I suppose it can also be argued that the subsidies to farmers in Africa for fertilizers and seed and pesticides had to be removed as part of structural adjustment because subsidies were not "sustainable." Unfortunately, this standard didn't seem to apply back home in donor countries; Western governments continued to subsidize their own farmers to the hilt while their IMF forbade African governments to do the same. At the same time, those same lending agencies and donors funded research and held countless conferences to delve into the perplexing question of why Africa was hungry.

In 1996, I had a chance to interview Ismael Serageldin, the vice president for Environmentally Sustainable Development at the World Bank, and ask him why, when there was so much concern about food security and hunger in Africa, the Bank and IMF had insisted on yanking off subsidies on farm inputs. He directed his gaze at my belly-button, not an endearing habit, and recited a well-rehearsed spiel, denying those subsidies had ever reached the poorest farmers who needed them.

Just before this interview, I had done a sweep of several African countries, interviewing dozens of those "poorest" farmers, and heard the same tale from each one of them — echoes of that lecture the toothless old woman in Ghana had given me in 1991. All said they had grown to depend on the purchased (and subsidized) farm inputs of hybrid seed, pesticides and fertilizer — thanks mostly to imported development expertise — and suddenly they found themselves unable to afford those very things they'd been advised to use. When I said this to the vice president, citing just a couple of cases, it was as though I hadn't spoken. With his eyes still roaming over my midriff, he picked up where he'd left off, spouting rhetoric about the importance of "sustainability" until I finally cut him off by asking him if subsidies to farmers in donor countries could be regarded as sustainable. He glanced at his watch and terminated the interview. I don't think he had run out of time. I think he had run out of rehearsed script.

Over and over again, however, I heard one huge complaint about structural adjustment that dwarfed nearly all the other objections put forward by the most strident critics of the reform packages — African intellectuals, non-governmental organizations, humanitarian agencies, church groups. Their overriding concern was the squeeze that structural reform put on health and education.

Just when Ghanaians and parents all over Africa were clamouring for schools, free and quality education more or less disappeared in the new atmosphere of fiscal restraint. If children were fortunate enough to live within walking distance of a school, their parents still had to scrape to come up with school fees and even cover the costs of teacher housing, teachers' salaries, books, desks, uniforms, and school upkeep. In the poorest parts of rural Africa, where annual income could be a hundred dollars, such education costs were simply impossible. But parents still tried.

In the Northern Region the state schools and colleges that were already standing were in a sorry state. I used to wonder if it was worth bankrupting the family to send children for years of schooling that might not even result in basic literacy and could destroy the child's spirit and curiosity. Many young people were torn between their desperate longing for a decent education and the stark realization that even if such a thing were possible in the deteriorating school system, they might still emerge from secondary school with no hope of employment. The civil service was being cut back at a great rate, industrialization was still a long way off.

Thanks to Iddrissu, who was living with us and attending senior secondary school in Tamale, I got a good look at how dismal things were inside one of the town's better state secondary schools. Missing were the most basic fixtures: chairs, tables, chalk, books, and even teachers. Iddrissu was preparing for his O-level examinations at the end of the year. He would bring home copies of examination papers from previous years, which were close copies of O-level exams from the UK, where all students would have had a far better education than was available in any but a few of the private schools in Ghana.

Iddrissu was expected to answer questions on the use of a microscope and correct procedures in a science laboratory, neither of which he had ever seen. I'll never forget the long hours I spent reading up on atomic isotopes in my own limited reference materials so that I could explain it to him in a way he would understand. I might as well have been doing a sleight of hand with chicken feathers to try to prove the powers of African juju to a pragmatic, hard-nosed scientist back home.

Those secondary school students had never been taught the basic, most essential facts, such as the biological causes of malaria and diarrhea and guinea worm, which were the most prevalent ailments in the region. In ten years of schooling, Iddrissu had never come across explanations of why there was night and day, of how to divide one number by another, of bacterial infections. Nor had he ever been shown a map of Africa or even West Africa, so that he would know which countries surrounded his.

I recall the science exam he brought home to show me because the "mastah" had given him a good score, even though the master had asked many questions that would have stumped me: "What is the darkest planet in the world?" and "What is the best element in a molecule?"

He came home with long pages of French homework to do but had no French text or dictionary with which to work. I asked him if the teacher expected him to pull the French vocabulary out of thin air. He said he didn't know. I asked him if others in the class were able to perform such miracles in French without a single book for reference. He said most of them didn't bother attending the class and hoped that when examination time rolled around, some unscrupulous education official would sell them copies of the exam papers in advance, at which point they would hire a professional cheater to provide them with answers, which they would memorize.

It all made me furious and poor Iddrissu would sit there and listen quietly while I ranted about what looked like the hopeless state of education. He was so happy just to be in school getting what was loosely called an "education." He didn't quite grasp where I was coming from, which was that privileged rich country across the great divide, where public schools and teachers were among the best on the planet.

Some teachers were permanently absent — such as Iddrissu's agricultural science master, who went missing for six months. Finally, in exasperation, I headed to the school to give the teachers a piece of my mind. The agricultural science teacher was nowhere to be seen, but other teachers I did locate gave me no opening to speak. They had their own grievances to air. They told me they were miserably paid and with those tough fiscal restraint policies of structural adjustment in place they said they had no hope of increases that might bring their salaries up to, say, a hundred dollars a month. They stated the obvious when they said it was nearly impossible to teach classes that usually exceeded a hundred students, many of whom barely spoke English let alone wrote it. Some had no money for school benches and lay on the floor during classes, taking notes only if they had found someone willing to pay for a pen and paper. The teachers themselves often had no chalk.

Out of either desperation or self-interest — or both — many teachers had begun their own innovative system of private education within the state system. They might appear in class long enough to tell their students that private classes were available after hours for any children whose parents could afford it. These out-of-school classes were small, usually just a handful of students, and they were also extremely common — not just in Ghana but in other West African countries I visited or lived in. Students and teachers alike told me they blamed this breakdown of the public education system on governments carrying out the edicts of the IMF and World Bank. They said that in the olden days, before economic reform, Ghana had had one of the best education systems on the continent.

To compensate for this, or to give the World Bank a line of defence against their critics, the structural adjustment program in Ghana was accompanied by something called the Program to Alleviate and Mitigate the Social Costs of Structural Adjustment, or PAMSCAD.

In the Northern Region, this small-budget program manifested itself most obviously in some skeletal structures that popped up throughout the region. I heard they were meant to be schools. In fact, they were really just bundles of roofing sheets and metal poles to hold them up, which were trucked into the region and dropped all over the place.

Local people told me that the theory behind PAMSCAD was this: if people in the region were genuine in their desire for schools, they would supply the labour and the bricks to complete them, find themselves a teacher and come up with the money to equip the school with blackboards, chairs, tables, chalk, maybe even a book or two. Someone may have actually visited the Northern Region to work out a plan for where these schools from heaven were supposed to be erected, but in four years in Tamale I could find no evidence of such a plan.

What I did see, in the strangest places and miles from any village, were those tin roofs supported by metal poles — abandoned and overgrown with grass. I saw only three that had actually been completed with mud bricks by villagers. The rest of them served as convenient shelters from the rain or the sun for the local livestock population. Even if rural people had been consulted, it is doubtful they would have been able to come up with the resources needed to finish and equip the schools, let alone convince the government to hire teachers to run them.

In Ghana, and just about everywhere we lived and travelled on the continent, I certainly heard a lot of dissenting voices raised against structural adjustment, primarily from everyone who worked with the poorest of the poor on the ground. But these voices were rarely heard outside Africa, or they were drowned out by the noise the IMF continued to make about the success of its policies in developing Africa — development being measured by numbers on a spreadsheet.

For the international lenders, if GNP rose by 5 per cent a year they said the country was making good progress. The distribution of the wealth from that growing national product didn't seem to concern the economists, even though annual per capita income in Africa had been dropping for years. When pushed on this point, many experts claimed it had to do with the burgeoning populations. This was indeed a big factor, but it certainly wasn't the whole picture; rapid population growth was as much a symptom of poverty and lack of development as it was a cause. Poor rural people continued to bring forth children they had no hope of educating, largely because as they told me, "We're so poor, children are the only wealth we can have."

The urban middle class, especially educated families, tended to have fewer children. My non-expert logic suggested to me that if the West were really concerned by the population explosion in Africa, they would pump money into education and make sincere efforts to jump-start indigenous industry that might generate wealth in Africa for Africans. This would be the most effective social trigger for reducing family sizes.

On my despairing days, and there were many, I started to see this whole set-up as a throwback to the feudal system of the Middle Ages in Europe. The only real difference was that instead of the medieval church, it was now banks and lending institutions that kept a whole continent enslaved by poverty — and debt.

By 1999, Africa's total debt to the West stood well over $300 billion US. Some of the world's poorest countries were paying more than half their export earnings just to keep up interest payments on their debts. And as Africans would tell me indignantly, the African people had had no hand in incurring the debt and had nothing in their hands to show for the money that had been loaned to their leaders over the years.

Most loans were destined specifically for infrastructure — roads, hydroelectric dams, oil or gas pipelines, water systems, airports, urban sanitation. All those things were needed, of course. Coincidentally or not, major infrastructure projects involved major construction or consulting contracts that inevitably went to companies from countries holding sway at the World Bank — American, British, French, German, Belgian, Italian, Canadian, and so on. So the "donor" countries that won the contracts got their hefty share of the money dispensed as loans to Africa — but not necessarily to Africans, who would have to repay them. Outspoken and informed Africans, such as Mali's former minister of culture, Aminata Traoré, refused to call our countries donors at all. She pointed out that they were taking out of Africa much, much more than they ever "donated." She preferred the word "creditors."

Jesse Jackson called Africa's debt burden the new economy's chains of slavery and the All Africa Conference of Churches called the debt "a new form of slavery as vicious as the slave trade."

When I wondered aloud in Ghana and elsewhere in Africa why it was that governments accepted the structural reform packages without a whimper, African politicians said the governments had no choice in the matter. Their reasoning went something like this — if any African government were foolhardy enough not to adopt the entire package of reforms, then international lending institutions and so-called "donor" countries could brandish their hefty economic clubs and withhold further financing altogether. And in the new age of democracy that was coming to Africa, which was strongly encouraged by those same donor countries, a sudden financial crunch and cash shortage could seriously destabilize a newly elected government.

Much of the debt had accumulated during the Cold War in the 1970s and '80s, when the leaders in Africa who had brokered the loans had been self-appointed. During the Cold War, most of these heads of state had been more accountable to foreign "friends," either the East or the West, who bankrolled them than they were to their own people. Loans granted during those years were seldom used for any kind of meaningful development, except to develop walloping great accounts in foreign banks for those same leaders. Much of that borrowed or aid money that crooked leaders had devoured, money that had gone into Africa supposedly for its development and now was owing to foreign banks and lending agencies, had boomeranged right back into private accounts in Western banks. African friends said hotly they should not be responsible for bad debts incurred by bad leaders kept in power for political reasons by one side or the other during the Cold War. I didn't argue.

For years, this neat little financial arrangement with corrupt African leaders had served Western interests. Take the case of Mobutu Sese Seko the late president of former Zaire, now the Democratic Republic of Congo. A good "friend" to the West during the Cold War, Mobutu's estimated personal fortune before he died was somewhere between $10 and 14 billion US (in whatever banks offshore), coincidentally about the same amount his country owed to foreign banks. After his death in 1997, his fortune was nowhere to be found. That didn't stop the lending agencies from hounding the people of the country that Mobutu had run as a personal fiefdom for three decades to repay the colossal debt.

In the '90s, African governments that behaved themselves, obeying the edicts of structural adjustment, were rewarded with more loans. Sometimes new loans were even offered in official "poverty eradication programs," adding to the debt load that kept the continent eternally impoverished. Many African countries spent more each year on servicing their debts than they did on health and education combined, so how could more loans do anything but dig them deeper and deeper into dependence and eternal poverty? To me, it looked like catch 22 or 44 — or any multiple thereof.

After some seventeen years of listening to Africans and reporting on what they said, my jaded take on structural reform was that it was a resounding success, if success meant you had been aiming to (a) help the small elite get richer, (b) pave the way for multinational companies wanting to "invest" (i.e. sell their products or services) in Africa, (c) open up Africa's hinterland to foreign mining and logging companies, (d) plunge the continent further into debt while upping the take on debt repayment, (e) preclude local industry and manufacturing by flooding the "liberalized" African marketplace with foreign goods and our cast-offs, (f) ensure that the infrastructure (roads, dams) were there to make it easier for foreign interests to get at raw materials and natural resources, (g) keep the rural people dirt poor, (h) keep the urban slums growing, (i) take the small urban middle class down a peg or two, from plain old cash-strapped to really poor, (j) create still more economic — and political — dependence, and (k) make good education and health facilities the exclusive domain of the well-to-do.

The structural adjustment programs did create a favourable environment for already well-heeled Africans to do business. But the well-heeled in West Africa were a minuscule minority and worse, the elite were such a small and tight-knit clique that few of them were ever forced to pay taxes on either their legal or their illicit incomes. That further negated any equalizing effects of structural adjustment and merely increased the already incredible gap between the very few very rich and the very many very poor.

With the sudden opening up of African markets to foreign goods, there was little incentive for indigenous manufacturing or local processing that would at least add value to raw materials. The enforced liberalization of SAPs did encourage the proliferation of service industries (primarily subsidiaries of multinationals) that catered mostly to the small wealthy elite or to expatriates. And unfortunately most of the money of the small elite wound its way back to Western banks anyway, once all the money transfers and imported Mercedes or marble floors or gold watches were tallied.

It would take rare and real patriots to invest all their money, expertise and energy in an African country where the currency is prone to devaluation and where banks were known to go belly-up because a president or a president's spouse or a president's right-hand man had used it as a personal lending institution. Only true patriots would stay at home when they had the education and skills to qualify for a position anywhere in the developed world.

But I knew some.

One was a doctor in Tamale who tired of the new ways of doing medicine in the country, with the strict (but economically sound) rules that came with the SAPs and did just that to health services — sapped them. Patients not only had to cover their costs up front before treatment but they also had to supply a lot of the materials needed. He told me about the incident that spurred his final decision to quit the system. One day a young woman came to him suffering from a fistula, a tear in the tissue wall between her urinary tract and her vagina. Such fistulas, which can also occur between the vagina and the anus, can destroy a young woman's life because she constantly leaks either urine or feces. They can have many causes — teenage pregnancies and poor birthing methods — and the end result is disastrous for her. Victims of such fistulas become outcasts because of the smell. The saddest part of the story is that the fistula can be repaired, *if* the patient were to have access to a well-equipped hospital with a surgeon who knew the procedure, and *if* the patient has the money to pay for the operation.

The doctor told me that the young woman had come to him in desperation to have the urinary wall repaired. He had been forced to turn her away because of strict rules about payment for health services. She returned a month later, having begged and borrowed from her entire extended family. He attempted the operation, short as he was on the most basic of materials and medical instruments.

It wasn't successful.

"To this day," he said, "I cannot forget how she wept. She banged her head against the wall and begged me to kill her and put her out of her misery. She still leaked urine and she was now in debt to her whole family and half the village, money she could never repay. She asked me to do the operation again, but of course, regulations forbade a second operation without her paying for it. It was tragic. I wept too."

I was deeply impressed and in March 1992, I wrote another of those letters from far away to Peter Gzowski at *Morningside:*

There are moments — entire days in fact, when I feel sure there is no hope for this continent. Between AIDS and explosive population growth, amidst the civil and tribal wars which are tearing nations and people's lives to bloody shreds, between the dreadful news reports of anarchy and the appalling statistics of suffering, I search for a glimmer of hope. More often than not I see nothing but dark clouds of doom. The problems — famine, corruption, disease, poverty, desertification — defy description, let alone solution.

Then along comes someone who blows away my carefully reasoned pessimism with the cool, refreshing breath of hope. The latest of these small (but bigger than life) miracles comes in the form of a thin, animated man. He's in his late thirties, has some grey flecks in his hair, and wears a smile that could swallow Africa whole. His name is David Abdullaye. He's a medical doctor and a native of Tamale. His father was a leper, his family as poor as the dirt which encompasses this town in northern Ghana. He now runs a medical clinic on the outskirts of Tamale. In it he welcomes the poorest of the poor — examines, medicates, feeds, operates on, and heals them. For free.

The waiting and recovery rooms are traditional round mud and thatched huts, eighteen of them, erected by individual villages when they heard someone was building a clinic for . . . them. These cool, dark huts make patients feel "at home." They prefer the "comforts" they know — thin mats spread on hard but clean concrete floors — to the beds inside the clinic itself.

Dr. Abdullaye takes me along on his afternoon rounds. Eight post-operative patients are on beds in the airy recovery rooms inside. Outside in the mud huts women are recovering from eye operations, from calcium deficiency brought on by meagre diets of maize porridge. One has a tropical ulcer on her leg, a sore two decades old that has begun to eat into her bones. The leg has to come off. Dr. Abdullaye tells me he's giving her time to come to grips with that, to prepare herself for an amputation with local anaesthetic — which is all he has. There's a young man in another hut floundering about trying to show us how he's regaining movement in his left limbs after a stroke. He's laughing at something Dr. Abdullaye has said in Dagbani.

"I told him I brought him a wife," he explains to me with a smile. "You."

I hang back, unsure and uneasy. Where do they resurrect their humour?

Another man has a two-year-old sore on his shin, which has festered and spread. His thighs are tattooed with neat rows of dime-sized pale scars. Dr. Abdullaye has taken skin grafts for the ulcerated shin. He unwraps the gauze, pointing to the graft which now almost completely covers the seeping red sore.

"Look," he says. "I've made the graft in the shape of the cross. If our intelligence doesn't take, maybe Jesus will help."

He draws my attention to a woman standing outside the hut. She's learning to see again after an operation to remove cataracts. She's standing with her eyes raised to the dusky sky, rubbing them with the backs of her hands. She's wearing a flaming pink blouse, shoulders thrown back. "We've just given her that shirt," says Dr. Abdullaye. "She's proud, wants us to see."

Then he sighs. I glance quickly at him. His face mirrors the ecstasy on the woman's. So *this* is his reward.

The clinic is well back from the main road, just a few hundred meters from a new housing complex belonging to the Northern Region electrification program, with its spot-lit tennis courts, clubhouse and, soon, swimming pool. The clinic could be — is — a world away. It is not hooked up to any power lines, deriving its light from donated solar energy panels. Energy here comes from the heavens, no development agency or corporation or World Bank loans. There is no sign indicating the presence of any kind of medical facility out in the flat, scorched scrub-land. People who come here don't read or need signs.

These are people who don't go to government or even to mission hospitals. Treatment there costs money they don't have. These are rural subsistence farmers, mostly. I see them every day trudging the roads with their head-top burdens, or I see them bent double in their fields. Franz Fanon gave them a name: The Wretched of the Earth. I'm not sure he got the whole picture though — he missed their humour and their inability to perceive themselves as "wretched." They are alive, and they are struggling, and they are grateful for even the smallest of blessings, for which they continue to thank God or Allah.

I think, as I circle the clinic, smelling the disinfectant, examining the small but sterile operating theatre, watching volunteer staff steam surgical gloves and pressure-cook operating instruments, that this place must look to these people as daunting — but inviting — as a bit of heaven fallen to earth.

"People think I'm crazy," Dr. Abdullaye says. "I gave up a job as district medical officer to start this free clinic for the poor. This was always my dream. I had no idea where to get the money to build it. But God," he says, spreading his hands to take in the whole structure, "gathers his own."

He tells me of the first operation he performed here, before the clinic was built. "It was November 1989. I removed a tumour from a woman's nose. Under that mango tree, over there." He points to the sandy, shaded area under a fruiting tree just in front of the blue and white building which houses the Shekhinah Clinic. I ask him what "shekhinah" means. "That's Hebrew," he says. "It means Glory of God." He relates to me a tale from the Old Testament about Hebrews setting off to follow God, who appears to them by day as a cloud, by night as a ball of fire.

His eyes are shining. Maybe a little too brightly. I wonder how long he can follow his cloud before he burns himself up.

He recalls, or rather he cannot forget, how it felt to suffer. He smiles as he tells about his struggle to beg, borrow and earn the money to pay for school, the years he spent scavenging rotten fruit from Tamale's gutters, to assuage hunger pains. He eventually became a Catholic and earned a scholarship to study tropical medicine in England. He was never tempted to stay and reap the benefits of a first world salary. He came home to work.

His clinic is built through charitable donations from people in Europe, and from individuals, many Catholic, here in Ghana. He doesn't solicit funds, doesn't accept donations with "strings attached." He carefully circumvents the traditional system here by which favours or gifts received are favours or gifts owed. There is no queue-jumping in his clinic. That discourages visits by privileged people for whom first-come-first-served and the poor-before-the-rich are unknown concepts.

David Abdullaye believes the clinic is not his but God's work, and that God will provide whenever medicine, materials or funds run out. He exudes faith in a God I have neglected, or never known.

The sceptic, cynic, non-believer in me is shaken. For a few moments in the Shekhinah Clinic I can forget all the reasons I have carefully constructed for believing that Africa is doomed. Dr. Abdullaye has restored my faith in the power of faith, and given me more grounds to believe that Africa's salvation lies in her own people — as long as there is a little help from friends outside. And above?

Chapter 8

No condition is permanent

*If we are not true to our most basic principles of multilateralism and humanitarian ethics, we will be accused of inconsistency at best, hypocrisy at worst. —
Kofi Annan, Secretary General of the United Nations, September 9, 1999*

It was Tuesday, November 2, 1992. Hot, sunny, and hope was running high. Ghanaians had been waiting for this day for weeks, or months, or perhaps for more than a decade — since 1981 when Flight Lieutenant Jerry John Rawlings overthrew the elected civilian president and installed himself as President of Ghana, for the second time. For the past eleven years Ghana had been ruled by President Rawlings' Provisional National Defence Council, and people had been wondering for years if that "provisional" had become "permanent."

But as people in Ghana liked to say and also to write all over their vehicles, "No condition is permanent." They firmly believed that November 2 was their day for change. It was the day they were to cast their ballots in the presidential elections. People told me this was a strategic date for President J.J. Rawlings — Ghanaians maintained that Tuesday and the number "two" were somehow connected to the president's own fetish spirits. I was more inclined to see the chosen date as a stroke of strategic genius, never lacking in Africa.

The Ghanaian elections coincided with the US presidential vote in 1992, meaning that the Ghanaian elections would receive precious little notice from the world at large. Why Rawlings and his strategists might not wish their elections to hit the world's news headlines would become apparent to me only later.

I was moving through Tamale and the outlying villages with a Ghanaian journalist whose name there's no need to mention. He had offered to "protect" me while I interviewed voters. Many feared that the presidential election would not pass without violence. In the weeks prior to the elections, tempers had been short and emotions frayed. I'd witnessed fistfights between people with stakes in opposing parties. I had thought it very gallant of this journalist whom I barely knew to offer to shield me from any violence that might erupt in the polling stations we visited.

We had been under way only an hour when I began to regret having accepted his offer. First, he tried to keep me away from long lines of would-be voters, many of whom were barely up to my waist and most definitely several years underage. When I approached them and began to interview them, he shooed them away. Told me they were just kids and that I shouldn't believe they were really there to vote, although it was patently obvious to me that they were — they all had voting cards in their hands and told me their man was "J.J.," or Jerry John Rawlings, the incumbent.

We also came across two polling stations that were closed and surrounded by armed security men. There too he refused to allow me to stop and find out what had happened. I didn't want to seem rude or ungrateful, but that's how I was feeling when we exchanged heated words about how he was crowding me.

By midday I finally twigged to the obvious. He had been sent not to protect me from getting hurt but to shield me from getting at the truth of what was going on that morning. I later learned he was paid handsomely for shadowing me that day. From the Big Men in Rawlings' ruling party, he received a colour television and a sum of money equivalent to about a year's salary that he received at the state news agency. Fortunately, I managed to ditch him at noon and get out on my own to see what was really happening. It was not at all as I'd imagined the advent of democracy in Africa.

Naïve as it now seems with the advantage of hindsight, I was one of many in Ghana — and all over Africa — who really believed that the metamorphosis from Dictatorship to Democracy was as simple as E for Elections. It seemed so straightforward — especially to me as a Canadian with dubious interest in civic duties even before I moved abroad and given up my right to vote.

Elections had always seemed to me rather tedious affairs hardly warranting a trip to the polls, let alone passionate emotions that could lead to violence. I'd grasped the basics back in high school when we spent a term or two studying something called "civics." Your name went on the electoral list when electoral agents came round to your house looking for eligible voters. This was easy in Canada where just about everyone had a valid birth certificate and was on government records somewhere or other.

Then on election day, you went to the nearest polling station (usually within walking distance in cities and usually in your own car in rural areas), you picked up your ballot, marked an "x" beside the name of your favourite candidate or party. Fortunately, you could read what was printed on the ballot because your parents, like most Canadian adults, dutifully paid taxes so that you could benefit from free education for twelve years or so. Ballot x'ed, you then just dropped it in the ballot box. Those would all be gathered up (by impartial people) and counted (impartially) and then results would be tallied (impartially) and presto — D for democracy. No matter who won, in Canada it was unlikely to change a whole lot in your everyday life. It wasn't absolute power that was up for grabs. The stakes certainly weren't high enough to kill for.

The biggest danger I faced growing up in Canada, I realize only now, is that it was too easy to take all we had for granted — not least of which democracy. It should have occurred to me in 1992 that it would all work very differently in Africa. But it didn't.

First, birth dates confirmed by birth certificates were a rarity. In many countries, much less than half of the population could read or write. With average annual incomes less than $300 Cdn. in most areas, people were generally so desperate for any cash at all that an affluent political candidate could easily buy their presence at rallies — and their votes — for a few cents and perhaps a T-shirt. And most of the continent had been ruled by dictators for some three decades and many of the younger would-be voters had been brainwashed by state media into believing that their head of state was a deity. Who's going to vote against God?

The Berlin Wall had been down for three years, Western powers no longer needed to coddle dictators who had been their allies during the Cold War. The Eastern Block was no more. The shards of the Soviet empire had better things to do than to buy friends in high places in Africa or to arm African rebel movements, although that didn't stop them from selling off massive amounts of leftover armaments to whatever militia, rebel band or mercenary group asking for them.

The "Communist menace" no longer justified Western democratic countries' friendship with oppressive despotic regimes. And so the West quickly backed away from the very men they had either put in place or aided and abetted to keep in power. This list was long. It included such figures as Mobutu Sese Seko, then president of Zaire, which would revert to its original name, Democratic Republic of Congo, in 1997 when Mobutu fled just before Laurent Désiré Kabila marched into the capital and seized power. In Africa, it was widely believed that the CIA had hoisted Mobutu to power in that enormous and resource-rich land. Mobutu's predecessor, Patrice Lumumba, had been assassinated, as the populist president Thomas Sankara in Burkina Faso would be a quarter of a century later. Both were guilty of the same crime; both had looked out for African interests and thus threatened the interests of Western powers on the African map. From independence right through to the end of the Cold War, African leaders who tried to serve the interests of their own people, and not those of powerful men on other continents, could not count on long lives.

For many years, humanitarian and non-governmental organizations, which had been mopping up the blood and soothing the hunger pangs caused by dictators in Africa, had been applying enormous pressure for change. Suddenly, at the beginning of the 1990s, the same Western democracies that for years had helped to stifle democracy in Africa, began to wash their hands of former "friends" on the continent. They discovered the urgent need for democracy — now that it served their interests to do so.

Donor countries — Canada, the UK, Germany, the US — were falling all over themselves to pump money into the elections that were going to lead to "good governance" in African countries. African leaders didn't comply willingly. In President Rawlings' case, he made a lot of noise about the West imposing multiparty politics that wouldn't work in Africa, before reluctantly ditching his military uniform and declaring himself candidate for president. There were many long and pedantic speeches from leading members of the ruling party who said "Western-style democracy" was not of interest to Ghanaians, whose only interest was satiating their "hunger" and not in such "frills" as free speech and voting. But as one of the World Bank's best "pupils" in Africa, President Rawlings and his regime had little choice but to comply with the sudden donor interest in democracy in his country.

People referred to winds of change and hope sweeping the continent. Democracy was going to usher in a new generation of presidents who would be accountable to their people. That is, African governments would have to at least *pretend* that they had the interests of their people at heart so they could be elected and re-elected, just the way our politicians did it.

The excesses of the past in so many African countries — the media restrictions, the heavy arm of the "security forces," the complete lack of transparency in government dealings and finances, a justice system tied to the whims of the president and his entourage, the unbridled megalomania of despots — all those would fade away as unpleasant memories of a bygone era all over Africa. All that was just an election away. Or so it looked. Back then. Before I saw how tricky elections could be when an electoral commission appointed by a ruling party could be "independent" in name only.

The "preparations" had begun long before election day, long before election day had even been scheduled. In fact, the ruling party was on the campaign trail long before political parties were legalized a few months before the polling and the opposition could finally hold meetings without fear of arrest. Yet Rawlings and his party had been on the campaign trail for many months, or even years. I think that's called an unfair head start. But, as I consoled myself, it was at least a start.

The opposition complained. Still, they had to join the race if they wanted to prove they were willing to confront Rawlings' omniscient party, which had transformed itself from the Provisional National Defence Council (PNDC) to the NDC, or New Democratic Congress. And at that point, after eleven years in power, Rawlings' NDC party by whatever name was an institution that could not be separated from any government office or organization in the country.

In the months prior to the presidential elections in Ghana, President Rawlings cavorted around the country in state-owned helicopters and military airplanes, sometimes piloting them himself. State television, GBC, brought us daily images of massive crowds, filmed through wide-angle lenses and exaggerating the turnout of supporters cheering for J.J. They didn't film the scenes I photographed in

Tamale. These involved huge transport trucks and fleets of smaller vans dispatched to fill up with idle youth, who leapt right in for the chance of a couple of hundred Cedis (worth about one Canadian quarter at the time) in exchange for nothing more than a free ride in the trucks to wherever J.J. Rawlings was campaigning that day. Nor did state media get around to covering a single one of the huge opposition rallies in town.

Yet, how was I to judge how popular Rawlings really was? The youth of the country, who constituted almost half the electorate, had grown up knowing nothing *but* J.J. Rawlings and the truth as it was served up to them on state-controlled television and radio, all there was at that point. I had good friends who admired him because he was not a demagogue. He was courageous (or crazy) enough to tackle sensitive, taboo subjects that more politically astute, lawyer-type candidates wouldn't touch with a ten-foot pestle — family planning and women's rights, for instance.

Many in the Northern Region distrusted the main opposition party, the NPP, which was headed by African historian, Adu Boahen. The NPP had a strong base in the powerful Ashanti region to the south. Northerners told me they viewed the NPP as an elite and urban party that would promote the cause of Ashantis.

In addition, the Northern Region was primarily Muslim whereas people in the south were mostly Christian. For those reasons, Boahen chose as his running mate a northerner — a very well known and respected lawyer in Tamale. Lawyer Alhassan, as he was affectionately known, swore to me that his party was going to win. His wife, a vivacious British woman who had lived and taught in Tamale for three decades, was already fretting aloud to me over the upheaval it would cause her when the time came to move to the capital, Accra.

Political posters now festooned just about every inch of mud wall in the region. "Gong-gong beaters" drummed up clouds of dust and election fever in neighbourhoods, pounding out propaganda for their political party of choice on their talking drums. It was hard to keep a cool head in the frenzy that heralded the new era that was said to be coming. Right up to polling day, I felt the euphoria that comes when it still looks like everything is going to change — overnight. I should have known better. I'd had warnings.

On the eve of the presidential poll, the international team of observers from the Commonwealth arrived. One of the Australian men, who parachuted in to observe the voting in Ghana's two Upper Regions, behaved and dressed as though he thought he had come for the filming of *Crocodile Dundee* — he seemed more interested in bars with cold beer and hot-blooded girls than in polling stations.

The two Commonwealth observers responsible for the Northern Region weren't a whole lot more "serious," as Ghanaian friends delicately phrased it. One was a man from Cyprus who spent his time haranguing anyone who would listen, about the "damn Turks" who had "no right" to be on his Mediterranean island.

The other was a stocky man from Tanzania, decked out in appropriate attire for, say, a bank in London, replete with smart pinstripes and gold watch. He told me he was based at Commonwealth headquarters in the UK. He was seriously upset about the conditions he was expected to endure in this northern outpost. He said that should Rawlings not get the 51 per cent of the vote he needed to win the first round of the elections, he, for one, would refuse to come back to observe the run-off. Not without some five-star hotels to keep him comfortable.

There were no Canadians on the Commonwealth team of observers, but there was a lone Canadian who had been sent, he said, to observe the elections for the Canadian foreign minister and to submit a confidential report for "internal purposes." He told me, in the privacy of my house, that Canada had refused to send anyone to join the Commonwealth team because the group was not considered "credible." This I found quite reassuring, given that I had leapt to the same conclusion. He said the British government, still staunchly Conservative at that point, was fully backing President Rawlings and his party, despite Rawlings' former reputation as a revolutionary on the continent. The revolutionary fervour — like Rawlings — had gone a little soft and paunchy around the middle in recent years and no longer inspired fear in the West.

The Canadian observer listed what he had already observed. The voters' lists were dubious, given that vital statistics were lacking in the region and that the independent electoral commission was anything but independent. The ruling party was too firmly entrenched in villages with their "revolutionary" defence committees and the First Lady's women's movement. Rawlings' men had founded a couple of fake opposition parties to obscure the picture for outsiders who came to observe the elections. Development vehicles provided by donor projects in the region (including Canadian ones) had been "borrowed" to run NDC campaigns.

He seemed well-informed and less prone than I to believe that despite the obvious and unfair advantages that Rawlings' party had, the actual voting would make up for that and reveal the true will of the people. This was a man who had observed a lot of elections in sunny places with shady politicians and the larger spectre of foreign influence and interests.

I suggested that the opposition party, so popular in the south, could still win the elections.

He smiled. "Rawlings will win," he said, as if it were a foregone conclusion and he had proof to that effect. Well, maybe it was and maybe he did.

A friend of mine, a journalist from BBC London who was being stalked and threatened in the days leading up to the election, had headed to the British High Commission to report her fears for her life to the representative of the British government in Ghana. She had already been smeared as a South African spy in one state-owned newspaper. She'd been told by another top man in Rawlings' inner circle that she should continue to report but to change the tone of her reports or else something might happen. It would happen not to her but to my son in Tamale, whose name and school they cited to her, just in case we still had any doubts that the Special Branch was not watching journalists very closely.

When she spoke to the British High Commissioner, he said that if she got into trouble with the Ghanaian authorities she had only herself to blame. She should expect no protection from the British government. Her conclusion: the Conservative British government of the time knew very well that Rawlings was going to win, and they were not going to worry about what went on behind the scenes to make sure he did — in fact they might even offer a hand behind the scenes. That old, better-the-devil-we-know approach to foreign policy that I've heard so many Western representatives in Africa evoke when explaining why they continued to support what were often unsavoury regimes on the continent.

I don't know why I hadn't read the signs and put all this together before election day, to see what was coming. While my BBC friend was being harassed in Accra, up in Tamale I had also been tailed in the days leading up to the elections. The only distinguishing — overtly menacing — thing about the two men who followed me everywhere was their fingernails. Those weren't nails; they were daggers. Except for a terrifying thief who had once come after me with a machete on the Cameroon coast, I had never seen any man anywhere with nails like that on all ten fingertips.

Those two men kept popping up wherever I went in Tamale. They'd be at our regular table in a small chop bar where a group of us met on Sundays to devour breasts of guinea fowl. Or they'd appear behind me in the market or tailing me on the road in a silver, unmarked sedan. I told myself not to panic — it was just standard procedure at such a tense time in Ghana's political history. After all, it was believed by many in Africa that all foreign journalists really were spies. It was normal that the security service put a tail on me. I had decided to ignore that sign, just as I had the obvious clues that the elections were not going to be run quite according to the rules.

In the afternoon of election day, I filed a preliminary report for BBC, pointing out the many obvious problems I had observed with the voting procedures in the region. These included underage voters, people who voted over and over again (the India ink applied to fingertips to identify those who had already voted could be removed easily with brake fluid), voters being chased away from ballot boxes by unidentified thugs, polling stations locked up tight while patient Ghanaians endured the blazing sun and queued up for hours, nourished only by the sometimes vain hope that eventually someone would open the doors and let them cast their ballots. The list went on and on. In my report, I called these "irregularities."

This report went out on BBC and was followed by a news story from Accra. In this, the head of the Commonwealth Commission in the capital, Accra, made a stunning proclamation to the world that the Ghanaian presidential elections had been "free and fair." That was a few hours before the polling booths were to close and before they had even opened in some remote parts of the Northern Region.

The Tanzanian election observer cornered me mid-afternoon, as I was heading out to do some more observation and he was heading in, to rest with a beer in the clubhouse on the compound where we lived. He asked me belligerently what kind of nonsense I had reported on the BBC about "irregularities." I began to list them off on my fingers.

He waved his arms about and said angrily. "Irregularities? Those aren't irregularities. What do you expect? This is Africa."

In some ways, he had a valid point. Those "irregularities" I'd seen during polling were trivial — *nothing* — compared with the evidence that poured in during the hours and days following the election, after the observers had boarded their planes and flown away. There were reports from reliable sources that government ministers themselves had been ferrying ballot boxes around, many of which had been stuffed with pre-marked ballots. There were more tales of intimidation of voters at polling stations and of highly dubious voters' lists.

But that wasn't all. There was also serious fraud I was to see that night after polling stations closed and in the days that followed as the results poured in — and kept changing. In one constituency, the first figures that went up on the huge blackboard mounted in downtown Tamale had an opposition presidential candidate winning by a margin of three thousand votes over J.J. Rawlings' NDC. That small victory — or defeat — was simply annulled using a rag on the blackboard. I watched it happen, then went to interview the regional head of the independent electoral commission. He told me there had been "mistakes" made and that he was now "correcting" them. But by then the international election observers had already gone home, declaring Ghana's elections "free and fair."

This rapidly entered the local and colourful slang lexicon in Tamale. At the market I would protest the rising price of tomatoes, at the pumps I would ask why the fuel price had leapt like that and they would smile, telling me the prices were "free and fair." Eventually this was shortened to "F and F," and used as a closing line in conversations about the ever-growing difficulties of making ends meet. "Ah well, it's all just F and F."

The Canadian observer had predicted that Rawlings would win with 53 per cent of the vote. He was wrong. When all results had been tallied (and retallied to ensure the right result?), Rawlings had won with more than 70 per cent of the vote. There would be no run-off, which would save that Tanzanian observer that dreaded second trip to Ghana's north. And the opposition would boycott the upcoming parliamentary elections slated for December, saying they couldn't fight for democracy when the playing field was as "tilted" as they alleged it had been for the presidential elections.

But for the donors, it was apparently enough. Ghana was now considered a democratic country with a democratically elected president. What nagged at me was the question of how Rawlings had come to power as a democrat. And why would donor countries that say they want democracy in Africa, paying enormous amounts for ballot papers and transparent ballot boxes, be so quick to whitewash and accept what are patently *un*democratic elections? Why would those observers so blatantly downplay election malpractice that would have anyone living in a Western democracy screaming foul had it occurred in their country?

I can't count the number of times I've heard it said: democracy couldn't work in Africa because Africa isn't "ready" or "mature enough." This familiar refrain has been sung by those ageing and ultra-conservative leaders in Africa who don't want to give up their opulent, deified existence or expose their foreign bank accounts. But at least their reticence to go democratic is comprehensible.

I've heard the same refrain chanted by academics and the intelligentsia outside Africa, where the theory was that democracy was a "Western" dogma being "imposed" on unwilling African societies for which it was simply not adapted. There were those who said that by pushing multiparty politics on Africa, the West was once again colonizing the continent. As if all those African intellectuals and professionals who had been clambering for political change and democracy for years, often at risk of their freedom and their lives, didn't count.

This suggestion that Africa wasn't "ripe" enough for democracy also came from French President Jacques Chirac. I felt he at least should have known better, since French interference in internal African affairs was one huge obstacle to democracy on the continent.

The most recent and stark example of this was in Brazzaville, capital of Congo. In 1997, the democratically elected leader of that country dared to challenge a giant French oil company's unofficial monopoly on his country's oil resources by talking to a giant American oil company. Suddenly the country's former (unelected) president, Denis Sassou Nguesso, was armed to the teeth with his own private army and the democratically elected president was toppled. But not neatly. Thousands and thousands died. Brazzaville was almost destroyed and two years later fighting continues. As far as I can tell, the *non-democratic* interference by the world's great democracies is all too often to blame for the mess of African politics.

Admittedly, there is plenty of room for discussion on how best to get representative governments up and running in Africa. Uganda's president Yoweri Museveni argued that multiparty politics were best suited to industrialized societies with large middle classes. He said they were treacherous in societies where 90 per cent of the populace couldn't read and where ethnicity was a dangerous political card played in a dangerous way by political party leaders. Speaking at an international conference on poverty, Museveni said that before Africa considered bowing to outside pressure for multiparty politics, the Swiss should open up their banks, expose some of the numbered ac-

110

counts and then restore some of those many billions to the rightful owners — the African people.

However, Museveni's reasons for keeping his country a "one-party democracy," surely an oxymoron, were suspect. So was support he received from his friends in the US and admirers at the World Bank, who backed him constantly despite his refusal to open up Uganda to multiparty politics. It looked to many on the continent that Uganda's president could get away with lots of things others couldn't because the US found him strategically useful. They counted on him to oppose the strongly Islamic regime in neighbouring Sudan and to counter French interests in the Great Lakes region of East Africa.

Many Africans suggest it is in fact the Western powers that once divided and ruled the continent — from an ocean away — that are still not ready for democracy in Africa. Genuine democracy might allow Africans to take control of their own resources for a change, and to rule themselves with their own best interests at heart. This would not be, at least not in the short-term, in the best *business* interests of the developed world. But back in 1992 when most African countries had yet to go "democratic," none of this was clear — at least not to me.

After I reported on Rawlings' "apparent" victory, the Regional Secretary of the Northern Region invited me to his office. He appraised me from over the frames of his reading glasses and then asked what kind of reporting I thought I was doing. "Apparent victory," he spat. "That means it was not a real victory. The Commonwealth team declared the election free and fair."

"Do you have a dictionary?" I said.

"Yes," he replied.

"I didn't mean it was not real. I meant that it had not yet been made official. That it was obviously a victory." I flipped through the dictionary. "See? Here it is. *Plainly visible for all to see.* That's what I meant."

"You did not," he said, using his finger to underscore another meaning of the word "apparent." "You see? Here it is. *Seeming but not real.* You are saying that the NDC victory was not real."

He was an elderly and a kind man, a true gentleman, who had told me on many occasions how he couldn't make it through the day if he didn't listen to the morning message of faith on the BBC World

Service. He didn't actually mean to make my life hell by taking me apart for almost every report I filed for the BBC and holding me up in his office for hours while we quibbled over the semantics of a single word. He was just terrified. For his position. For his reputation with the new — democratic — powers that be. And he wanted to maintain calm and peace in the Northern Region, which had already suffered so many ethnic clashes. He wanted to keep both his job and the peace. Poor man, in the end he wouldn't manage to do any of those things.

The peace that prevailed in the Northern Region was fragile. In the '80s there had been three outbreaks of inter-ethnic fighting and there were two major outbreaks in the four years we were there. There was nothing done whatsoever to prevent another, even worse, outbreak. The government went on making a pretence of peace — sending in the military to stop the fighting and then holding its official commissions of inquiry to investigate the causes of the fighting. Causes that everyone in the region understood quite well already. And if at first I didn't understand any of the ethnic problems, no matter; they would school me in those too.

Chapter 9

Petty, petty details

When the white man came we had the land and they had the Bible. They taught us to pray with our eyes closed and when we opened them, they had the land and we had the Bible. — Jomo Kenyatta, Kenya's first president

In the spring of 1992, people came to me with dire predictions about the extent of the ethnic trouble that was brewing. They seemed to think that if the government wouldn't do something to prevent it, perhaps the BBC might help by attracting international attention to the unresolved conflicts that simmered away in the region. But I was reluctant to report rumours and at that point that was all I had to go on.

Then Ghana's president came to Tamale and in one of his speeches declared that if he could, he himself would arm the subordinate ethnic groups to stand up and fight for their rights in the region. That certainly didn't do much to cool things down.

After that, the rumours of war intensified. The next fighting, people said to me, would be on a scale not witnessed in Ghana's history. Next time, they whispered, the fighting would involve the largest ethnic group in the region, the Konkombas, who had no political standing, no land, and grievances enough to raise an army. They had already fought against the Nanumbas, a so-called paramount group headed by a paramount chief. And now — so the rumours went — they were ready to fight the Gonjas, another of those powerful ethnic groups with a paramount chief.

Taking great liberty with what is an extremely complex issue, I had more or less boiled it down to this. In the Northern Region there were four ethnic groups — the Gonjas, Nanumbas, Dagombas and Mamprusis — that had officially recognized 'paramount chiefs.' Paramount chief was the anthropological term for a traditional ruler who presided over a fairly centralized and hierarchical social and political system. This paramount status came with a lot of advantages. Paramount chiefs had seats in the regional and national Houses of Chiefs, a powerful traditional form of government running parallel to the modern state. Paramount chiefs also owned land.

The trouble was, in the Northern Region there were about two dozen ethnic groups that were called "acephalous," literally people with no heads. Their opinion leaders, who in fact behaved like chiefs or headmen, had no officially recognized status. Worse, people of these acephalous groups were generally treated as second- or even third-class citizens. There had been several uprisings among some of the smaller acephalous groups over the years. But most recently, it had been — and still was — the populous Konkombas pushing for change, asking for paramount status. Or rather, demanding it.

Both Gonjas and Konkombas told me that the other side was busily arming itself, preparing to "defend" itself against the other.

Then one day a young man showed up at my door saying his leader wanted to see me. His leader? Nana Felix Atorsah II. I knew Nana Atorsah, the young and charismatic self-proclaimed "paramount chief" of the tiny Nawuri ethnic group, which officially and after forty years of struggling for it still had no legal claim to such a high-level chief. I'd met him during an official enquiry held into ethnic clashes between the Nawuri and their Gonja overlords back in 1991. During that enquiry he had filled my ears, offered me a litany of injustices, as he perceived them, in the way the government (or the British colonists before them) had handed out "paramount status" in the region. He went on at great length about the time being ripe for granting paramount status to all the acephalous ethnic groups in the Northern Region, about the need to put an end to the "unfair advantages" enjoyed by the four paramountcies.

Not coincidentally, the big Canadian and German development projects in the area had been advised by the authorities in Accra to focus their work (and naturally their funds) in the four districts where those four paramount chiefs had their palaces. This meant that nine other districts — and twenty-one other ethnic groups — were neatly excluded from millions of dollars and Deutsche Marks. This didn't help appease all those so-called "lesser" ethnic groups in the rest of the region, which had no paramount status and thus no seat in the powerful National House of Chiefs — and no land to call their own.

Nana Atorsah II had told me he wanted all of this changed. Even if it meant going to war. He's already done so once. I wondered if he had summoned me this time to tell me he was about to do so again. It wasn't until I was in the car on my way to the rendezvous with Atorsah that it occurred to me he should have no idea where I lived. But of course that was also silly. There were no secrets in Tamale. Nana Atorsah was said to have close connections with the Special Branch, as the secret service was called, as well as with the Committees for the Defence of the Revolution, the "CDRs" left over from President Rawlings' tired old "revolution." And of course I was kidding myself if I thought I was either anonymous or inconspicuous in that town.

Atorsah was waiting for me in a dusty, low-slung mud dwelling set well back from any discernible road. To get there I took an adventure walk over gullies and open sewers and strewn litter. Gone were the magnificent indigo *boubou* robe and the chief's hat adorned with small leather fetishes he claimed had been his father's, with which he'd impressed the hell out of me when he had addressed the official enquiry. Now he was caked in dust, clad in second-hand clothes that were the mainstay of the day-to-day wardrobe in the country: jeans and T-shirt. His eyes were hidden by a baseball cap. He looked smaller than I remembered, like a different person entirely. I looked closely and he smiled. Only then did I catch a hint of that proud, arresting man who had made my head swim throughout the enquiry. He said he was on the run; a dozen security men had come to his house in the capital, Accra, to arrest him and several of his advisers. He'd hitched a ride in the back of a truck loaded with yams. He told me he'd disguised himself as a yam farmer and he wanted me to file a report to the BBC saying the authorities were trying to arrest the Nawuri paramount chief.

Rather than make any foolish promises that might turn me into his mouthpiece, I asked him why they were trying to arrest him. He admitted that he'd been "travelling through the Northern Region" and "talking to leaders of acephalous groups" but insisted he was doing this only to help "keep peace." I held my tongue and allowed him to continue. He said the only reason the authorities were trying to arrest him was because the Gonjas were preparing for war and they wanted him out of the way.

I asked him if perhaps the authorities knew something that I didn't. Surely if he was instigating people to arms they had a very good reason to arrest him? It was easier to be a hard-nosed, straight-shooting journalist with an Atorsah who looked like a farmer of yams than it had been with a crown prince wearing a fez adorned with dozens of powerful fetishes, or juju.

He replied, every dusty inch the modest farmer he was impersonating, "Not at all. I am trying to keep peace. I've come to speak to the regional secretary and warn him." He said he had to remain incognito in Tamale because if he didn't, the Gonjas would kill him. He said the Gonjas were gearing up for war and that this time the fighting would not be a small thing. I took note, filed a cautious report and felt quite relieved when I learned through the yam vine that Atorsah had left town again. My relief was short-lived.

The war erupted in June 1992, just as everyone had warned me it would. And as predicted, this time it involved not only the relatively small Nawuri people against the Gonjas but the formidable Konkombas too. The Konkombas were the main producers of agricultural products and pottery, a hard-working and long-subservient people without any claim to land or paramount status. They were also extremely traditional in their approach to warfare. Between the age of about ten and their "first time with a woman," young Konkomba males constituted a kind of warrior class, armed mostly with traditional weapons that they used effectively when hunting, or when fighting their enemies.

When the Konkombas took on the Gonjas in a three-day war, it was a horrific and bloody fight that left hundreds dead and thousands homeless. The Gonjas fled by the thousands to Tamale. In breathless terror, they spoke into my microphone about Konkomba atrocities: pregnant women being bashed to death against trees by Konkomba warriors. Gonja women at the makeshift refugee camp in Tamale showed me how they had in the panic stuck nails through their small sons' ears, inserted earrings to try to fool the Konkomba attackers into thinking boys were girls. The Konkombas, they said, had a policy of exterminating all males in a village, lest that child grow up to be a warrior. That was why they also took no chances with pregnant women, lest the offspring inside might be a future warrior.

It was impossible to find a Konkomba in Tamale to hear their side of the story. There were no Konkombas around. They had gone into hiding in the bush.

I needed some official view on the events. I went to see the regional secretary, that very gentleman who wanted so desperately to argue semantics with me, to talk about faith and not politics. I might have saved his time — and my own. I started by asking how many had died, saying that I'd heard the death toll was sixty-six.

He leaned across his desk and retorted, "You journalists. Why do you always want to know these petty, petty details? Anyway, you British should concentrate on your own wars. Look at what's going on in Ireland. What business is this of the BBC?"

I didn't bother telling him I was not British and that were I in Ireland, I would report on that conflict too. I didn't bother trying to remind him that the only reason he thought this no business of the BBC was that it directly concerned him and his position. And I unkindly logged his words "petty, petty details" for quoting on the radio.

Next morning before dawn I linked up with a friend and fellow journalist, Iliasu, to head out to Salaga to see if we couldn't get some firsthand information.

There's been more than enough lurid coverage of ethnic slaughter in Africa on television over the years since then, so I will not go into detail here. Just about everyone knows what it looks like when people take up arms — AK-47s, Kalashnikovs, bows and arrows, machetes — to set about massacring an "enemy" tribe. What is so rarely explained is what lies behind those terrifying television images. There is just no room in our fast-paced media for complex histories like this one, which defies being told in fewer than many thousand words, let alone a couple of hundred words and a byte of sound or two on the evening news. There is no time to explain what lies behind terrifying television clips of land disputes or ethnic antagonism — exacerbated first by colonial and later by African governments supported by foreign powers. There is also no word on how such slaughters might have been prevented. There is always, however, room for sensational and gory details, which so skew the outside world's comprehension of Africa and her people. Always room for bits of footage in which Africans shoot or hack fellow Africans to pieces.

Fortunately, I didn't have a television camera for the visits that Iliasu and I made into the war zone, into villages where there was unearthly silence, a smell that defies description, and cadavers (or bits of them) — all too painful to summon or belabour here. The purpose of our visit was not to sensationalize; it was to collect some accurate information, a few of those "petty, petty details" on how many had died in the three-day war between Konkombas and Gonjas. A hundred? Several hundred? Who was counting? Not the regional secretary and not the government, not as far as we could tell.

Iliasu and I had no intention of standing there in that hellish silence and stench, taking down numbers as the military stacked up the bodies. They told us that in just this one village, they had so far collected over a hundred bodies. They had masks and nerves of steel. I had neither. I turned away, gagging and trembling like a woman possessed. Iliasu and those soldiers were made of tougher stuff than I was. I couldn't get away from there fast enough. Years later, those few moments in that dead village still haunt my waking hours.

Next we visited the Kpembe-wura, the Gonja divisional chief who had taken refuge in the town of Salaga. He told us he had lost fourteen sons in the battle. The military had moved in to stop the fighting, but now the soldiers told us they had little hope of controlling the Konkombas and the situation was extremely tense.

"You know the Konkombas," said one soldier. "You can't fight them. They live in the bush. They know the bush. They're here and then they're there." He used his fingers pedalling the air to show us what he meant, made little clucking noises with his tongue. "The Konkombas are like guinea fowl."

He and a whole battalion were camped out in Salaga and didn't seem inclined to enter any territory where the Konkombas might be still armed and waiting for them. Mind you, I heard loud discussions about the shortage of fuel for their vehicles, so they may have been holed up in that makeshift military camp for purely logistical reasons.

In Salaga, people were complaining bitterly about the military presence, necessary as it was given that the government had come up with no solutions to the problems of chiefs and land in the area. They accused the soldiers of helping themselves to all the roaming cattle they could find, roasting the beef on open fires and gorging themselves on the spoils of war.

The Kpembe-wura allowed me to photograph him inside his makeshift palace in Salaga, with his youngest son seated beside him. Looking tired and very old, he told me this would be the first photograph for him. He was allowing it only because he had decided, after the battle, that he was beyond handling the powerful fetish powers that came with this district chief status. He sat staring impassively into the camera, with his youngest son of just five beside him on his concrete throne, surrounded by carpets and pillows. He said that with his other sons now gone, that small boy would be his heir to the throne, the royal skins.

I asked him if peace had been restored to the area, as the government had been claiming. He said, "There's no peace here, only soldiers."

This was only months before the elections were to be held and the government was handling the whole thing like the explosive potato it was, not touching the ethnic issue at all so as not to lose the votes of any ethnic group.

Just before the elections, I met with members of the Konkomba Youth Association. Several of them worked with the international missionary organization, the Summer Institute of Linguistics, which works worldwide to promote Christianity by translating the Bible into local languages. For the past two decades, these Christian missionaries and linguists had been working to educate some of the acephalous groups, particularly the Konkombas. The general idea seemed to be to get the Konkomba language down on paper, teach the Konkombas how to read and, mostly, to make sure they were reading the Bible in their own language. With the Konkombas becoming Christians, there was yet another potential element for conflict in the ethnic tinderbox of northern Ghana — the paramount groups were largely Muslim.

The result of twenty years of missionary education was a generation of Konkomba youths, highly educated, motivated, and all too aware of their long-time subservience to the paramount chiefs of the overlord groups. As I sat there in the offices of the Summer Institute of Linguistics that night, listening to four young — Christian — Konkombas talking, a spasm of fear worked its way from my stomach outwards to raise goosebumps on my arms. The youths were animated, their eyes bright, their hands slashing the air as though they were already wielding weapons. Their leader put it this way. "We outnumber all the other ethnic groups in the region. We are no longer going to submit to the indignity and injustice of paying tithes to anyone. We are demanding recognition for our chiefs and a seat in the House of Chiefs. If not, we will fight."

It was the same battle cry I'd heard from Nana Atorsah II.

I asked them why, when they were so numerous, they couldn't use the upcoming elections to ensure that Konkombas had several MPs in the new parliament that would be formed. Surely that would be the safest and most peaceful way to bring about change, and to fight — peacefully — for a change in their status.

"Oh, we will go out in force and vote in the elections," said the Konkomba youth leader. "And we the Konkombas will then have our own parliamentarians, and when we do, they will make noise in Accra and the government will be forced to grant us paramount status."

I nodded. This wasn't exactly the way the African activists and donor countries pushing for democracy and multiparty elections had foreseen it, I was sure, but no need to bring that up now. I also guessed this was not the kind of militant religious fervour, turned ethnic, that the missionaries had intended. At least I hoped it wasn't.

"The way it is we cannot accept," he continued. "The whole regional administration here is filled only with princes from the paramount groups, the Gonjas or Dagombas or Nanumbas or Mamprusis. It's time we minority groups also had our part of the cake." He made a nasty sound. "Imagine. They call us a minority group but we outnumber them all. If the Gonjas still want to claim they own all the land, if they base their land ownership on ancient conquests, then we will do the same."

"What do you mean?" I said.

"Look, if after the elections things don't change and we don't get full recognition of our chiefs and get a paramount chief, we will fight. And since we outnumber the Gonjas, we can fight until there are only ten of us Konkombas left. By then we will have killed all the Gonjas and then we will just start to reproduce to fill up the region. We don't mind. We know how to reproduce in numbers."

"That doesn't sound very good," I said finally.

"It's not good. But that's how it is. You know what the Gonjas and Dagombas are suggesting to the government? They're saying that we and all the other so-called acephalous tribes in the region should get paramount status. That doesn't bother them as long as their paramount chiefs are promoted to be kings! That we will never accept." He hammered a fist into his open palm so hard that it sounded like a gunshot and made me flinch.

"Never!" he said. "We are warriors and we will fight."

We had already left Tamale when the next war — the worst one yet — finally did break out in early 1994. People in Tamale wrote to us about it. The dead numbered in the thousands, the destruction was in the millions and the new outpouring of hatred was not quantifiable. Dagomba friends, people who had socialized and joked with Konkombas while we'd been in Tamale, now wrote to me about the "evil" Konkombas. They went on to allege that one of the men who had spearheaded the weapons build-up was a Konkomba man who had worked on the Canadian development project and lived on the compound with us. One woman suggested that I was probably "in with the Konkombas" because I'd known this man.

I didn't know him well, but I knew his wife and his five children. His daughter, whom I'll call Juliana, had all but lived with us for four years, travelled with us when we took trips north to Burkina Faso or south to the coast. Juliana and my daughter shared everything, their secrets, their girlhood worries, even the lice that had to be treated in their hair about once a week.

People now wrote to tell us that Juliana's father had stocked weapons in the Canadian freezer that came with his Canadian-made house on the Canadian development project compound.

We wrote back, frantic for news of his wife and family — particularly Juliana. None of our correspondents in Tamale was willing or able to say what had become of the family.

My daughter was morose and bewildered. She wrote letter after letter, but we had no address for Juliana's family. We'd heard on news reports, read in press clippings and letters from friends in Tamale that all Konkombas had fled because they were no longer welcome in Tamale. Konkombas married to Gonjas or to Dagombas had to run for their lives or run the risk of being poisoned by the Gonja or Dagomba extended family. In Tamale town, even those suspected of being Konkomba were killed.

It wasn't until 1995 that friends who were travelling in Ghana finally tracked down Juliana and gave her our address. That is how we learned what had befallen the family during and after that horrific war in 1994. The family had been evacuated by the military to their camp where they had lived as refugees for some months, under heavy security, until they could be smuggled out of Tamale and south to Accra in a military convoy. Juliana's father had abandoned them, taking up with another woman. He'd left his wife and five children destitute. They were surviving only through the good graces of the evangelistic church to which they belonged. Juliana wrote about these woes to my daughter, who insisted we send money to help out. We did. But it never seemed to arrive.

Then we lost track of them altogether, those close friends who had shared peaceful years and good times with us in Tamale, who are now living in exile in their own country because their father was alleged to have helped start a war — a war that didn't change a thing except to end or destroy the lives of thousands of people.

Nothing has been done since then to change the situation in the region to ensure a more equitable distribution of the land — or privilege. All remains just as it was and the soldiers are still in place, even in 2000. The government in Accra has taken no action, and in Ghana there's been more press coverage given to President Rawlings' purchase of a presidential jet than there ever was to the ethnic bomb waiting to explode in the Northern Region. The threat of war is always there.

But now the world has bigger fish to fry, bigger wars to fight in more politically or economically "interesting" parts of the world. So even if fighting breaks out again in northern Ghana, it is doubtful the world will notice. And if they do it will probably be a couple of lines of print at the bottom of a page of a newspaper, and the conflict will likely be blamed on "ethnic hatred," when it's really a case of serious injustices and inequities in power and land ownership accorded different ethnic groups by history or by politicians of the day.

If governments won't act to even things out, I suppose it's inevitable that one day people will take up arms to fight wars that they can ill afford.

Chapter 10

Calling all dreamers

Suddenly, our time in Ghana was about to end. Four years had elapsed, just like that. I don't know what we expected as we prepared to pack our lives up in boxes (again) for a move to a new country. Nothing probably. I couldn't see beyond the gloom of impending departure. Despite all the political hanky-panky, the ethnic intrigue, the lack of amenities in Tamale — or maybe because of those things — I'd come to love living there. It had become home.

I simply could not imagine finding the energy to start a new life somewhere else when I had the one I wanted right there in Tamale. I could not imagine leaving that magical regional capital in northern Ghana that sported only the one traffic light at the only almost-major intersection, as a sign that it was indeed part of the fast-paced road into the twenty-first century. Or twentieth. It didn't matter. Timelessness was one of the things I loved most about living there, some eight hundred kilometres north of the crashing waves and the slave castles on the once famous or infamous Gold Coast of colonial and slave-trading days.

Months before we were to leave, I began to put together my scrapbooks and started to catalogue my premature nostalgia for Tamale. One of its many charms had been its size and relative isolation from the world. It had been so easy to ignore global happenings and to tunnel instead into the fascinating local world of mysteries and intrigue. When the Gulf War was in full Technicolor on televisions all over the world, there had been no television reception in northern Ghana. When in 1999, I happened to be in Timbuktu with a group of journalists from around the world, I was the only one there who had no idea that I was supposed to recognize instantly one Peter Arnett, Mr. Gulf War, formerly of CNN, who was in our midst. He quickly forgave me my ignorance and set me straight. But that also me realize how blissfully unaware we'd been back in 1991, missing that round-the-clock television coverage that showed the world (well, most of it) what Desert Storm actually looked like, with the missiles and the explosions and oil fires.

Like most people in northern Ghana, the only images we had of global events were those we conjured in our heads from reports we heard on the radio. As elsewhere in rural Africa, Ghanaians were often glued to their radios, tuning in to national and international shortwave radio to follow current events. They were extremely well informed about what was what out there in the rest of the world, a world that didn't know they even existed.

Their take on world news was absolutely their own; they had an uncanny ability to see through the hype of headlines or detect the slant of newscasts coming from anywhere, be it their own capital or Washington or Moscow. They listened to accounts from all sides and decided for themselves who was hero and who was villain. During the Gulf War, many people in the Northern Region became fascinated with the character of Saddam Hussein, who could so upset the superpowers and whom they tended to view as heroic little David taking on brutish Goliath. The hottest new hairstyle in Tamale, a short brushy look for men, was known as the "Saddam Cut." When you spiked the volleyball over the net, you were launching a "Scud missile." And baby boys born during that war had a good chance of being named after the Iraqi president.

Most of those earth-shattering world events seemed very far removed from our lives in Tamale. We talked about the rains and whether the harvests might be good this year, about the complexities of the ethnic fighting and land tenure problems, about which important men were messing around with which girls in town, about witches and witchcraft and whether the dewitching shrines in the region were anthropological artifacts or still very real necessities in the late twentieth century.

We marvelled over local mysteries along with everyone else. There was the python, believed to be sacred, that had taken to sunning itself on the roadside in front of the library, day after day. The library had an amazing collection of mouldy books dating back to colonial times, which was the last time any acquisitions had been made.

We exchanged tales of a mysterious creature — or spirit — that terrified Tamale for two nights. It hunted down livestock, severed the heads and then dismembered its dead prey with almost surgical precision, eating only the intestines. A local veterinarian told me this had to be some kind of wild cat. Local fetish priests hinted at something much more sinister and uncontrollable.

We played the local lottery along with everyone else and followed the lucky numbers on Saturday nights when they were announced in Accra. We shared the joy of the neighbouring village when nearly all the men living there won the lottery. Turns out they had all obeyed the advice of their "Professor Lotto" and all used the same "lucky number," which they obtained from the rear license plate of a vehicle that had tipped onto its side in front of their village. Vehicles that had been in accidents were said to provide lucky numbers in the lottery. That passenger truck had the words "Everything By God" painted across the back, just over that lucky license plate that had brought good fortune to the village.

The next week, a tow-truck sent to right the vehicle also capsized into the deep ditch on the roadside, and once again, the villagers used its number plate to select their lotto numbers. Against all odds I'm familiar with, this also turned out to be a winning number on the following Saturday night.

This was no million-dollar lottery. The winners had enough to buy at most a new bicycle. Yet a new bicycle in the village was no different from a new Rolls Royce to a 6/49-winner back home in Nova Scotia.

That good luck for the village meant bad luck for most of the lottery dealers in Tamale. They had to put up only a nominal sum to be permitted to sell tickets and from these sales there were expected to pay any winners. When an entire village won, the lottery dealers wound up losing not only their earnings but everything they owned. There were emotional and occasionally tense scenes when the winners went to claim their due.

These were the kinds of stories that confounded and fascinated me in Tamale, the kind of stories I loved to delve into and report on. They didn't even scrape the surface of what was there to be discovered, but they hinted at the magic that swirled around us in that northern enclave. A journalist friend, Iliasu Adam, who hails from Tamale, called his "the town of unresolved puzzles."

Still, as Karl reminded me almost daily, it was time to stop chasing after stories and to stop missing Tamale even before we'd packed up. It was also high time that I faced the fact that we were leaving. He came home from work every day and asked me how the packing was going, when it was plain to see I had not placed a single thing in a single box, hadn't yet managed to scrounge any boxes. He was getting concerned that I was falling to pieces. I was. I didn't want to leave, so I certainly didn't look forward to going anywhere else. All that and those we'd be leaving behind preoccupied me much more than any expectations of what we would find, what kind of life awaited us in Kenya.

Kenya had never been high on my list of priority destinations, if such a list existed in my head. Actually, so far in our lives, we had just gone where the harmattan wind blew us from one West African country to another, where jobs awaited one or the other of us — this time I was the one signing a contract to work in Kenya. So far, we'd found ourselves in little-known places that didn't ring a lot of bells with people outside Africa.

Kenya was a major tourist destination. Everyone had heard of Kenya. Everyone had seen television programs about the magnificent game parks and the "big five" that ranged there — elephants, lions, buffaloes, rhinos and leopards. Kenyan tourism advertisements called on "dreamers" to come and savour "sun-drenched beaches," "the bluest of seas, warm with the Indian Ocean current," "four-wheel drive safaris through the tall grassland . . . with cheetah and lion just alongside." These tantalizing dreams were said to come true in Kenya, with "long, icy cocktails in the cool evening breeze," with "nights that are filled with romance" and "life in the very lap of luxury, with every whim attended."

That sure didn't sound like the Africa I knew and had come to love. It neglected to mention the greatest attraction of all in any country — its people.

There were daily charter flights from Germany to the coastal city of Mombasa. Hundreds of thousands of European tourists made their way to Kenya every year for a few days on those sun-drenched beaches and a few days of safari through splendid national parks. All of this, in my perverse way of thinking, was already a major strike against living in Kenya. Perhaps that marvellous country — with that snow-capped mountain plonked right on the equator, its vast national parks teeming with the kings of the beasts, that beautiful coastline — was just too obviously appealing for my contrary and reactionary personality.

Life might be too easy and too comfortable there. Worse, we might actually get too used to that perfect upland climate in Nairobi and all that postcard beauty. We might be lured by the physical luxury into forgetting all the human and social charms of West Africa, where people were the mainstay of our happiness and basic amenities seemed like great luxuries that made us feel blessed when they were there. In Tamale, my definition of a good day, a day when the stars were all aligned in our favour, was a twenty-four-hour period during which: water ran from the taps; current came from the electrical sockets; and the telephone line (we had just got a few months before our departure) was alive and humming.

I fretted. I tried not to think ahead. Taking a leaf from the books of so many people in Tamale who could not afford to think ahead because they were too busy trying to figure out how they would make ends meet that very day, I too concentrated on taking each day as it came. I clung resolutely to the past and present. Indeed, Ghanaian friends eager to comfort me kept saying they knew that we would be coming back, that it was just a matter of time. It was in God's hands and God would most definitely bring us back because it was obviously what we wanted.

European friends took a more pragmatic tack, speaking to us about the assuredly wonderful future that lay ahead in Kenya. Some who knew East Africa said they envied us the move to Kenya. "You'll love it there," they assured us. It was, they said, "more developed" and "very beautiful." One German man who had spent two years on the Tanzanian coast (justified by his job on a rural development project) could hardly contain himself when, usually deep into his sixth or seventh or eighth beer of the evening, he launched into a monologue on his glorious years in East Africa. He thought East Africa vastly superior to West Africa, the climate and the people far more "civilized."

Next, he wanted to tell me about the almost limitless recreation opportunities available to development people fortunate enough to be posted in East Africa. He had got his pilot's license there and flown a small plane out over the Indian Ocean. He'd explored Zanzibar from the air, scuba-dived around the coral reefs. He'd savoured the delights of bright lights in the cities, Dar es Salaam and Nairobi, the luxury lodges in Kenya's Masai Mara and Tanzania's spectacular

Serengeti. "So on weekends you can get away on safari in decent places. Not like this, this Mole Game Park here. Pathetic." And with a wave of his cigarette and a puff of toxic smoke he dismissed the park and the entire Northern Region of Ghana as worthy of his contempt — or perhaps even beneath it.

I didn't react. I admit that I couldn't explain my contentment in northern Ghana, not to myself and certainly not in so many words to a man who loathed the place. Even my mother, who had listened to me praising Africa for endless hours, contradicting so much of the African news she heard, read or watched on television, had trouble understanding our affection for northern Ghana. She and my father had come to visit us twice in Tamale, and on the last visit she had quite inadvertently let slip her real feelings about the place.

It was an extremely hot day, not unusual, and we were driving past a place known as the "police park," which had seen better days as a grassy playground for children when it was marked off as a park right behind the colonial police barracks. In modern times, it had become an enormous public toilet and there was nothing that could be said to excuse the stench. I told her to wind up her window. She did. It was hot. Very, very hot.

We drove along in silence for a couple of minutes before she said, "You know, the good thing about coming to visit you here is that it makes me so happy to go home again. Really," she continued, "with all the beautiful places there are in the world, don't you wonder why you landed here, in a place like this?"

I laughed, then murmured something vague about the wonderful sense of community here in northern Ghana, the richness of the cultural landscape, the wonderful and witty people who had become such good friends. I came up with implausible words like "human-scape," which I said truthfully was second to none anywhere we'd lived and which was, admittedly, in inverse proportion to the rapidly deteriorating and unspectacular landscape that surrounded us.

Although she hadn't said it in so many flattering words, I knew she had also been quite impressed by Mole Game Park. It was difficult not to be impressed by the decaying motel and the long, rough drive it took to get there from Tamale. My parents had been sitting (too) quietly in the back seat of the van on the way home, next to the children. I recall glancing at them a couple of times, worried that the hot wind blasting through the vehicle was really becoming too much for them. My father's face was a bright red and I could see he was suffering a good deal of discomfort. But for a long time they said nothing. Not a hint of a complaint. A different generation from mine altogether.

Eventually my father, the intrepid investigator of all things electrical and mechanical, began to investigate. He discovered that the heater, which had never been used before to my knowledge, was now jammed on full. In addition to the shimmering heat of the air around us, they were getting a full blast of heated air from the engine of that hard-working van as it navigated the jolting craters on the dirt track that linked Mole and Tamale. Once again, though, the trip to Mole had helped my mother put things in perspective. When she was in Tamale, she dreamed of the relative luxury and comfort of her life in Nova Scotia. After Mole, she was thrilled to be back in the relative comfort of Tamale.

It's true that Mole National Park in Ghana could not compare with those famed East African safari parks. There were none of those things associated with East African safari lodges — the long, lean Maasai dancers decked out in full hunter regalia, their faces caked with ochre as they pranced about on shining tile or hardwood floors in lodge dining rooms while guests ploughed their way through mountains of bush meat and tropical fruit served up by subservient waiters in smart uniforms. It has to be said that Mole wouldn't win even one fallen star from Michelin for accommodation or cuisine. In fact, Mole was undeniably short on even the basics.

Like so many things in Ghana, Mole National Park had been established in the heady days of early independence under the country's first president, Kwame Nkrumah, who was never short on vision, not even after his ambitious government had squandered the country's cash. The lodge at Mole had been put up in those days, erected out of concrete and dreams. Shortly thereafter, it had started to go to seed. In 1990, the first time we visited the park, it was patently clear that the lodge was suffering from the all-too-common problems of decay, neglect and the economic catastrophe that had struck Ghana in the 1970s under President Ignatius Acheampong, and then hung on in much of the country.

The swimming pool had fallen into the same state of total disrepair as nearly all the pools — some even Olympic sized — in state hotels throughout the country. In Mole, the pool was either completely empty or else half full of green and pungent water pumped up from the elephants' waterhole some two hundred metres below the lodge. It goes without saying that the staff had no chemicals for treating the water, that the pump had long since ceased to work, and that there was no budget to reverse the situation. Certainly not then, after almost ten years of vicious austerity measures in place on Ghana's public sector.

The lodge itself had been built in the angular and God-defying architectural style popular in the late '50s and early '60s. This seemed to me to have been a time when things man-made and artificial were more than just fashion but rather monuments to some kind of unholy faith in secular Western society. This society believed, for a few fleeting seconds in the geological time frame, that human beings could conquer nature and play at being God without any consequence. That notion still persists among some high-wheeling economists, who think human genius and technology will get us out of the hot water we're in with Mother Nature, and spare us the heat we've generated on this planet. Humility, moderation and a bit of human kindness might have been more the ticket, but these seemed to have gone missing from the world's financial capitals towards the start of the twenty-first century.

The Mole lodge struck me as a kind of memorial, a museum of human folly in Africa and elsewhere. It symbolized so much that had been done wrong on the continent by foreigners and by Africans themselves, by governments that still seemed to believe that "modern" and "progressive" were synonymous with anything not African or made by human hands. The idea seemed to be that nature could be overcome with enough concrete and air conditioning.

There had been no attempt to use local building materials such as the thatch and clay that were well adapted to the conditions and the climate. No attempt either to pretend that the low-slung concrete motel actually belonged there or should try to fit the African landscape. The long rows of rooms, each marked by a jagged roof set at an angry angle towards the heavens, had been erected on the edge of a crumbling and rocky cliff. A front veranda running along the cliff side of the lodge allowed guests a magnificent view of the savannah to the west. That was where the wildlife roamed. During the day, the veranda and the rooms received the full brunt of the blazing sun, making the lodge just about the hottest place on the face of this earth, at least of the hot parts I've sampled.

I can't even begin to explain why it seemed like such a magical place. But it was, especially late in the day when the sun dipped mercifully into the scraggy tops of the trees on the western horizon. That was when the elephants below began to trumpet and appear in clearings around the water holes. The cliff was a tranquil and lovely spot to sit with binoculars in hand to savour dreams of the African hinter-land as it once was. The wildlife officers who ran the park itself and guided visitors on foot or in vehicles through the reserve were experi-enced, knowledgeable, conscientious, and just plain good company, paying great attention to excited children, as was the African way.

The motel staff were affable and when you could find them, they could on occasion even be helpful. When the official vehicle was working and when someone had a few Cedis for petrol to get to the nearest village market, there was an evening meal served. The once extensive menu had been considerably simplified over the years. There was rice with tomato sauce and chicken or guinea fowl, and any permutation thereof. The one or two hours one had to wait served as a very effective "appetizer" and greatly increased apprecia-tion of the meal when it finally appeared.

Only two people that I know of ever fell ill after such a meal, a German friend from Tamale, who admitted that he had always suf-fered from a weak stomach, and his Thai wife who had never accept-ed the generally lackadaisical approach to food hygiene in the region.

The only other complaints I ever heard about the food or ser-vice came from tourists who failed to succumb right away to the charms of the place. In my view, their mistake was coming to Mole Park with great — or rather the wrong — expectations. Maybe they'd conjured their dreams of Africa from those adverts "calling all dream-ers" to Kenya. Maybe they had imagined themselves moving about in herds, singing extracts from *The Lion King,* which is what I would see later in lavish lodges in Kenyan national parks. But those dreams were not applicable in Mole, where nature had gained the upper hand over human gadgetry and amenities.

I sometimes wished one of the park staff would offer lectures on what a miracle it was that the national park existed at all. The park it-self encompassed about six hundred square kilometres of well-treed savannah that had been kept, against huge odds, largely intact over the years. That itself was an amazing feat in an impoverished part of the country where land- and meat-hungry villagers would have every right to feel that they should hunt and cultivate on that land reserved for animals — and for visitors from far places. The ethnic fighting in the Northern Region was evidence of the growing pressure for land, which was the most precious commodity in the region, as it was all over Africa. Yet there was Mole Game Park, miraculously being held in trust for wildlife, the plants and biodiversity. But more obviously and immediately, it was reserved for well-fed tourists who descended to enjoy the rugged beauty of a wildlife reserve on land that had been confiscated from villagers just three decades earlier.

On our last visit to Mole, I met a team of young Americans and Ghanaians working on an externally funded project, modelled on projects that were ongoing in eastern and southern Africa. They were trying to develop "income-generating" activities in villages around the borders of the park. They said they were negotiating villagers' rights over the use of waterways within the park while "educating" the surrounding villagers on the many benefits the park could have for the region, were it to become a major tourist attraction. As in southern and eastern Africa, it was difficult to explain to small-scale farmers living in abject poverty on the outskirts of a wildlife park that even though the elephants had come and destroyed their crops — or worse trampled a child — they were not permitted to kill the elephant.

In some places in Africa, Kenya's Abedares National Park for example, a chain-link fence was being put up around the park to help keep the wildlife in and poachers out. But that did little to smooth out hard feelings among the villagers and was probably not the sustainable solution. The best solution might have been, in fact, to cautiously hand ownership of the park over to the local people who would then stand to benefit themselves, directly, from tourism revenue. This had a few big risks, in the form of Big Men who could simply turn a former national park into a private and personal "income-generating" project. This had happened in Kenya in some reserves that fell outside the jurisdiction of the Kenya Wildlife Service. They were supposed to be run by "communities," when in fact it was unscrupulous and high-level politicians in the ruling party who really did the running of (and the plundering of the income from) the game reserves.

Still, there were good examples of how community self-interest could be an effective incentive for conservation in Africa. One of these was the Virunga Triangle made famous by Dianne Fossey and the mountain gorillas that roamed the mountains where Uganda, Rwanda and the Democratic Republic of Congo (formerly Zaire) met. At one point, when President Mobutu's regime was still in full control of the country, the park guards on the Zaire side of the border had been among the worst poachers of mountain gorillas. That had been their way of augmenting meagre salaries that came from the capital in Kinshasa.

In 1995, I would visit Bwindi Impenetrable National Park on the Ugandan side of the border, the same park that was the scene of the much-publicized killing of tourists in 1999. At the time of my visit, Mobutu's regime in the former Zaire was rapidly crumbling and government salaries had not been paid for more than a year. People in the Mountain Gorilla Project in Uganda told me that the forest guards in Zaire, who had once been paid by the government to "protect" the gorillas while they were busy poaching them, had suddenly become the most fervent conservationists around. Left with only the gorillas as a source of income because they attracted eco-tourists willing to hike those hills for a glimpse of the magnificent and highly endangered apes, the guards ceased their poaching and began instead to fight poachers in earnest. Surely there was a lesson there for other national wildlife parks in Africa.

In any case, in Mole the project to "sensitize" the villagers to the value of the park and the wildlife struck me as suspect, and most certainly belated. I could see little in the way of monetary incentives there for the villagers in the region. And I wondered about the rumoured plans to privatize the lodge itself — whether improvements that could come with privatization would put the place out of reach of Ghanaians themselves. Even as it was, broken down and dirt cheap, few Ghanaians actually had the means to get to Mole or rent a room in the motel.

I thought it was somehow fitting that the accommodations were not luxurious, given the context. Mole Game Park still had a flourishing population of wildlife and it was still fun trekking in the early morning or late evening behind a well-armed park guard and guide, to try to find kob antelope, elephants, monkeys, warthogs, baboons, and even lions and leopards. On days when the tsetse flies were too numerous, we would drive through the park. It wasn't sleeping sickness that frightened us off when the flies were swarming; it was the actual bites they took. They removed substantial chunks of flesh when feeding on their mammalian prey and the children came back to the lodge looking like war victims, with blood all over. But never mind, it was real and not part of any touristic dream.

We loved it, that national park that a few expatriates, whose views on Africa had been shaped in East Africa, called "pathetic." They were the same people who assured me we would be much happier in East Africa.

Apart from the pain of leaving the town we had come to love in a completely unreasonable way, there was another reason why I was leery of heading off to the other side of the continent. I would be taking up a "real job." Fixed hours and a permanent position would take up all the time I had previously had to nose around in out-of-the-way places and to hang about under palaver trees listening in for morsels of African wisdom and insight, which was one of the biggest delights of living in Africa. I would have a real salary, be paid even for days when I wasn't feeling very creative or productive. But I would also have to head off to an office every day, account for all my hours, write what I was told to write, limit myself to science rather than life in full colour. This return to the "real world" worried me.

It shouldn't have. It would be easy to adapt to the job and all it entailed. What wouldn't be quite so easy was adjusting to some other aspects of Nairobi life, once we'd said our weepy goodbyes and moved to the capital of one of the world's most spectacularly beautiful countries — Kenya.

Kenya

SUDAN

ETHIOPIA

UGANDA

Great Rift Valley

SOMALIA

KENYA

Lake Victoria

Nairobi

TANZANIA

INDIAN OCEAN

Mombasa

Chapter 11

Lose your car not your life

During the last few weeks there have been a number of hijackings of UN and Diplomatic vehicles so it is timely to remind all Staff Members and their Spouses what they should do. There is no 100% effective way of preventing your car from being hijacked but by taking some preventative measures, you will reduce the risk of it happening but if it should happen, by taking certain actions, you can make sure that it is just your car you loose [sic] and not your life. — Bulletin from the United Nations Kenya Security Coordinator, 1994

Kenya, 1993

I was lucky. I was attacked only once in Nairobi, on a main road leading to the International School of Kenya at one o'clock in the afternoon. I was jogging, alone. It was silly. I'd been warned many times not to go running alone anywhere in the city.

I'd taken the precaution of removing my rings, earrings, watch. I was wearing an old, threadbare T-shirt that sported a drawing of a Nova Scotian lighthouse, running shorts and a pair of sneakers that were as tired as I was after the five kilometres I'd done at that altitude. I had my head down and was lost in my own thoughts, far from that city road that ran through remnant coffee plantations in the Kenyan highlands, when I ran up against a large stick. I glanced around, stunned.

There were two of them. One blocked my way with that big baton firmly braced across my stomach. Another had closed in on me from the right. A quick glance behind and ahead showed there were no cars coming in either direction, and no other pedestrians on what was normally a busy road.

"Stop where you are!" said the man holding the stick. Perhaps he hadn't noticed that the stick had already stopped me good and short.

"Why should I?" I said, feigning indignant bravado.

By way of reply, the second man pulled out a knife from under his red T-shirt. It was a very big knife, along the menacing lines of a machete. He held this meaningfully against my stomach. Another hopeless glance up and down the street. Still no cars or pedestrians. It dawned on me a bit belatedly that I might be in very big trouble. Thieves didn't *usually* kill people, not expatriates anyway. That could cause too much commotion with the police. But lately there had been some horrific cases of beheading and stabbing in the city. I shut up and didn't fight as they frog-marched me off the road and deep into the coffee bushes on the side of the road.

They frisked me thoroughly, lifted my T-shirt and pulled at my shorts, hoping perhaps I had a money-belt or something valuable hidden under my clothes. They eyed me in silence for a few seconds. Their eyes were as soft and compassionate as volcanic glass.

The man with the knife pointed at the ground. "Your shoes," he said.

I looked down at those old battered Nikes, dyed red after hundreds of kilometres on muddy paths in Kenya's highlands. "My shoes?" I said in a very small voice.

"Take them off."

I bent down and began untying them. I noticed the holes in the toes, compared the state of my running shoes with the almost pristine pair the man with the knife was wearing. I thought to myself: this is ridiculous. Up I bobbed, thinking I might just point this out to my would-be shoe stealers. I said, "But this is ridicul . . ."

The knife against my ribs shut me right up. Ridiculous is not the appropriate word when there is a knife blade pressing into your bare skin, in the vicinity of your heart. I tugged at the shoes, my hands trembling so badly it was impossible to untie the laces. Then I stepped out of them. The two men eyed me a little longer, as if trying to decide if it were worthwhile doing anything else with me. Then without a word they scooped up the shoes and disappeared into the leafy depths of the coffee plantation. Abandoning me to delayed waves of fear. Leaving me there in socks. I turned and started to run home — five kilometres over gravel and mud with socks for shoes. It wasn't until I came through the gate and Dalmas, the day watchman, looked aghast at those muddy socks and asked me what had happened, that I burst into tears.

Once the initial shock was over, I realized how lucky I'd been. If the same thing had happened in, say, Central Park, things might have been quite different. I might have kept my shoes, but I would likely have been raped or killed or both. These guys who took off with my shoes weren't evil or perverted; they were just young men who had turned to petty theft to make ends meet . . . or maybe they knew someone who desperately needed a pair of shoes. I don't know. It didn't matter. I'd come out of it unscathed.

I consider myself extremely fortunate to have experienced nothing worse than that during four years in Nairobi. What was far more frightening in Kenya — and what struck me most on my arrival in Nairobi in 1993 — was the fear of organized crime, which seemed to be orchestrated from on high. These criminals were not pickpockets or shoe pilferers wearing second-hand clothes and wielding machetes. These men wore ties and jackets, brandished pistols or AK-47s, which could be had for about ten dollars in Nairobi, cheaper than a garden hoe. These criminal gangs carried out daring and sophisticated raids on heavily guarded private homes and diplomatic residences. They also hijacked cars, without the slightest apparent fear of the law. They seemed immune to arrest and prosecution. For this reason, the fear they invoked was pervasive.

Was it reasonable, this fear? In some ways, yes it was. The statistics spoke for themselves in Nairobi. On some weekends twenty vehicles were taken at gunpoint; murder rates were high enough to mimic inner city madness in an American drug and crime capital. Every day it seemed we heard of a Kenyan friend or a relative of a friend who had been a victim of theft or even brutal murder. People who had precious little that they could afford to lose had, of course, fewer means to protect themselves from thieves. Despite the splash it made in the media — even the international media — every time an expatriate or a diplomat was gunned down, it was the Kenyans who suffered most from the crime.

In the good old days, it hadn't been like this. Nairobi had been — so everyone told me — a paradise. There were hints of the old grandeur and the splendid natural beauty in the roads that snaked through deep and lovely valleys and up over hills, covered by magnificent flame trees with their dazzling red blossoms interspersed with the pastel mauve crowns of the jacarandas. At an altitude of 1,700 metres, it could be cold enough that in the evenings we would cosy up in front of the fireplace, shivering. During the dry season, the sun could be counted on to recreate the effect of a perfect summer day in the northern hemisphere. It was a refreshing change from the oppressive and enervating heat of much of West Africa.

In colonial times, and even afterwards, Kenya had been a favoured destination of the rich and famous who immersed themselves in their tight-knit little webs of petty jealousies set in private clubs or on their enormous farms. This was land that belonged by right to the local people of course, but such trivialities rarely seem to matter to the fun- and sun-seekers.

The best known and by far the most "modern" of places we had lived, the Kenyan capital had — on the surface — everything going for it. It could, if you had the money to keep your distance from reality, be the stuff Hollywood drums up to depict dreams of Africa. The Kenyan tour-makers were not averse to playing this to the hilt to please visitors who came looking for *Out of Africa* revisited.

The Isak Dinesen (Karen Blixen) home had, after the filming of that movie, been turned into a museum as part of Kenya's extensive and impressive museum and parks system. Inside, you could spy through the doorway into Blixen's bedroom on the farm she had owned on the outskirts of Nairobi, in a neighbourhood now called Karen, with those famed Ngong Hills as backdrop. The clothes spread out neatly on the bed were not the famous writer's; they were Meryl Streep's and Robert Redford's, leftovers from the film that had been shot on location. Hardly a single safari tour to Kenya failed to take visitors to tour the house and have a look at this movie set that evoked colonial dreams of Africa.

Nairobi had once been known as the City in the Sun. These days, people called it the City in the Slums. There were rutted mud paths where paved roads had once run; there were mountains of rubbish and there was traffic to die in. There was homelessness and there were sprawling shantytowns, true slums with all the social ills that festered in narrow, stinking alleyways of ghettos anywhere. These neighbourhoods in Nairobi were quite different from the squalid quarters in West African cities where we'd lived, where poverty was merely material and there was still a wealth of traditional values and social norms, where decency and neighbourly relations still prevailed just as they did in rural areas. Nairobi's slums, alas, suffered from modern urban problems — social alienation, drugs and serious crime.

Crime, in fact, seemed to be everywhere, giving rise to another new nickname for this city — Nai-robbery. In the city centre, gangs of glue-sniffing ragamuffins, some barely past the toddler stage, would attack unsuspecting tourists or pedestrians. They had many tactics. While some pleaded for handouts, others would come up from behind and grab at necklaces or earrings. Others came armed with small plastic bags full of what they said was human excrement. Of course they had nastier words to describe the genre of biological weaponry they used on their victims, who were told to hand over all jewellery and money or be smeared with the contents of the bag. There were other cases reported in the media of street gangs who armed themselves with old syringes, which they claimed were infected with HIV. Some used knives or guns. But most of the thieves on the streets just grabbed bags and necklaces (or running shoes) and ran. All were effective ways of getting victims to part rapidly with their precious belongings.

Our arrival in Kenya was badly timed. In September 1993, the expatriate community was in an uproar over a car hijacking and murder that had occurred close to the United Nations complex, the global headquarters of the United Nations Environment Program. A Danish UNEP man, who had been following a female colleague's car, watched as armed hijackers approached the woman in traffic, forced her out of her car and prepared to get in and drive away. He leapt from his car and approached. When the hijackers asked for his car keys, he made the fatal mistake of tossing them into the luxuriant bushes on the side of the road. They put him face down on the pavement and shot him in the back of the head, then took off in the woman's vehicle.

Colleagues at the research organization where I worked told me their own tales of horror. Some of them had been hijacked more than once — at the gates of their homes, some in broad daylight in town. Some had been shot at. Others had watched hijackers drive off with their children in the car and then had to wait until the children were dropped off somewhere on the outskirts of the city and were able to call and tell them where they were. This was an effective way of ensuring victims were not hasty in alerting the police before the hijackers had got out of the city — or wherever it was they went with all those vehicles. The recovery rate of vehicles was very low indeed, not even 10 per cent.

There were as many stories of who organized the crime and how it worked as there were stories of hijacking. Some people swore they had seen with their very own eyes the underground warehouse in the city where the stolen cars (mostly luxury four-wheel-drive vehicles) were taken and dismantled. One person swore to me that such a warehouse was located on the premises of State House in the capital.

Popular opinion was divided on who was behind the organized crime in the city. The people's list of possible godfathers included (a) one of the president's sons, who was also allegedly a big player in shenanigans at the port of Mombasa and generally believed to be up to no good at all, (b) a former minister of energy, who was widely believed to have had a hand in killing a former minister of foreign affairs, but had somehow managed to escape trial and had resurfaced recently in the Office of the President, (c) none of the above because it was really the work of the police themselves, (d) all of the above.

As for how it was done and where all those vehicles were going, well, that was equally mysterious. Once again, there was no shortage of barroom and roadside theories. There were those who said the parts from the vehicles were then put into large trucks and driven (a) through the Masai Mara Reserve and across the border into Tanzania, towards their ultimate destination in Zimbabwe, or (b) to Mombasa, where they were loaded onto southbound ships destined for South Africa. Others said many of the stolen vehicles were simply repainted in one of these secret subterranean garages, then quickly driven out of the country for use by (a) either rebel or (b) government forces in (1) Rwanda, (2) Uganda or (3) Somalia. It was impossible for the average person to garner evidence to prove or disprove any of the permutations and combinations of alleged culprits or causes behind all the crime. But that didn't deter average people from speculating. "Where there's smoke there's fire," people would say to me. "And where there's fire, there's often an arsonist."

In just one week in September 1993, the institute where I worked lost three Toyota Land Cruisers (at that time the favourite of the armed gangs, to be replaced later by Land Rover's luxury safari vehicle, the Discovery). There was a meeting with the heads of diplomatic missions in the city and the president, who maintained the anarchy was their fault — the "donor" countries had forced multiparty politics on the country. He said something to the effect that all of this crime and the ethnic fighting that had broken out in the Rift Valley were exactly the price he had warned the donor countries that Kenya would pay for multiparty democracy. The heads of missions shut up and went back to their corners.

But many Kenyans themselves alleged the anarchy was being orchestrated from on high. They claimed men at the top, mostly from the Kalenjin ethnic group, were instigating ethnic fighting and targeting the financially powerful Kikuyu people, by arming and dressing ruthless bands of men as Maasai warriors. Popular reasoning said that the new Kalenjin elite that ruled the country loathed the Kikuyus, allegedly out of jealousy over their wealth and success and harboured grudges built up over the years when Kikuyu President Jomo Kenyatta ruled the country. In any case, it was undeniable that all of this chaos was convenient ammunition against democracy, which the president maintained was the root of the problem.

There was something fishy about the timing and the cycles of the troubles — both the ethnic fighting and the car hijackings. Each time car theft reached almost epidemic proportions, or a foreign diplomat was killed, the diplomatic corps and the UN would start making noises about moving their missions out of Nairobi. Donors started hinting at drastic cuts in assistance to Kenya and closing development programs. Even the Bretton Woods institutions started balking at dispensing loans for balance of payments, often delaying them ostensibly because of huge financial scandals. Then there would be meetings with high-level Kenyan officials (or the president). And each time things seemed to calm right down again — for a while anyway. Car hijacking would ease up for a few weeks or months. The same was true of the "Maasai" attacks on the Kikuyu.

When we arrived, Nairobi was jammed to overflowing with the flood of expatriates posted there to handle, from the "safety" of Kenya, the chaos in Somalia, soon to be usurped by the horrendous genocide in Rwanda. We couldn't find a vacant house to rent and my new employer booked us into the New Stanley hotel in downtown Nairobi for six weeks. Its main claim to fame was an ancient thorn tree on the sidewalk restaurant, dating back to a golden era some four decades earlier when Ernest Hemingway used it as a favourite haunt. But by the time we stayed there in 1993, the Thorn Tree Cafe had become a tiny island of greenery in a sea of concrete and the chaos of downtown. Almost every night we heard gunfire from our second-floor rooms, even over the blasting music and roaring engines of the matatus, Kenya's version of the bush taxi. Without a place to call home, without a friend within several thousand kilometres — and with the fear — the first six weeks in Kenya ranked right up there with the worst times of my life.

The undercurrent of terror in that city and indeed the whole country, could, if you allowed it to, overwhelm you and make each excursion to the city centre or out of the city a safari to hell. It would have been easy to fall into the terror trap and avoid going out at all. Regular bulletins from the United Nations Security Coordinator in Kenya that reached all of us who were working for international organizations weren't exactly reassuring. It took me a long time to get over the effects of the one advising us on how to deal with car hijackers:

> If the worst happens and you are confronted by armed men, do the following:
>
> Forget bravado and do as you are told — be prepared to loose [sic] your car.
>
> You will be nervous and hyped up but so will the thieves so don't do anything to increase this, i.e. argue or stare angrily at them and don't talk to them unless they demand it or for a specific reason (see below).
>
> React as calmly as possible and make all your movements slowly and deliberately.
>
> Keep your hands in sight and if you do have to release a seat belt, tell the thieves — they might think that you have a gun.
>
> Do not wait to be told to get out of the car but get out slowly and calmly leaving the keys in the igni-

tion and any other property you might have e.g. a handbag.

You should tell your passengers to behave in the same way. If there is a child or baby in the car tell the thieves that you are going to help him/her out before you do so.

DO NOT ACTIVATE ANTI HIJACKING DE-VICES OR FUEL CUT OFFS — IT MIGHT COST YOU YOUR LIFE.

Walk away slowly from the car and count your blessings that you are alive and unhurt.

Targeting of cars — thieves will often want a particular car and they will watch your house, observe your routine to see when the best time to take the car is. Always be observant and encourage your Family, Staff and Watchmen etc to be likewise.

When I wasn't wallowing in my own fear, I was trying to understand what had gone so terribly wrong in this magnificent country, which at independence, seemed to have all it needed to become a successful and wealthy nation. The infrastructure had been there — the roads, dams, communications, hospitals, schools, colleges, universities. The education levels had been among the highest in Africa and the first president, Jomo Kenyatta, had ensured that education was not just a privilege for the rich.

Kenya had a thriving agricultural sector, producing tea and coffee and cut flowers for export — even if much of this was in the hands of foreigners. It had an equally promising tourism industry — even if much of that too was in the hands of foreigners. Not enough to explain what on earth had gone so wrong in this beautiful country full of hard-working, humorous, educated, religious and ambitious people.

When I asked Kenyans to help me understand what had kept their country from leaping over that great divide separating "developed" from "developing" countries, I nearly always got the same answer, in one form or another. "The problem in this country is the men who govern us. They've killed the golden goose, eaten all the meat and now they are going at the bones."

While I was reporting from Ghana on the parliamentary elections on December 28, 1992, I recall clearly hearing the reports from

144

Kenya where multiparty presidential elections were being held for the very first time. I also clearly recalled the international observers' comments that they could not condone the elections as "free and fair" but that they believed the outcome (a landslide victory for the incumbent) more or less reflected the will of the Kenyan people.

The president had in fact railed long and loud against multiparty elections. He had ruled a one-party state without any popular mandate for too many years (since his predecessor had died in 1978) to want to open himself up to public opinion and popular will now. He saw no need for elections but was coerced into holding them by the "donor countries" (the West), in the spirit of the post-Cold War period when it was no longer necessary for the West to prop up distasteful dictators in the name of the Free World. Donors were demanding a transition to democracy, which of course required elections.

The president capitulated eventually. Even at home the pressure for elections — the true source of democracy in Africa — was too much. In 1992, elections were held. Not free and fair, but what the heck? Now any country that wished to justify a military deal or trade with Kenya could defend their "friendly" relations by saying Kenya was a democracy.

Unofficially, the Americans regarded Kenya as a bastion against what they viewed as incipient Muslim fundamentalists in neighbouring Sudan and Somalia. They were even said to have appropriated a piece of the Kenyan coast for their defence installations against the Middle East. I recall in 1996 a motion by the African-American lobby in the US to have Kenya's status as favoured trading partner downgraded because of the country's dismal human rights record. The reaction? A Republican senator stood up and said that was impossible; the US had just signed a major military agreement with Kenya, which might be put at risk by such a move.

The British also had military cooperation agreements with the country, along with enormous investments in Kenya — Barclays Bank owned a good deal of agricultural land in the Rift Valley, for example. On one occasion, Linda Chalker, British minister of state in the Foreign Office and minister of international cooperation, landed in Kenya and met with the press to express her concern about corruption and human rights violations in the country. The reaction was swift and angry. The president said it was unacceptable that "this woman" would come to Kenya behaving like a "schoolmistress" to lecture on how Kenya should be run. He followed this with quick references to the many millions of pounds of profits Barclays Bank had made in Kenya the previous year, and the military agreements Britain and Kenya shared, and he warned if the British government continued to insult Kenyans this way, they would be the losers. After that, the British were very quiet. If there was one thing Kenya's leadership knew how to do, and do well, it was to call a "donor" country's bluff just what it was — a bluff.

In the four years I was in Kenya, the only time I heard the Canadian diplomatic mission make a peep about anything was when two Canadian tourists were sexually assaulted. Canada had already cut its bilateral development assistance to Kenya as part of sweeping cutbacks a few years earlier, but that didn't mean Canada wasn't up to its neck in Kenyan muck. A Canadian firm had worked hand in hand with a much-dreaded and shadowy former minister of energy to construct a major oil pipeline from the coast. This same former minister was rumoured to have his hands in a lot of the most gruesome and undemocratic activities in the country and still remained the people's prime suspect in the murder of a former foreign minister.

I learned that, despite his reputation, he had managed on occasion to get himself into Canada, where he showed up at high-level receptions in Ottawa acting like a special guest. I asked the official from the Canadian embassy who was responsible for visas why it was that such a man could get a visa when highly trustworthy African friends of mine with legitimate business in Canada were often refused. He replied that the man had somehow managed to enter without a visa and that it had almost caused a diplomatic scandal. He refused to explain how that could happen and would not comment on my suggestion that this former minister might have very high-level connections in Ottawa.

While we were there that same Canadian company, which seemed to specialize in contracting itself to work for questionable African regimes on suspect construction projects, won the contract for and was building a multimillion dollar international airport in the president's own region. Even the World Bank complained about that one, questioning the source of the financing at a time when Kenya was performing poorly economically, not to mention its dismal record on human rights.

Still, the work on the airport went ahead, with no one knowing who was paying for it. Rumours circulated in Kenya that the Canadian government might have to step in to pay the Canadian company because the Kenyan budget had not provided for payment on this superfluous airport in Kalenjin territory, home to so many of those at the top. The Canadian High Commissioner finally tried to extinguish the rumours by putting out a denial in the Kenyan press.

That didn't satisfy Kenyans, who loved to rib me about my country, that prided itself on being a paragon of democracy and justice, tarnishing itself in the opaque world of high-level Kenyan politics and business. They especially liked to tease me about a former Canadian High Commissioner to Kenya who, when his term finished, decided to leave the Canadian diplomatic service and to stay on as "financial adviser" to the president. Wasn't much I could say, although I tried to laugh it off with quips about Canada being a free country.

But all of this was high-level shenanigans, the foreign affairs and business dealings that went on way over the heads of the common person, or the *wananchi* as they were called in Kiswahili. And in Kenya, wananchi didn't seem to count for much despite all the president's tedious declarations to the contrary. Almost daily he could be found in yet another part of the country, attending a church service or visiting a school, after which he would hand out enormous sums of money as gifts. This was called the *harambee* spirit of sharing and giving that had been developed in the early years of independence to encourage Kenyans to work together to build their country.

By the early '90s, when those at the top were holding a harambee every few days and dishing out money as though it multiplied on trees, or perhaps in the many casinos they allegedly owned in Nairobi, the question everyone asked was: where did our leaders get this money? "It's ours, they stole it and now they give it back to us — as charity?"

Mostly the wananchi kept their heads down and tried to make ends meet or just to stay alive. They watched and they listened and they analyzed from down below what they figured was going on at the top. There were a very few names that were whispered every time tragedy befell, or every time people got wind of another massive case of fraud, or missing public funds, or scandal, or "mystery" killing. One of these was that former minister, who had recently re-risen from simple MP to minister without portfolio in the Office of the

President. Since he had already proclaimed himself a "total man" in parliament, that is how the media often referred to him. Later, after his name was brought up in a scandal involving a chambermaid in a hotel in Auckland, New Zealand, during a Commonwealth meeting there, he became known as the "Bull of Auckland."

But real names connected with real crimes hardly showed up in the newspapers, not even the high-quality *Daily Nation*, because despite the new liberalization of the print media that had come with democracy, even they weren't that courageous or foolhardy. Publicly attacking figures as shadowy and terrifying as some of those Big Men was not a mark of courage. It was simply an invitation for trouble. There were always ways of getting back at opponents or journalists who spoke out.

There might be another "random" break-in. "Common thieves" might come with the sophisticated tools to drill through thick stone walls and cut through security bars over windows and maybe even decide to kill rather than just steal. And the police might have another unsolved crime, with no suspects identified but lots of broad hints about nasty foreigners (Somalis and Ugandans were favoured scapegoats) committing "random" crimes in Kenya. Meanwhile, Kenyans saw many of these as straightforward hit jobs.

People in Kenya actually used the words "evil" and "sinister" to refer to some of the men who governed their country. I had no way of knowing if any of the men at the top could be as ruthless or Machiavellian as the wananchi, the opposition and the street media made them out to be, but I was not about to try to find out either. I had a job. I was no longer a reporter, and in Kenya, I was glad of that.

Chapter 12

Crime and no punishment

A woman is shot dead at point blank range sitting in her car outside a Nairobi kindergarten and police officer . . . calls it "a normal robbery." Apart from the insensitivity of the remark and the hurt it must cause to the woman's family, are we now so inured to violence that we can regard such an atrocity as a commonplace event? — Daily Nation newspaper, February 2, 1995.

What was amazing to me — and also worrisome — was that over time I began to get used to living with the fear. The trick was a bit of fatalism and involved accepting the fact that if armed men decided they wanted into your house, then there was little you could do. I figured your best hope was that should they break in, they would do so when your night watchman was deep asleep (so they wouldn't feel obliged to decapitate him) and that they would get what they wanted without waking you up.

Most up-market homes had metal doors separating the living quarters from the bedrooms. These were popularly known as "rape gates." The theory was if the thieves could get a television and perhaps a stereo from the living room, they might just sneak away satisfied and not risk breaking into the rest of the house in search of valuables such as cash and jewellery, which were generally kept in bedrooms.

This was a fine theory, I suppose. I always figured you could do what you wanted to protect yourself in Nairobi — hide behind thick walls, rape gates and windows covered with thick iron grillwork — but nothing was a guarantee against armed gangs. I thought any armed men in their right minds would simply point their guns through the bars over the bedroom windows and demand that you open up, if they wanted a real haul of valuables or, if they were hit men on a job, a particular person. And of course anyone with a semi-automatic rifle aimed at them through a bedroom window would be quick to comply and open up — at least anyone in their right mind.

For a time the UN office in Nairobi was recommending that staff of international organizations install, for a mere $1,000 a month, sensor systems in their homes that would wake them the moment someone entered the house. The security notice informed us that 90 per cent of all thefts occurred while house occupants were deep asleep so the losses were not discovered until the morning, and that such sensor systems would ensure occupants were alerted to theft in progress. I contemplated the usefulness of a system that would wake me up to the fact that there was a gang of masked, armed and trigger-happy men in my house. Surely that knowledge would make me scream in terror and they would come on the run to kill me — if I hadn't already died of fright. We decided to ignore the UN recommendations.

As a lucrative business in Nairobi, I guessed that security didn't rank far behind car hijacking and armed break-ins. We didn't want to get fanatic, although the security we did have would have looked that way to just about anyone in Canada. We had the usual security package for anyone with the money to have belongings worth protecting, and the money to protect them. This included thick bars over all windows and doors, sirens mounted within the house that could be turned on to frighten thieves (or occupants, if switched on by mistake), the services of a day and a night watchman with access to a buzzer that would summon a van of back-up men (carrying batons) within minutes.

Being a watchman in Nairobi was not all that different from being a witch back a few hundred years ago in Europe, when your innocence could be determined only posthumously after you had drowned in the lake into which you were tossed. It worked like this:

if thieves did come and the watchman stuck around to do his duty and press the alarm and try to defend the house, that same unarmed watchman stood a very good chance of being killed on the spot by the thieves. If he took to his heels and ran away, there was a very good chance the police would name him as the prime suspect. He would be captured, tossed in prison and subjected to the beating and torture that human rights groups claimed went on in those jails. It wasn't much of a job, but in Kenya, job seekers didn't have much choice in the matter. The unemployed were everywhere and they were desperate. It was an employer's market.

Our watchmen worked for the Kenyan branch of a British security firm whose services my employers hired. They were kept on temporary status with the firm, which meant they earned about $50 a month for working twelve-hour shifts, seven days a week, fifty-two weeks a year. One day I called the firm and complained, saying it was akin to slavery the way the guards were made to work. I said they should get at least one day off a week and also receive annual holidays. The head of the operation, who identified himself as a former British policeman, told me that full-time staff did get annual holidays, but the guards didn't want to reduce their working week to six days because they wanted the extra money.

"Extra money?" I said. "What extra money?"

"They're paid for seven days or nights a week. If they take a day off, we would have to cut their salary," he said.

"You're joking. Cut it to what? Are you trying to tell me that somewhere in that big monthly paycheque of $50 there's a day of double-time payment for the seventh day?"

"New out here, are you?" he said.

"What do you mean by 'out here'?" I said.

"Look, things work a certain way here in Kenya," he said, pronouncing the name Keen-ya, as many white Kenyans and a few tin-eared expatriates were wont to do. "When you're new here you don't understand these things. Look, we have men who have worked for this firm for twenty years. And we have hundreds of men who would love to come to work for us. Our guards like working for us. Once you've been here longer, you'll see. American, are you? Americans often have these kinds of ideals. Those'll go away fast in Keeenya, believe me." He guffawed into my ear and I hung up with a sigh.

So it was up to us to work out our own private system with the watchmen, which gave them one full day and night off each week.

Many of our neighbours had killer dogs in their compounds, terrifying brutes that drooled and growled and exposed their fangs through iron gates when anyone dared to pass within a hundred metres of the house. We had cats and no room for a killer dog. Instead, we got a flock of smelly but very noisy and aggressive geese. Karl assured me that geese were great watchdogs. He said the Americans had used them as such during the war in Vietnam. I decided not to push the point that the Americans hadn't won that war.

We were fortunate. We could afford security. We could and did keep our distance from the uglier realities of Nairobi. We heard all the stories, read about them daily, and got used to living behind walls and closed gates.

In 1996 when I was relieved of thousands of dollars worth of my belongings, it would not happen in Kenya. It would happen in Canada.

It was late spring in 1996 when I went to Canada to do some publicity for a book. The friend who picked me up at the airport in Ottawa wanted to stop for a few minutes at Dow's Lake to show me a bit of the nation's capital, which I didn't know nearly as well as I knew many African capitals. We'd parked the car, covered my suitcase and carry-on bag with a jacket, and taken a stroll onto the jetty. When we returned to the car, the suitcases were gone and the lock on her car had been sprung, leaving a few dents as evidence.

Gone with those suitcases were the laptop computer that belonged to my employers in Kenya, all the back-up disks, my own camera and tape recorder — just about everything I valued enough to lug it with me between continents. Worst of all, though, was the loss of my immunization card with records of all the shots I'd had over the years. Without that, I would not be able to get back into Africa. I would have no choice but to renew all the mandatory immunizations in one single visit to Health and Welfare Canada's traveller's clinic.

First, though, I wanted to report the theft. This was Canada and I was sure the police would do something to recover my stolen property. For years, from Africa, I had romanticized Canadian police as being always caring, trustworthy and at the service of the public.

The uncooperative young woman on duty that Friday night in the Ottawa police station stared insolently at me. She said, her tone petulant and her voice raised a little more than necessary, "Look, we're always telling you not to leave anything valuable in your cars.

We've had a terrible problem with bikers since the *Sûreté Québec* chased them over here to Ottawa. We've warned you repeatedly not to leave anything in a car."

"You're not always telling me," I said. "I don't live here."

She shrugged, looked at me blankly.

"I live in Africa," I added for no good reason.

I had the impression I'd just named a Canadian province that she didn't want to admit she'd not heard of. I said it again. She shrugged again, then told me sternly she couldn't help me and theft from cars and homes was so common in the nation's capital that the police didn't trouble themselves with investigations any more. She said my valuables were probably already in pawnshops and the empty suitcases had no doubt been chucked into the Rideau Canal. It took a good deal of patience — backed finally with shouting — before she would give me even a police report with a rough list and estimate of the value of the stolen goods. She said that was not routine in Ottawa. I said I needed it for Africa. She muttered something about that being my problem, before filling out a form I could at least give to my employers to prove I had not delivered their laptop to those pawnshops in Ottawa.

When we flew back into Nairobi a month later, it was with a whole new perspective on the crime there, and even on the police. In Kenya, with the injustices and inequities of the system, theft was somehow more excusable and forgivable than it was in the capital of one of the world's richest countries, deemed year after year by the United Nations as the best place to live on the planet.

Except for the time I had been arrested in Cameroon many years earlier for extreme insolence to the police (guilty as charged, I actually called them "crazy"), I couldn't recall a single time any African policeman or woman had been less sympathetic than that policewoman on duty that Friday night in Ottawa. In Kenya, after I was relieved of my shoes and reported the stolen Nikes to the police, they had consoled me by at least pretending that they felt sympathy and they were going to investigate the case.

It had taken about two and half years, but I now realized we had subconsciously come to terms with our new home in Kenya. In fact, we were very happy there. At the end of the summer break in 1996, we said our usual sad goodbyes to friends and family in Canada but were happy when we landed again in Nairobi. The children had their friends; I had an interesting job with great colleagues and friends and Karl had contracts that took him into fascinating — if depressing — parts of Sudan and Zaire.

We drove cheerfully through the gate in the London taxi that had brought us in from Jomo Kenyatta airport. Dalmas, the day watchman, saluted us with a solemn smile, clicking his heels as he always did. Despite his stunted salary and shoddy treatment at the hands of the security firm that employed him, he took his work very seriously indeed, comporting and carrying himself as the proud professional that he was. I asked him in passing if all was well. He nodded. He helped us cart in the suitcases, including my new one with all new contents, before taking me aside to ask me how we were, how our families were back there, how our holiday had been.

I thought about telling him about the theft in the capital of my native land but decided it was too early. Greetings are ritualized and everything is first painted up rosy, before any real exchange of information is made. In reply to his questions, I told him my family was well, my father well, my mother too, that everything in Canada was just hunky-dory. "And here?" I said. "How is everything?" He told me his family was fine, that everything was fine but I could tell by the look on his face that it wasn't.

"What is it, Dalmas? What's happened?"

"Madam," he said, faltering. "We are fine. I am fine. But there is something I need to say to you. It pains me sorrowfully. It is about the cat. You left us with two cats to care for. I must say that now you return to find only one cat." The children were listening in. There were immediate outbursts of tears.

"Yes," Dalmas said. "One of them was struck there on the road. We located the dead body of the cat the next day. I am sorry."

The children were wailing like hyenas.

"I am sorry too," I said. "But she was only a cat."

They wailed louder. I told them to stop it.

"Yes," he said, nodding. "But I feel I have let you down. You left me with two cats and you return to only one."

"Dalmas, it's not your fault and really, there's nothing to be said or done about it."

He hesitated, then said, "There is another thing."

"What?" I said.

"Peter has passed away."

The children suddenly went silent. Peter, his wife Eli and his daughter Agatha lived with us, had done for two years since we'd moved into the house. He had been tending the garden. Eli was the housekeeper and like a mother to me. Agatha was like a big sister to the children.

"Peter?" I said. "How? When?"

"A week after you left. He was ill."

"He had those swollen glands on his neck," I said. "But those had been taken care of at the hospital. He wasn't sick when we left. He seemed fine. He'd been treated at the hospital. How could he just die?"

Dalmas shrugged. Not an I-don't-know shrug but something much bigger, that spoke volumes about his acceptance of God's hand working in those mysterious ways, which he — for one — was not audacious enough to question. What mattered was that Peter had died and that Dalmas, who had viewed him as his surrogate father, was devastated by the loss.

It was a tearful homecoming. Peter's death overshadowed everything else and the children spent a lot of time with Agatha, trying to console her in their childlike way, over the loss of her father.

A couple of days later, I was sitting on the back porch, mourning for Peter and staring up at the trees and that magnificent blue expanse of sky that seems like a view of eternity from up there in the highlands of Kenya. Dalmas, ever vigilant in doing his rounds of the house, approached me.

He was tall, lean and he wore that private security uniform with unsurpassed aplomb. He stood in front of me. At attention.

We exchanged a few more thoughts about Peter, and about Eli who had gone home to western Kenya to observe forty days of mourning among her family and her people.

We were silent for a few minutes, then I said, "Dalmas, tell me something. Why when you were telling me the bad news did you tell me about the cat before you told me about Peter's death?"

"Because Madam, I know that white people love animals more than they love people."

I almost laughed, but saw that he was deadly serious.

"Is that what you really think?"

"But it is true. We see many white people here who do not have children because they prefer to have dogs or cats. There are all those white people who live with the elephants and the rhinos and don't like people at all or have any children. White people are like the Kikuyus. They don't love children too much, not like we the Luos. Look at the Kikuyu man who owns this house here. He is so rich that he comes every day with a different Mercedes. He has so much money. But he has only three children and only one wife. We Luos, if we have money, we get more wives and have many children."

"But that's why the Luos are not known for having much money, maybe?" I said. "Big families are very costly. The children have to be educated. And land is scarce out in Western Province where the Luos live. Isn't that so?"

He mulled that over for a little bit.

"I suppose so. But you see, we are not like the Kikiyus or you whites. We want money only so we can have more children. The children are what makes us wealthy, not the money."

I'd been outdone neatly. Again.

"It's been a rough summer, Dalmas," I said finally. "I didn't mention it yet because of Peter and so on, but while I was in Canada, I was robbed. I lost everything I left here with."

He looked startled — too startled, as though I'd just announced the end of the world.

"I mean, it wasn't serious or anything. I wasn't attacked. I left my suitcases in a locked car and someone broke open the lock and stole them." He still had that look of terror.

"Wait, Dalmas, it wasn't so serious. It was only material things I lost. No one died. No one was hurt. Why are you looking like that?"

He began to stutter. "You mean? You mean?" He took a breath. Shook his head. Studied his black and polished shoes.

"What, Dalmas? I was robbed. No big deal. What's wrong?"

"Do you mean . . . ?" he stuttered. "Do you mean that there are Africans there in Canada too?"

Now it was my turn to be uncomprehending.

"Yes, of course there are . . . " I suddenly grasped what he was trying to say, what he was thinking. At least a bit of it. I laughed. "Yes, there are Africans in Canada but it most certainly wasn't Africans who stole my suitcase. It was common criminals. The police said it was motorcycle gangs, who steal and sell drugs. I don't know."

His mouth was working around the words. "You mean? Madam, are you telling me that white people can be thieves? That white people . . . steal from white people?"

"Of course they do. What did you think?"

"But I thought only Africans were thieves." He had removed his official beret and was rubbing his head, obviously troubled and perplexed.

There it was again. That complex that cripples minds throughout so much of Africa, so long after the colonial "masters" left (at least officially) the continent. The complex that won't go away and weakens claims that it is time to stop accusing colonialism for the ills on the continent. The inferiority complex has been hammered into Africa for many generations and is still there, a legacy that continues to plague the continent decades after independence — and for how much longer, only the gods can say.

"Well, it is good to learn this thing," Dalmas said then, giving his palms a good rub together. "As at now, I will stop all the white people at the gate too."

"Not the ones you already know," I said. "Same as you let in the Kenyans you know, you can also let in the white people you know. No need to quiz everyone. I don't want to live inside a prison."

He laughed. "Madam, don't say this," he said. Then he made a sweeping gesture to indicate the lovely house and garden he guarded, and of which he was inordinately proud. I glanced around me, took in the high walls, the security alarm buzzer, the windows and the doors, all covered with bars and firmly closed with huge padlocks.

Dalmas said, "This is not a prison, Madam. This is a rich man's house."

He was right. There was a difference. Both had bars to keep the occupants locked up but one was very comfortable and the other was most definitely not. But in that country, with that system of justice or rather injustice for those who were the majority — the voiceless and the powerless — it wasn't clear which of the two was more likely to house the real criminals.

Chapter 13

Bottoms-up development

Until now, the project's activities and purpose are in line with the given policy criteria. Presently, there are no deviations between the planned and implemented activities. However it was experienced that the planned activities have been defined too narrow in its scope in order to achieve the expected outputs in a co-ordinated and process oriented way. They still aim at achieving the project purpose — even at activity/output level — but they include now more information on the process for achieving the expected outputs. — Semi-annual Progress Report, for Second Co-ordination Meeting, 1996

As it turned out, the best thing about living in Nairobi was not the many amenities to be enjoyed by those who could afford them. Nor was it the lovely climate and splendid colours of the sky, the flowers and trees. It wasn't even the proximity of marvellous national parks for weekend getaways. All of these were indeed great luxuries that no one with the money to take advantage of them could fail to appreciate, not even a champion complainer like me. But what really made Nairobi feel like home, what made work and life a pleasure was, as always, people — friends of the family, work colleagues, and the friends on the information "team" I was part of in the research organization.

Actually, a couple of my bosses liked to tell me I was not an exemplary player on their team. I'm sure they felt they had good reason to say so, starting with my reluctance to attend all those many seminars organized for staff on "team-building" or "time management" or "morale building."

In principle, there was nothing wrong with seminars that were meant to turn us all into happy worker bees by building on our team-playing skills. I did feel there may have been a few too many of these exercises, some of them a little infantile for grown-up and well-paid professionals who presumably had the qualifications they needed before being hired as international professionals. My enthusiasm for these exercises was further dampened by the fact that they did not address the real cause of the morale problem, which started at the top and not the bottom. At least that was my perspective, from somewhere in the middle.

I felt there were serious inequities in the treatment and payment of staff. Three tiers neatly separated the international professional staff from both the so-called national professionals (people hired locally) and the support staff, not just in Kenya but on the three continents where the institute worked. No team-building exercise in the world was going to alter the fact that many of the national staff felt sidelined, under-appreciated and underpaid. I figured that all those expensive seminars simply missed the point.

That was not the main reason for my poor attendance, which lost me so many brownie points with my immediate boss, his boss and then the overall boss (international organizations are big on bosses). Mostly it was because there simply wasn't time. The information team produced the tangibles — the books, scientific papers, magazines, brochures, proceedings — the things that the public could put their hands on to see what the institution was actually doing, a lot of which was very worthwhile and merited a lot more publicity than we could give it.

These tasks seemed more urgent than seminars that had people sitting for entire days in an auditorium trying to decide what colour sprang to mind when they considered the institution, or playing games to discover their hidden strengths or weaknesses as team players. But then, I may have thought that way precisely because I didn't attend those team-building exercises.

The team I was on had their hands pretty full, actually, trying to publish the research results in a way that would make them useful to farmers, development agents and people in high places who set policies on agriculture, trees and how to manage natural resources. That meant translating development gobbledegook into plain old English, the way we speak it closer to the "grassroots level," which was where the development was needed, after all.

I was taking an immersion course in buzzwords, which had become like Gospel in international organizations concerned with "development assistance" (the correct term is "international cooperation"). This development doublespeak seems specially designed to try to foil the straight thinker and straight talker. Although this language has spread like a kind of verbal AIDS throughout the development community, it is generally much more exaggerated in the uppermost development circles, particularly in board rooms of international organizations or in planning divisions of bilateral development agencies.

The further removed one is from people on the ground — the disadvantaged people that development funds are supposedly dispensed to help — the worse it tends to become. And there is generally an inverse relation between how much of this jargon is used by an organization or a project or an agency, and how much is actually accomplished on the ground. Many development organizations and activities are extremely fruitful and valuable, and this is immediately obvious when one reads their straightforward progress reports.

Those who have little to show for all the money spent (or feeble grounds for soliciting more funds) tend to be the worst offenders when it comes to padding their reports with gobbledegook. I offer an (almost-fictional) example:

The Global Initiative on Alleviating Rural Poverty through Sustainable and Environmentally Sound Utilization of Natural Resources in the Sub-humid Tropics (GIARP-SESUN-RISHT), which is co-ordinated by a global steering committee (GSC) of high-level experts (HLE) representing a broad range of international agricultural research organizations (IARCs) and bilateral development agencies, and being implemented jointly by national agricultural research systems (NARS) working together as a multidisciplinary team in full collaboration with a broad and dynamic network of partners from IARCs and non-governmental organizations (NGOs), which aims to build a solid but resilient framework for achieving the overall goal of enhancing income-generating opportunities for resource-poor persons in the sub-humid tropics on a long-term and sustainable basis with a fully gender-sensitive and participatory approach, is being supported financially by the Consultative Group on International Development (CGID) and Global Developmental Facility (GDF).

The first thing to be said about such passages is that they boggle the mind — which may already be boggled or even dead if such stuff has been read (or worse, written) every day for several years. But with patience and perseverance, sometimes it can be boiled down, usually to a simple sentence that comes somewhere near the truth. That sentence, for example, I take the liberty of translating roughly like this: A bunch of very handsomely paid international civil servants (all men except for the one woman who takes the minutes of the meetings) are squabbling over positions, titles and perks so that when the funding comes in to keep their castle in the air, they'll get their hands on it before any of it trickles down to the impoverished farmers in the tropics.

In the thesaurus of development rhetoric, no one ever "does" anything — projects are "launched" or "implemented." Initiatives are even "initiated." You don't alleviate poverty; the alleviation of poverty is achieved. Passive voice prevails.

There is a whole whack of overblown words for simple surveys or studies, which are never "done" but are "carried out" or "undertaken." There is a whole slew of "approaches" and "strategies," which are adopted to achieve or attain a set of objectives or goals or aims. These can be equally nebulous but impressive all the same. You may, for example, "envision" one of the objectives of your institution as the "enhancement of environmental resilience."

The people who are supposed to benefit from these development activities are called the "target groups," which unfortunately summons for me images of a sorry bunch of shackled innocents facing a firing squad. This may in fact be how African villagers feel when once every year or so the Big Men from abroad, perhaps members of The Executive Board or someone from the *Corps Diploma-*

tique, cruise into their little village in a fleet of air-conditioned four-wheel-drive vehicles and a cloud of dust to see for themselves how things are going in any one project or initiative.

Fortunately, most impoverished farmers in Africa and elsewhere are a very hospitable lot and know how to turn on the charm and the smiles for their visitors. I've heard the odd visiting dignitary decide, on the basis of those smiles and the ritualized gratitude, that a project was a great success. I once heard a scientific consultant conclude after his first visit to the continent that African farmers were awfully happy people with simple lives and no big worries. How did he know this? Why, they all smiled and waved at him from the roadside.

Some of the dilemma over terminology is quite understandable. What word, for example, can be used to describe those farmers who constitute the target group? Are they "poor farmers?" This doesn't work because they are not poor at farming; they may well be excellent farmers who just don't have any capital or land to work with. Are they "small farmers?" That doesn't work either, because their farms may indeed be minuscule, less than an acre in fact, but they themselves may be large and imposing human beings physically. In the end, they have to be called small-scale or subsistence or resource-poor farmers. Perverse and averse as I was to so much of the terminology, I did agree to those terms. I worried that the simple word "farmer," read by someone far from Africa, might evoke mental pictures of a wheat farm or a ranch in, say, Alberta, rather than an accurate image of a dirt-poor family in rags, bent double over their hoes in tiny fields, with an income of less than a couple of hundred dollars a year — in a good year. The latter was a fairly accurate description of the farmers who were benefiting (in theory) from the research.

Over the years and quite undeservedly, gender became the butt of a lot of backlash and back-room humour. The term "women in development," which was in vogue in the 1980s, all but vanished in the '90s. It had offended about half of the population in Africa, nearly all the men, even the many who were well aware that women in Africa produced 70 per cent of the food, did 90 per cent of the labour in and around the household, and were the most responsible when it came to handling family income to ensure the welfare of the children.

The trouble was that it seemed to ignore the men and that was no solution. Suddenly the new term was "gender sensitive" or "gender equity" and it was a must for any project funding proposal or project report. It might be dropped like a subliminal message into just about every line in a project document, or added after the fact when an astute proposal writer noticed it was missing. It appeared so often in development literature, in fact, that it came to be highly suspect. The same can be said of the term "environmentally sound" or "environmentally sensitive."

Even if it is not, nearly every development initiative simply must claim to be "fully participatory" or "grassroots" or "village-level" or "bottom-up." "Top-down" is out, out, out. One genial, bumbling and extremely well-paid scientist for whom I worked in Nairobi once wrote in one of his reports that the global initiative he headed had "adopted a bottoms-up" approach to research. I deleted the "s," assuming he'd merely made a typo and that he was still recalling the rollicking good times he'd had on his recent official mission to Peru — something to do with a scuzzy nightclub, wild and willing girls, and shaving creme. When I gave it back to him, he neatly penned the "s" back in, telling me pedantically that he was better versed in the terminology than was I. I demurred. He insisted. But then I looked at his face, still florid from whatever he'd been drinking the night before, and acquiesced. And so his report went out, describing the initiative as bottoms-up, which probably wasn't inaccurate.

Then there are the liberties taken with a whole lot of words that are miraculously pluralized to exaggerate what has actually been accomplished in any particular project — there are "outputs" and "impacts" which lead to "sustainable development," sometimes even "environmentally sustainable development." No one ever defined for me the word "sustainable" — as in, will this development "impact" be sustainable until the sun burns up? Or was all this sustainable just until we in the developed world self-destructed and brought ruin to the developing world too, by overheating the world's climate, depleting all the natural resources on the planet or "initiating" a global war?

When I tried on occasion to sneak in the word "lasting" to replace the sixth "sustainable" in a single paragraph, I had my knuckles rapped and earned myself a lecture on the Theory of Development.

Donors, I was told, may not accept any funding proposals or reports that are not weighted down with incomprehensible acronyms and mouthfuls of mumbo jumbo. Translation into simple English is a no-no, perhaps because that would be too revealing. "Institutional capacity building," for example, really means that a donor will take on some of the more immediate costs of keeping any particular na-

163

tional institution or organization from going belly-up, for a while anyway. Or else it means that civil servants in any government ministry or a national research or educational institution, who might pull in less than $100 a month as a salary and have virtually no budget to work with, might get a "topping up" of their salary and a car and perhaps a fuel budget and maybe even a computer so they can actually do their job — or start a private moonlighting business so they can make ends meet to feed and school their large extended family.

A favourite pastime of the hidden heretics (HHs) in international organizations is decoding acronyms, which proliferate like fruit flies in development documents (DDs). Following fickle faddish favourites (FFFs) in terminology is also a source of some amusement for the cynics. These are terms that came into vogue for a while in development theory, and then rapidly transformed themselves into yet another euphemism for something else that donors are interested in "developing" in Africa.

For a while "food security," as one example, was synonymous with food aid, a handy way for Western nations to funnel off a little of their excess harvests and keep their farmers happy, while nicely adding to national budgets for international development. Massive amounts of food aid are sent to areas that could well be supplied from surpluses produced by African farmers elsewhere on the continent. But who wishes to quibble about such details when people are said to be starving somewhere? Only the hidden heretic (HH) would be so mean-spirited.

In the mid-'80s I saw canola oil flood the local markets in Burkina Faso, undercutting the market for locally produced peanut oil. I asked Canadian officials in Ouagadougou what on earth all that Canadian oil was doing there. They said that a couple of years earlier when Burkina Faso had suffered a drought, the Burkinabe government had asked for food aid from Canada, which it could then sell on the market to bring in much-needed income. Unfortunately, that food aid, the Canadian surplus, had come two years too late and landed in Burkina Faso during a year with a bumper harvest of peanuts. Yes, it was unfortunate that the Canadian oil completely undercut the market for locally produced groundnut oil, and thus discouraged farmers from growing peanuts in coming years, and thus helped contribute not to food security but to food insecurity. But no, there was no way of stopping such food aid once it was in the pipeline.

Eventually it seems that the voices of development workers on the ground in Africa, and the small and highly knowledgeable lobby group that understood the politics of food aid, were heard. The term "food aid" suddenly disappeared from the vocabulary of the donor community. The new and acceptable term was "food security."

This became synonymous with a whole new set of factors and a whole new list of terms. "Modernizing" agricultural methods, food aid that was delivered as Food For Work (FFW), sustainable land use, reversing land degradation, enhancing nutritional security — you name it, they claimed they were doing it.

But then suddenly, one sunny day in Nairobi, I learned from the overall boss that "food security" was also on its way out. He was freshly back from a trip to Washington where he'd been brushing up on the latest in lingo at the World Bank. He called me into a meeting in his office to draw up an outline for the "medium-term strategic plan" for the institute and informed me that from now on, I was to ditch the term "food security" altogether and replace it with the words "nutritional security."

I was feeling prickly, as I often was those days, and I balked at his order. I suggested to him that traditional diets in Africa with all-natural foodstuffs and many varied nutrients coming from tree fruits and leaves and oils, supplemented with high-protein beans and fish, probably offered a lot more nutritional security than the average fast-food, fat-full and chemical-sugar diet in mainstream North America. I went on to say that traditional farming systems had served Africa very well for a long time. Then I said that a lot of the food and nutritional *insecurity* might well be blamed on the much-touted Green Revolution that had converted African farmers to crops like hybrid maize and reduced tree cover and diversity on their farms, wiping out soil fertility and poisoning waterways and human beings along the way. He regarded me as though I'd just written *Satanic Verses*. He wasn't having a bit of that. I was to use the phrase "nutritional security," no more ifs, buts or criticism. He'd been to Washington. He'd been at the meeting at the World Bank and their word was Gospel.

Which brings me to the subject of those meetings. All of the theories, frameworks, concepts, strategies, and phrases had, of course, to be discussed in depth in endless meetings of experts on any one subject all over the continent, and even off it. These meetings were not simple "meetings" of course. They were called seminars, conferences, symposia, summits, colloquia, workshops, fora, strategic or goal-oriented planning sessions, round tables, days of reflection. Each generally came attached to an epithet indicating whether it was (a) global, (b) continent-wide, (c) regional, (d) national. So far I've not seen one claiming to be universal, but surely that too will come.

The costs over the years of these meetings are incalculable, but maybe that's the point. They were easy ways to dispense with budget excesses quickly before the end of any fiscal year. I imagine that if one tallied the total — all the airfares, hotel bills, per diems, person-hours, little side trips to favourite tourist attractions by participants — and then divided it up and distributed it evenly to every African man, woman and child, the continent's economy would have long since got the jump-start it needed to develop itself. And there would probably be enough left over to cover the costs of building an entire network of roads or railways, that would finally make it possible to move goods easily from one part of Africa to another without resorting to a camel or a donkey on a mud walking path. Africans might finally find it possible to communicate with each other and trade among themselves.

When I had left the institution and returned to the life of freelance reporter, this time in Bamako, Mali, I occasionally tried to attend a few of these meetings (a meeting by any fancy name is still a meeting) to see if there was something to report. The subject matter was often interesting and the discussions important, dealing with many of the real problems that plague Africa and its development. But many years down the line, it simply wasn't clear to me that all the recommendations or action plans that had emerged from the meetings had ever gone anywhere or had much impact — many "impacts." And there were so many of these conferences that had I wanted to cover even a few of the ones going on simultaneously in Bamako every single day, I would have had to clone myself many times over.

By the year 2000, when the Internet has made it as far as Timbuktu, I wondered how many of those discussions could just as easily have been handled using telecommunications and video conferencing or e-mail or chat-lines. But there seemed little incentive for reducing costs this way. Some conference-goers had come to enjoy the healthy per diems accorded them. African civil servants often used these to help make ends meet. And many international experts quite enjoyed jaunting about the world, often in first or business class, feeling like VIPs.

I don't wish to paint a completely negative picture of development work, and certainly not of the many hard-working and knowledgeable people who are involved in countless invaluable efforts to improve basic living standards on the continent. The biggest problem is not, in fact, what is said or done about development. Much of the development work being done is well intentioned, effective and essential.

The trouble is that the small achievements and the development work are inconsequential next to the much bigger issue of what is *not* being done to remove the obstacles to Africa's development. This would require fundamental changes in the approaches taken, not by the development people on the ground, but by the leaders in the West or the North or whatever one wishes to call the political and economic heavyweights of the industrialized world, starting with the Group of Seven and their free-wheeling enterprises.

The prerequisites would include more transparency and honesty in international affairs, respect for African know-how and culture, decent prices paid for African commodities and natural resources, sincere and knowledgeable encouragement of genuine democracy, justice and economic unity on the continent, removing hidden political and economic agendas, an easing of the debt, and an end to arms sales.

That's a tall order that would require more than jargon and meetings that produce sound recommendations, which usually get shelved. It would mean creating that long-awaited and much-discussed New World Order, by balancing a few of the economic and political inequities that keep the so-called developing world at the mercy of the so-called developed world. On this planet that is now so glibly termed a Global Village, surely equity and a "fair deal" should be the very first goals.

In private, African friends have told me they don't understand the schizophrenia of the developed world. On one hand, they see competent and knowledgeable development people sent out to work on the ground with or even under them, with sincere goals of helping them to help themselves, people who love Africa and never want to leave it. They hear representatives from the developed world calling for democracy and economic progress and righting the wrongs of hundreds of years of colonialism and neo-colonialism. They see international human rights groups making valiant efforts to improve governance and reduce injustice in Africa. They hear Western individuals and lobbies, often church groups, academics and non-governmental organizations, arguing to have the African debt burden eased.

At the same time, Africans complain to me that they see those same donor countries backing corrupt and crooked leaders in their countries. They watch the West accepting the results of blatantly dishonest elections, selling arms to countries where even the few schools and health clinics that are standing are in sorry shape, dispensing loans to corrupt governments so that African countries go deeper into debt while those same dollars bounce back into Western banks.

They see private firms from those countries handing out whacking bribes to get at a particular mineral, precious gem, logging concession, oil deposit, construction contract. And most recently, just when the donor countries are making the most noise about democracy and peace, they see multinationals from the rich (democratic) world, aiding, abetting, and even arming violent factions in civil wars.

Africans who ask me about these mind-boggling contradictions don't receive an answer. I can't help them. I don't understand either. Or maybe we're not meant to. Maybe that helps explain why so many truths about development in Africa are shrouded in jargon that is just about as transparent, substantial and easy to stomach as pink cotton candy.

Chapter 14

Unsung heroines

Jennifer was one of the "resource-poor" farmers that the research institute was aiming to help, which was why I had come to Zambia to see her and others in the village who were working with the researchers. We were sitting at the edge of her maize field, in a tiny village outside a tiny town in Zambia's southeastern corner. Jennifer was telling me, matter-of-factly, a bit about herself.

"I was born in 1962. I have five children. Two died. The first, born in 1975, died at one week. The second was born in 1977. She's alive. Elube Phiri. In 1979, I had Inid, who died at four of diarrhea. In 1980 I had Harrison, who lived. Then in 1983 I had Charity. In 1985 I had Dorothy and in 1987 I had Wilson. The five of them go to school."

We were sitting on the ground, profiting from the bits of shade cast by a small plot of trees she had planted around her maize field as a tree fallow, which she hoped would enrich her soil. With the removal of farm subsidies in the past few years, she said she could no longer afford fertilizer for her maize. Well, she said, she could but only if she sold her one goat. And the goat provided her with milk for her children. And if the rains failed, as they often did these days, her maize seed would be wasted and so would any fertilizer. Buying the maize seed was expensive enough.

She had grown up working fields of — and eating — millet and sorghum. Maize was relatively recent. Hybrid maize seed packages and suppliers claimed this improved seed would yield about one tonne of maize per hectare, a much higher output than millet. Of course the packages recommended that fertilizer and pesticides also be applied, but didn't mention the costs of those, or the costs of this Green Revolution agriculture on Africa's small-scale farmers. The maize sapped more nutrients from the soil to produce that yield than would the traditional millet crop, nutrients that would have to be replaced by chemical fertilizers. But these days such fertilizers were no longer affordable and the soils were getting poorer all the time.

Jennifer said this land wasn't hers. As a girl in the family, she could not inherit land from her father. "When I got married with Mr. Phiri," she said, "he took me to his village and we cultivated, but he didn't like staying in his village. So we came here to cultivate in 1978. Then we stayed together for some time until 1990 when Mr. Phiri went to Lusaka and never came back to get the wife."

I wondered if her use of the third person when she referred to her runaway husband — and to herself as "the wife" — was some kind of psychological trick to make it all a little less personal.

She continued. "We parted in a good way. But I don't know what was in his heart when he left, because he's never come back. I don't know if he's dead or alive because there's been no communication for a long time. When he left for Lusaka he said he was going to visit a relative. He wrote to say that he had found employment. Then he wrote another letter in 1991 saying he was now coming to pick me and the children. That was the last letter he sent."

After that, her brothers loaned her two hectares so she could farm and support her children, on her own.

She said that in a good year she could just about cover the most essential costs. The children's school fees and uniforms and books cost her roughly $50 a year, which is about what she could make from selling off surplus harvests after keeping enough to feed her children. When rains weren't good, there was no surplus, barely enough for the family. She bought them school uniforms — mandatory — every two years.

She said education was the most important thing of all. "I went up to grade four and I got married in 1973."

I stopped her, checking the dates. If she was born in 1962 and married in 1973, that meant she married when she was eleven years old?

"Yes, it was bad that I married at such an early age. My thinking was not mature."

I waited a few seconds, wondering whether to ask the next question. Images passed through my mind of what might befall African writers or researchers who marched into a village back on my own continent, prying into someone's personal affairs the way I was hers. Even if they didn't get clobbered senseless, I doubted they would get away with so much as a scrap of information. Still, on I went. "Did you choose to marry that young?" I asked.

She shook her head. "I was forced into marriage because of the stepmother. The father was a polygamist. He had two wives. My own mother was second wife. She died. The other wife also died, so there were ten of us children. I was number seven. My father took a new wife. I couldn't get along with his new wife. The stepmother never had children herself. It was difficult for her to look after the children. It was a difficult situation. The stepmother wanted me out of her way. So they sent me to marry."

And what did she, Jennifer, want for her children?

She pulled a twig off the tree beside her, and slowly picked off the delicate leaves, one by one. Not looking up. "I do not want my children to suffer the way I've suffered. I want my children to go to school because when they are educated they can look after themselves properly. They can work in the city. These years there is drought. Our soil is now depleted from all these years of cultivation. The old men say that there used to be trees here to make the soil good. But now the trees are gone and we cannot buy fertilizer. That's why I am planting these sesbania trees as improved fallows."

Would she remarry if she could?

No, no man would have her now. Everyone in the village knew her story. She was regarded as a failed wife, and thus a failed woman in their eyes.

Would she move to the city if she could, get away from those kinds of rural judgements?

She said she might not like the city, herself. Not that life was easy here in the village. She had to get up at three in the morning to get water from the well when the level was high, before the whole village had been to fetch a morning supply. She had to travel far for firewood with her children. And the farming was a question of whether God was going to be generous that year with the rain. But she would stay here because there was a sense of community in the village. She told me about the group of women farmers she had joined and was now leading, which met in a local church several afternoons a week. There they shared information they were getting on ways to improve their farming, shared funds for small community projects, shared their woes and their dreams too. It was small groups of hard-working, like-minded, unsung heroines like these, found in almost every village in every part of the continent, that gave Africa so much of its remarkable strength and resilience.

"Here, people help each other," she said. "That's how we survive. In the city, it is not like this." Then she sat for a photograph of herself, with her children whom she was sending to school so they would never have to suffer the way she did. They were all smiling and jubilant at this chance to pose for the visitors. And as the shutter clicked, it occurred to me that all through that conversation we had had, which was really just a litany of almost insurmountable problems she faced every day of her life, Jennifer had not once given even a hint of just how much she had suffered. There was no sign of self-pity or despair. Just a calm acceptance of her fate, the willingness to deal with it — and her ability to smile.

There was something wrong with a stereotype that had been pieced together over the years by outsiders looking in at Africa — or rather at African women. I tried to summon the image in my mind, the one I had brought with me to Africa many years earlier. It was a composite of misconceptions and it rose in my mind's eye as a bent and tired female form — hapless, helpless, despairing and defeated. A pitiful victim.

Jennifer, like just about all the African women I met in the most difficult circumstances imaginable (or even unimaginable), was none of the above. Sure, from my perspective, she looked like a victim of unfair social rules. But that was my perspective, not hers. And were I in her shoes, I would probably not have survived or done so as a bitter and hapless victim. But that was my problem and not Jennifer's. In reality, most African woman I know are jovial, humorous, tough, and full of faith and the drive to make things better, if not for themselves, then for their children, despite all the odds stacked against them. They certainly don't need our misplaced pity. They deserve respect and admiration. Theirs is a complex world and they know best how to survive in it — and to change it. And the best motor for change is education. Alas, even that is fraught with obstacles today.

Jennifer's tale was just one of dozens and dozens I'd collected on the job and over the years from women all over Africa. There were tales of pre-teen girls being married off to eighty-year-old men. More stories of teenage mothers who had to quit school when their teachers impregnated them and then denied any culpability.

I knew a Ghanaian woman, a third wife, whose husband had beaten her every time he wanted the money she earned by growing and selling vegetables. A young Ghanaian man told me how his father had beaten his mother because she had secretly sent him, her son, to school, using the money she made peddling vegetables in the market to cover the school fees.

Another woman friend, who dared to call her husband on his infidelities and to point out to him that for two years she had been a veritable handmaiden and prisoner in his house, was beaten for voicing her jealous concerns about his gallivanting with girls. Once the stitches on her face had been removed, she was tossed out of the house, penniless but not without scars from that marriage.

After all these endless tales of woe, I didn't know where to catalogue the offhand remarks of a young Cameroonian woman who told me that she expected her husband to beat her — if he didn't, it meant he didn't really love her.

In fact, I didn't really know what to do with any of the stories from a dozen countries. Nearly all dealt with suffering on a scale that I could not begin to grasp. Nearly all illustrated that staying power of African women. And all the stories spoke volumes about the need for human rights legislation to be extended at last to include women in African societies.

Those stories of men using brute force on their wives also told a cultural tale about norms and accepted behaviour. Boys would be boys, or rather human beings would be human beings, and most would do whatever society allowed them to do (and often even what it didn't allow them to do). Over the years, I had watched numerous European and North American men quickly dispense with all the rules they'd been obliged to obey back home as soon as they landed on African soil. In Burkina Faso, a German ambassador hadn't even attempted to hide his affair with a lovely slip of a very young woman from Senegal, whom he moved into his official residence, while his wife and four children took up lodgings in the staff quarters out back.

In northern Ghana, I listened to Canadian women weep about their husbands sleeping with the "housegirl." Housegirls, in turn, told me how they had been forced into bed by their white employers. I knew German men who left their wives at home and came to Africa on short contracts that were really just month-long orgies with teenage African beauties. And many destitute teenage African beauties were not about to say no, given that it was universally believed (and generally true) that all white men carried wads of money about in their pockets.

Then there were all those fatherless children whose white fathers had simply flown away when the construction project or development contract finished, never to be heard from again by either mother or child. As I saw it, there was no inherent difference in people anywhere on this big, round earth — it was what society told them they could or couldn't do. When in Rome and all that . . .

The real problem, given my belief in UN charters that said all human beings should be equal before the law, was that in much of Africa, they were not. The actual laws in many African countries still did nothing to protect women from physical abuse. In rural areas, there were traditional rules and rulers and family and elders; all helped enforce the submissive role women were to play. At the same time, they also helped protect women from unsanctioned abuse and violence. That intense family interest and power of persuasion helped forestall fatal incidents and keep domestic excesses in check. In urban areas these traditional checks and balances were breaking down. As much as neighbours might try to mediate when they heard violence in a house, they simply didn't have the clout that fellow villagers and family would have in preventing violence against women.

So there was that need for laws. But laws alone would not be enough. It was unlikely — unthinkable in most cases — that a young, shy, tongue-tied, dependent wife with no formal education and no knowledge at all about her rights would dare to take her wounds to court, heaping shame on herself and her family and probably risking worse beating in future. If, of course, she could afford the cost of transport to the court or knew where to find it, and if she had any idea of how to go about finding legal advice or the money to pay for it. Precious few young and unschooled women did.

In many parts of Africa, I had heard it said that some people still felt it was a "waste" to educate daughters because an education might "spoil" them for the role laid out for them as submissive, hard-labouring wives and mothers. An educated girl might stand less chance of marrying than her unschooled counterpart. A woman with formal education might be more inclined to "cross" a husband by demanding things of him — his help around the house, her right to hold down a job, her right to speak her mind in public, even her right to an opinion.

To make matters worse, many girls who did go to school found themselves at the mercy of male teachers, who could and often did demand all sorts of extra-curricular favours in exchange for a passing grade. Some teenage students found themselves pregnant because of the teacher's special interest in their education, and had to drop out of school.

For all that, more and more girls were being educated and more and more women were clamouring for change. Not that educated women did not suffer abuse at the hands of their educated husbands, any more than they would in, say, Canada. Indeed, I had women friends in West Africa who were highly educated and who were regularly beaten up by their highly educated professional husbands. This happened largely because of male jealousy of a wife who had an impressive office and perhaps a service car and commanded respect among the public.

Included in this list were some women cabinet ministers, ironically one who headed the ministry that dealt with social affairs and women's issues in Burkina Faso. She once told me that in rural areas where tradition was strong and women theoretically most subservient, she had no problem commanding respect as a woman minister. She said her biggest problems were in the city, among her male peers with top posts and university degrees — and with her own abusive husband.

But women like her could and often did leave their husbands to go it alone as single mothers, raising and schooling their children themselves. They had education and employment, the tickets to independence, or in the language of the women's movement, they were "empowered."

That was not so for a woman living in rural Mali or Zambia or a village in northern Ghana, who had no formal education and little hope of earning money of her own outside the house. Such women were less likely to stand up for their rights than a woman who was on an educational par with her husband and had learned to express her own opinion in public, or at least learned that she had a right to an opinion. Most rural women usually had no idea what human rights were.

A woman tossed out by her husband would not always be welcomed back in the folds of the family. Without money or family support and with children to feed and educate, women with no other options sometimes turned to the only form of income-generation available to them — selling the only assets a woman is born with, for a pitiful return.

I felt deeply troubled and torn about the gender issue in Africa, and loathe even to wade through those tales of suffering that filled notebooks on my shelves, loathe especially to publish them, go public on the issue. Not that I wanted to deny the reality of women's poverty and women's total lack of rights, just that I wasn't sure my foreign voice had any place in the choir of criticism within Africa, tempered African voices calling for changes, but changes that they would make themselves, for themselves. Not to please the outside world with a tendency to be pejorative and judgmental.

The flamboyant late president of Burkina Faso, Thomas Sankara, had been outspoken in his condemnation of some aspects of Burkinabe society. He'd stood up and lambasted the men of his country for treating their wives, the mothers of their own children, worse than "livestock." But that was an African speaking to fellow Africans. And Sankara had been assassinated in 1987, not least because of his radical ideas and actions for the oppressed in his country, which threatened Big Men at home and in distant capitals.

The negative images of how African women were treated were all too common in our media. One of the objectives of many western journalists I met, who were in Africa for the first time, was to do stories that probed the sensitive issues of polygamy, female circumcision, enslaved teenage servant girls, and forced or arranged marriage. There was nothing wrong with such stories — African writers and singers were treating these issues themselves for their home audiences, and often suffering ostracism and vicious criticism for their efforts.

But articles in our media on these issues, stories in isolation, didn't tell the whole story. They didn't offer any balance. One of my goals had always been to try to get at the "other side" of the story, the side that could not be immediately apparent the moment a camera-person or a special correspondent stepped off an airliner and put foot for the first time in Africa.

Apart from that, I had met as many African men who broke the negative stereotype, men who were responsible and caring husbands and fathers and who needed no laws to keep them that way, as I had African women who told me horrific tales of abuse at the hands of their African husbands.

On one hand, the publicity given to female circumcision and women's rights over the years in Africa, much of it funded by foreign organizations, had brought about a good deal of change and helped give African women a voice they had not had before. It was true that the issues were now coming out into the open and being discussed, usually heatedly. Laws governing the family that allowed women no rights at all, forbade women from owning land and from making decisions affecting the welfare of their families were all being discussed and, in some countries, reformulated. But inside the homes, tradition carried more weight than did laws in a magistrate's office, and change was not coming as fast as many Africans wanted.

There were times when I couldn't help wondering if it might come a little faster without some of the most audible and visible pressure from outsiders. Foreign intrusion gave reactionary male (and some female) elements the ammunition they needed to label all talk about women's rights as just more "neo-colonial" preaching from that "hypocritical Western world." They then lumped up all the social and economic reforms that were sweeping the world — some negative and some positive — and portrayed them as one huge "Western" package being "forced down their throats."

Family planning programs funded by the West were portrayed as "plots" to keep down the world's black population. AIDS was said to be a disease invented in CIA laboratories to kill off Africans. In one New Year's speech, the Kenyan president had questioned the Western interest in fighting AIDS in Africa with the use of condoms, saying this helped encourage immoral and non-Christian sexual behaviour. The next day his health minister went even further, alleging that the condoms sent to Africa were actually infected with HIV.

These reactionaries or traditionalists or fundamentalists or whatever you wanted to call the men (and some women) leading the wave of backlash against the emancipation of women, often labelled outspoken African feminists as puppets of the West, "sent to trouble our society." That way, they were able to garner support for their campaigns to block the elimination of traditional practices many people viewed as harmful and no longer relevant to the societies where they existed — such as female circumcision or the automatic handing over of a wife to her brother-in-law in the advent of her husband's death.

The latter was still the practise in western Kenya, and at one time it had served widows well. A widow and her children would not be left to their own devices should a husband and father die, because the deceased's brother would immediately take them under his wing and take his former sister-in-law as his wife. But towards the end of the twentieth century, when deaths related to AIDS were common in that part of the country, the practise had outlived its purpose and become a cause of the rapid spread of HIV in the region.

I had some press clippings detailing the reaction among a few parliamentarians when a proposal was brought forward in Kenya for a new law that would allow a wife the right to say "no" to her husband. This proposed legislation would make the unthinkable possible — if a man forced his wife to have sex with him, he could be prosecuted for rape. The reaction among some of the male parliamentarians was telling. One member stood up and said that this was contrary to tradition; there could be no such thing as a husband raping a wife because a wife could not say no. Tradition said so. Kenyan women friends laughed their heads off and said that this meant tradition condoned rape of wives.

Tradition was a favourite card to pull when a conservative man wanted to defend the old ways, defend his total dominance over his wife, or wives. In most West African countries, men were still the legal heads of household. Although I knew many independent and strong single African women raising children on their own (by choice), there was often a stigma attached to a woman who didn't have a husband, and a woman without children might be considered no woman at all. For rural women who had to suffer ostracism in the tight-knit community of the village, this might make it preferable to remain with an abusive husband than to try to go it alone.

I had on tape a conversation with a very prominent Imam in Mali, who asked me more questions than I ever got around putting to him. He wanted me to explain to him why the West wanted "to wipe out African traditions with its feminism and condemnation of traditional practises such as female circumcision." Without taking a breath, he then asked me to explain "why the same West that sent arms to Africa that were used to slaughter children was pretending it cared about the welfare of little girls whose mothers wanted them circumcised?"

He wasn't done yet. He went on to remind me that the United States had refused to sign the Ottawa Treaty on landmines, and it continued to produce and sell landmines. Those landmines, he said, continued to cause untold suffering among civilians in countries such as Angola, by blowing off girls' arms and legs, so "how could that country even pretend to have an interest in the socially sanctioned removal of a girl's clitoris?"

I sensed that there was a flaw in his reasoning, that the people who defended landmine production in the US were unlikely to be the same people with an interest in eliminating female circumcision in Africa, but he allowed me no time to argue and I was there to interview him — not for a debate.

He made it a political issue and alleged that Western intelligence was behind many of the evangelizing missions in Africa, where the aim was to "brainwash" Africans and "wipe out their culture."

I could not argue with him that the Central Intelligence Agency did not have any agents disguised as missionaries or volunteers in Africa. I had no proof, one way or the other. But over the years I had met a number of Americans in various development agencies who were rumoured to be undercover, even deep-cover, CIA agents. Friends in Nairobi had alleged that a US ambassador to the United Nations Environment Program was just such an agent.

There was also a telling news item I'd heard a year earlier. After American nuns had been massacred in Guatemala by militias that later alleged the women had been CIA agents, a bill was eventually proposed that would forbid the US intelligence agency from using charities and non-governmental organizations as cover for its agents. The bill was killed, which meant that legally the CIA could continue the unethical and dangerous practise of placing its people in what were meant to be benevolent organisations such as the Peace Corps and Christian missions.

None of us on the outside was in any position to identify agents disguised as harmless and well-intentioned development workers. So I had no proof to either confirm or refute the Imam's conspiracy theories.

I can't pretend that the Imam's attitude and simplistic arguments didn't rankle. They did. The West is not a huge uniform mass. Many people in Europe and North America were busy lapping up African culture — its textiles, its music, its films, more than were many Africans themselves. The Islam that the Imam was espousing was no more an indigenous African religion than Christianity was, and both had been used for centuries to denigrate African customs and beliefs. As he spoke I kept thinking about the late Fela, the notorious and much-loved Nigerian musician who had made a name for himself by decrying all forms of imported religions that supplanted traditional African faith in their own spirits and gods. Before he died, Fela had spent a good deal of time in prison for his heresy.

While I could not fault much of the logic the Imam used, his defence of female circumcision as something women wanted and needed did conflict with tales women in Ghana, Burkina Faso and Mali had told me about their struggle to keep their daughters away from their native villages. They said if they let their daughters visit the family in the village, it was inevitable that the old women with their knives would get them. These were the elderly women who were in the business of "upholding a girl's virtue" and perpetuating tradition by slicing off the clitoris and sometimes the labia and sometimes sewing the whole thing up after that, so that even menstrual blood could barely flow through. Hence the term: female genital mutilation, or FGM.

In 1999, statistics said that 94 per cent of all Malian women between the ages of fifteen and forty-nine years were circumcised. They also said that 75 per cent of those circumcised women were in favour of this traditional practise. Abolishing the practise was often considered a priority for development projects conceived by outsiders. And yet within Mali, when I asked women to list their main problems in order of importance, female circumcision rarely appeared on that list. That was hard for me to grasp, but it made it starkly clear to me that it was also not for me to judge. The only woman I knew who openly and loudly condemned the practise as a great evil to be eradicated was the head of a Malian women's association. And she, not coincidentally, was a great favourite of foreign donors that pumped money into her efforts to eradicate FGM.

Body mutilation was by no means confined to Africa or traditional peoples any more; the penchant for piercing had already moved below the belly button back home and, so I'd been told, reached the clitoris. My daughter and her friends ogle and admire tattoos. It wouldn't surprise me if, just at the time that Africans dispense with all their traditional cosmetic surgery because it's no longer considered healthy, relevant or "civilized," young people in Europe and North America decide it's time to start filing their teeth, binding their feet, flattening their foreheads, extending their lower lips.

Women's development and gender equity in Africa was anything but a black and white issue that could be boiled down to women pitted against men. There were conservative women's groups who clung to the need for female circumcision and the traditional role women played in the house. There were courageous men all over who espoused the unpopular rhetoric of women's rights, and insisted their daughters get an education so they would not be at the complete mercy of a man later in life.

One of the most soft-spoken gentlemen I ever ran across was a Sudanese colleague in Kenya. He had three beautiful young daughters, all of whom he and his wife steadfastly refused to have circumcised. The result? He'd lost many of his friends back home in Khartoum who told him he was the author of a dreadful future for his daughters. They told him his daughters would never find men willing to marry them, unclean as they were and liable to infidelity because they had not been circumcised. I laughed, although I shouldn't have, and told him I figured that with daughters as bright and stunningly beautiful as his, the young men would be lined up around the block for those girls. He didn't laugh. He smiled ruefully and said that might be the case, but not in Khartoum. For that reason, he was unlikely to move home to Sudan for a good long while, not until his daughters had been happily married off to the men of their choice, in a land that appreciated a "whole" woman.

The long and short of it was that I was confused and distressed. I knew I had only a vague notion of how much some African women friends suffered at the hands of traditions that allowed men to beat them up with impunity. I came from (and could always return to) a country where women's rights were entrenched in the constitution, which protected all Canadians as equals.

I recalled a conversation that I'd had once with a Cameroonian man who had spent six years studying in Canada. He'd waxed lyrical about how much he loved my country, how beautiful it was, how easy life was there, how good the education, how kind and open the people were. Then he glanced at me slyly and added, "In fact, if I could choose any country in the world to live in besides my Cameroon, it would be Canada. Canada would be perfect except for one thing."

"What's that?" I said. "The cold winters?"

He shook his head. "No, winters were not a problem. The one problem you have in Canada is all those feminists. Honestly, I simply couldn't put up with the women and their feminism."

In hindsight, I suspect he had been trying to get a rise out of me. He succeeded, probably beyond his wildest hopes. For someone who made a living reporting on events and people in Africa, I had absolutely no right to react badly to anyone making derogatory and unwarranted (in my view) attacks on my country. But that didn't stop me. I reacted terribly. My stomach knotted, I felt my indignation rising as a hot flush on my cheeks and I retorted very hotly, "Well, I'm glad you came back to Cameroon, then. If you feel that way about our society, then I'm glad you didn't stay there. I'm glad you brought your anti-feminist views home to Cameroon where they belong."

He was still smiling. "And you're here on my home territory," he replied. "So I hope I'm not going to hear you delivering any feminist lectures in my country."

One day not long after that, I picked up a Malian newspaper and read an editorial complaining about the way, in that journalist's eyes, the Americans and the West were busy imposing their brand of morality on the rest of the world. Naturally, there were the usual questions about why America considered itself such a moral paragon. Then there was the standard criticism of Western society, as it appeared from an African perspective that often focussed exclusively on the social ills in the West just as the West did when it looked at Africa. The editorial cited teenage murders, drug abuse, child pornography, broken homes and families, sex as a marketing device for a commercial world that seemed to be out of control.

There were also some legitimate questions raised about why the US thought it had a right to bypass the United Nations and bully the rest of the world into submission, if not with rhetoric and sanctions then with Cruise missiles. There were also questions about what would happen should an African country ever decide that it had a right to bludgeon the rest of the world into adopting its traditions and religious principles. The journalist had offered a small piece of sound and traditional African advice in a proverb: "Before you go to your neighbour's house to pick out the piece of straw in his eye, better you stay home long enough to remove the dust from your own eyes."

Chapter 15

A slum and a silver lining

We are fine despite the hardship here in Kenya. Otherwise things are not that bad. — Letter from Kenyan friend, September 1998

I knew I should be happy about the news, but I wasn't. Certainly Karl looked happy. He had just been offered a contract, but clear across the continent, in Mali. He said now I could quit my job and stop moaning to him about the international bureaucracy that I squirmed in every day and go back instead to just writing about it.

Had I been moaning that much? I shouldn't have been. I was, I realized, quite happy in Kenya and, when I wasn't locking horns with a couple of bosses who brought out the worst in me (or vice versa), I loved my work. I had become a veritable disciple of some of the institute's branches of science, particularly the idea of domesticating "wild trees" in tropical forests. This wasn't so complex. It meant bringing valuable tree species out of the forests (which were disappearing) and onto farmlands where they would grow in mixed stands (the term was agroforests), which produced lucrative products, helped towards that famous "nutritional security," and protected the environment — all in one go.

So my work was satisfying, and life in Nairobi was comfortable. I had no grounds to complain. African friends liked to count for me my blessings, just in case I had forgotten them (I often had). We had health and money to educate the children. We had a lovely house with running water (most of the time) and electricity (most of the time) and the phone could work for weeks on end, until the enterprising men in the local exchange remembered it was time for a regular, orchestrated "cut" in the line that they could fix with a flip of the switch, for a small fee. We had quite a few of life's luxuries too, at least luxuries in the African context — television, VCR, stereo, computer, car (that worked some of the time). I had a job that led into farmers' fields and into woodlands all over Africa. We had friends. We had much to be thankful for.

I couldn't deny any of it, as much as I would have liked someone to agree with me that I had solid grounds for self-pity when one of those disaffected and disenchanted moods hit me. These usually struck with the realization of just how long I had been living so far away from my people — my family and my "tribe" in Nova Scotia.

"So I'll have to go early," Karl was saying. "In two months I'll go to Mali. You can follow me with the kids when you're ready. When you've finished your contract."

Already, I realized the good news I'd been waiting for wasn't making me happy at all. I didn't want to move again. So I started to complain. To my husband, because no one else would make even a pretence of listening. My job would have to go. So would the impressive title I had at the research institute, a title I had pretended all along didn't matter a whit to me. We would have to say goodbye, yet again, to a whole set of friendships.

"But why are you complaining about leaving?" said Karl. "For four years you've been complaining about being here."

"I have not," I said, indignantly and not truthfully. "That was just the first year. It always takes me a year to get used to a new place. You know that. Then when I do, I want to stay forever."

"Have you forgotten what you said just last week? You said. . . "

He ignored my hand gestures meant to shut him up.

"You said Kenyan politics were unpalatable . . . "

No denying that I had blurted that out a few times.

And on he went, my husband, speaker of truths.

"You said you were tired of the unwritten apartheid in Nairobi, tired of this privileged neighbourhood, and all the killer dogs slobbering and growling through the iron bars of those medieval gates."

I had said as much, yes.

"You said you were tired of living behind high walls, tired of looking in the rear-view mirror in case car hijackers were on your tail."

I sighed.

"You also said you've been waiting for me to get a contract so you could quit working there and go back to journalism instead of pumping out propaganda you loathe."

I sighed again. "It's not propaganda. I don't loathe it. I've learned a lot."

"You said you wanted to quit. You've been threatening to quit since the day you started."

True, and not true. My German husband had never had much patience with my waffling and trying to see things from all sides, something I think he saw as a flaw in my Canadian character. Emotion had to be snuffed out or stuffed away in the suitcases, along with the stacks of sun-faded clothes and things we would lug to wherever it was we would land next.

I decided to try a different tack, not because I really wanted to block our move to a new country in Africa but to register the pain it was going to cause all of us, and he was the nearest and best target. I wanted to make my disclaimer now, just in case something went terribly wrong in our lives once we left Kenya and moved to Mali.

I could think of a thousand things that could go wrong. I was good at that. Maybe it was all the years in Africa, maybe it was my age, but lately I'd become starkly aware of life's fragility. I could no longer imagine why anyone would ever want to risk their neck for thrills on the end of a bungee chord, or the strings of a parachute, or atop a ski-board. Thrills were to be had for free every day in Africa — crossing the road, navigating a bridge made of narrow broken planks, attending a concert or soccer match. In Africa, anything that involved huge crowds could easily end up being smothered by tear gas, and security forces trying to "restore order" more often than not evoked mass panic and sometimes fatal stampedes.

Living in Africa was a constant reminder of how close death always lurked. And there was the awareness that in that context, where people lost loved ones or family members so often and for reasons having to do with poverty alone, any mishap in our family would seem inconsequential by comparison.

Moving to Mali, we would have to forsake the magnificent Kenyan highlands with their almost perfect climate — never too hot, often good and chilly but never too cold. In Nairobi there was almost no malaria or cholera or any of those other ailments that came with the tropical heat at lower altitudes in Africa, particularly in West Africa where urban sanitation was generally in a state of partial or complete dysfunction — or just plain non-existent. Those stinking open sewers or worse, no sewers at all. The mud paths that doubled as urban thoroughfares spawned polluted little streams, or worse, pools of wastes that sat there stagnating and breeding flies, mosquitoes and clouds of noxious gases.

From the lofty distance of Nairobi, all I could think of were those open gutters of festering sewage, those breeding grounds for a dozen diseases that could kill within hours. In hindsight, I found it amazing I'd lived for so many years in that other reality in West Africa, hardly batted an eye about taking the children as infants to places where we had no power, no water and no medical facilities. They were older now — nine and eleven — and toughened little kids whose immune systems I liked to imagine had been well fortified over the years. That meant they were in far less danger of dying quickly of an attack of malaria or dysentery, but much more at risk on the emotional and psychological front. I thought I'd just better make that clear to my husband, lest he overlook this point.

"Yes, but it's so hard on the kids," I said. "They've just got over the last move and stopped missing Ghana. They're happy here. They like their school. They have good friends. Here they can take piano lessons."

"They'll make new friends," he said, sighing himself now. "The international school in Bamako is small, but it seems okay. There is no shortage of music or musicians in Mali. You know that. Salif Keita, Ali Farka Touré, Oumou Sangaré, world-famous Malians. The kids can find a music teacher. They can learn how to play the *kora* and the *djembe*."

I grunted. No need to allow him to think he'd won me over that easily.

He continued. "There are lots of great things to look forward to in Mali. It's safe in Mali. Peaceful. Mali has a fantastic history. It was the centre of great empires. We can go to Timbuktu. The people are very proud of their heritage and . . . "

"Okay, okay," I said. "I know. I've accepted it. Really I have. We'll go there. But this is the one move too many. Six countries in fifteen years are enough. For the kids and for me."

He smiled. He knew. It was settled; we were going to Mali. After that? Well, who knows? At that point it didn't matter.

Two months later, Karl had already left Kenya and headed to Mali to set up shop. The children and I stayed behind — the children to finish out the school year and I to finish up my contract and to prepare for the move, sort through mountains of papers and all those notebooks I had collected over four years in Kenya.

One was labelled simply "Frank Plummer." It was full of scribbled notes about Frank, his family, his thoughts on medical research and AIDS, and the vast amounts of money spent on finding treatments rather than on understanding the syndrome and preventing it. It also had pages full of my impressions of the morning I had spent with him in Pumwani, one of Nairobi's more depressing slums areas.

The morning Frank took me to Pumwani, I was ashamed to admit I hadn't been there before, that I had almost no first-hand experience in the city's teeming, sprawling slums where about a million people live — perhaps a third or even a half of Nairobi's population. Frank, on the other hand, obviously felt quite at home in the shantytowns that most of us preferred to forget about. Frank worked in Pumwani as a medical researcher, when he wasn't at the hospital overseeing laboratory work, or back home in Manitoba trying to drum up more funding for research that might lead to prevention of AIDS, or attending international conferences to gain support for the same cause. Pumwani was, after all, a veritable laboratory for the infectious diseases he studied.

As he eased his Nissan Patrol into those alleyways, Frank told me Pumwani was one of the city's oldest slums, settled in the 1920s when the British housed their labourers there. He called it a "rough place," even for those who lived there. I won't try to pretend that I wasn't disturbed by the riotous squalor, the crowds, the claustrophobic *slumminess* of Pumwani. I was more than disturbed; I was appalled. I'd been living a very cosseted life in Nairobi that had spared me much of the reality.

There was a strong smell of sewage; I had the impression that all 15,000 inhabitants of this small ghetto had gathered in the one alley we were trying to negotiate that cloudy morning. Everyone was trying to sell something — old shoes, old curtains, old bed sheets, old brassieres. The only things that didn't look old, used or cast off were the mountains of fresh mangoes and tomatoes on the roadside market. The alley was thick with hawkers and makeshift stalls. Behind those stalls were the houses, wattle-and-daub structures that needed to lean on each other to remain standing. Behind those, there were mountains of rubbish that not even the resourceful people who lived here could re-use or recycle.

I kept my window wound right up to the top. I was terrified of thieves. I glanced over at Frank, who was busy winding his window down, sticking his head out like a farmer on a tractor in rural Canada about to have a wag with the neighbours.

"Excuse me," he said to the horde of young men blocking our path and armed with their wares, stacks of second-hand blue jeans. "I'm afraid I have to get through," he said, sounding every bit the country gentleman from the Canadian prairies that he was. The hawkers seemed to appreciate his good manners. They were, I suppose, unusual in a Big Man in a Big Car in their part of town. They took up the call in Kiswahili, warning everyone ahead that a car was coming through. The path cleared. We pulled into a littered yard in front of a small bungalow badly in need of a coat of whitewash.

"This is Majengo Clinic," Frank said. "Majengo means slum in Kiswahili. This is where we do our work with the *malaya,* or sex workers. We have 1,800 registered patients here. They're all malaya. They're not like prostitutes who work the bars downtown at night. The malaya work only in the daytime, selling sex to men who are on their way to work or passing by. They close up shop at dusk, when it's time to cook for their children or their husbands. Some of them are married or at least living with a man who may not even know they do this for income. They have houses, usually just one room with two beds: one for themselves and their children or steady boyfriend at night, one for their daytime clients. They have four or five clients a day. They charge twenty shillings for sex with a condom, thirty without."

I was busy taking notes, as my mind ground away on the arithmetic. Twenty shillings for sex. That worked out to less than half a Canadian dollar. It wasn't just life that was undervalued there.

Frank led the way into the clinic that was separated from the bedlam of the Pumwani market by a low wire fence. An amazing lack of security, in a city where security was typically measured by the diameter of the bars on windows and the height of walls around compounds. Frank had been working there for more than a decade, heading up a research project on sexually transmitted diseases. The project was a joint effort of the Universities of Manitoba and Nairobi.

Originally he came to study chancroid, a sexually transmitted disease that causes genital ulcers. It's rare in North America, common in this part of the world. But an epidemic of chancroid in Manitoba in the 1970s sparked interest in the disease at his university in Winnipeg. So Frank moved into a clinic in Pumwani, working with malaya. In 1985, not a single case of AIDS had been documented, not officially. But that year, on the off chance that HIV had made it into Nairobi slums, the research team decided to test their women patients at Majengo Clinic — just in case. The blood samples were sent off to the United States for testing and it was months before they came back.

"I remember the day," Frank said. "It was May. We opened up the envelope and learned that two-thirds of our patients were already HIV-positive. We couldn't believe it. After that," he said with a shrug and a wry smile, "there wasn't much choice but to work with AIDS."

Inside Majengo Clinic, Frank introduced me to the nurses, who were busy with files, and to a few women sitting quietly on a bench in the foyer that doubled as an office and waiting room. The nurses said how glad they were he had come. They had a patient in the treatment room and wanted his advice on what to do for her.

Frank led the way into the cramped but tidy treatment room where two Kenyan doctors were examining the patient. She was young, not yet thirty. She wore flip-flops and a low-waisted brown dress of polyester. She was having trouble standing and leaned against the bed. Frank and his Kenyan colleagues exchanged observations, noting that she had lost coordination in her right arm and leg. When they gently urged her to try to take a step, her right leg dragged behind her. The young doctors, Joshua Kimani and Ephantus Njagi, moved in to help her keep her balance while nudging her for answers with gentle questions. Speaking in Kiswahili, they asked her to try touching her nose with her finger. She tried but couldn't do it. I turned away.

The doctors switched back to English and told Frank that thrush had appeared on her tongue. They noted the bacterial infection around her eyes. Joshua said she had already been treated for tuberculosis. I glanced at her again, taking in her lifeless eyes. She was hacking up phlegm, using a faded wrapper slung over one shoulder to cover her mouth and wipe her face.

I averted my eyes again and gazed out the window, amazed that the riotous marketeering just a few feet from the open window didn't seem to bother anyone inside the clinic or even attract anyone's attention, except mine. I watched a dented van pulling up into the cacophony that was the alley just outside. The van was purple and green, with the words "Christ Crusades" emblazoned in silver letters on the side. There was an enormous plastic fish, also painted silver, on the roof. Deafening music came from loudspeakers inside the fish. The van door slid open to reveal a wall-to-wall selection of Christian music cassettes and videos. You could buy just about anything in Pumwani — Levis, fruit, sex . . . even faith.

Frank and his two Kenyan colleagues were still discussing the case, deciding that her loss of coordination indicated neurological problems, a sign that she was moving into the final stages of AIDS, the final days or hours of her life. Any further treatment would be far too costly for the project to cover and accomplish very little except to prolong her life and her suffering a few more days. The project paid for the patients' basic health care, in exchange for monitoring and studying the sexually transmitted diseases among the registered patients. That included the 1,800 sex workers here, 1,600 mothers with children in Eastleigh Clinic nearby and 1,400 patients in a special treatment clinic downtown.

The doctors escorted the woman out of the office, preparing for the next patient. I asked Joshua Kimani what else the project did for the women, besides paying basic health care as they succumbed to AIDS, taking their blood, and monitoring the rate of transmission of HIV and other sexually transmitted diseases. He said Majengo Clinic organized community projects to help the women find alternatives to the sex trade. This brought the malaya together in large groups, where they learned how to protect themselves from further infections. Perhaps even more importantly, they learned that together they had a voice and that unity gave them a little power. If all the sex workers in Pumwani refused their services to men who wouldn't wear a condom, the men would eventually be forced to go for safe sex. By protecting both men and women, the epidemic could be slowed. This was a give-and-take project, not, as Frank put it, "safari research" that gave nothing back to the communities in which it worked.

Joshua told me that 95 per cent of the patients in the clinic were HIV-positive. The remaining 5 per cent were women who had had intense contact with HIV for years — yet remained negative. It was this statistic that had inspired me to take a day of leave and to venture away from my side of town and into the slum with Frank. It was also the reason that Frank Plummer's name and the names of his Kenyan and Canadian colleagues featured large in medical journals and at international AIDS conferences. Those fifty-eight women with resistance to HIV — a small silver lining in that obscure Nairobi slum — were making and shaping medical history.

In the early '90s when the research team in Nairobi documented their resistance, those women were the first known cases apparently immune to HIV infection. Kelly MacDonald, another of the research team, who divided her time between Toronto and Nairobi, explained the resistance to me using the simplest terms. With apologies to her for what may well be a seriously deformed lay translation, I took her explanation to mean that resistance to HIV began with human leukocyte antigens, individual cells' defences that kicked in against infection before HIV could touch the body's immune system. And this, in turn, seemed to be linked to a certain genetic predisposition, which the researchers were studying in the resistant women.

I asked Frank if he would take me to see a malaya at home, where she lived and worked. He agreed, glancing down at my flimsy open sandals and suggested that next time I remember to wear a more serious pair of shoes. I nodded; I wasn't going to say out loud that I didn't foresee any next time.

We picked our way on foot (in my case, on tiptoe) through the crazed confusion of an African market in full swing, past dizzying displays of second-hand clothes. We stopped in front of a corner dwelling, a house of clay separated from streams of sewage only by a neatly swept stone porch. Frank said this was where Charity lived and worked. He called hello and she pulled aside a printed curtain and ushered us into her house with a gracious smile. We ducked to enter her room. It was dark and cool inside; the room was just big enough for two beds and one chair. Frank greeted her in Kiswahili and introduced me.

She was poised and soft-spoken, bright-eyed and beautiful. More like someone I might have expected to find in a convent than in a hovel where sex was for sale. The room was meticulously swept, clean and ordered. This was not the dwelling of a woman who had given up hope or pride. A stack of freshly washed bowls sat in one corner, under a faded colour print of a city square that looked distinctly like a shot of downtown Beijing. I wondered where she had bought that. Probably in Pumwani, where it seemed you could buy just about anything.

After a few minutes, I realized that I had nothing to ask her, nothing that wouldn't be injurious and out of line. I waited until she and Frank had finished exchanging pleasantries and news about mutual acquaintances — some malaya, some researchers on the project — and then nodded to let him know that I was ready to leave.

As we made our way back to the clinic, Frank told me Charity was one of the malaya who benefited from a small loan to help her get set up in business — selling second-hand clothes in Pumwani. It was hard to say if she had abandoned the sex trade altogether.

"There are only so many pieces of clothing that can be sold," he said. "It would be hard to match the money she could bring in selling sex, which is around $10 a week. That's more than a male labourer makes in Nairobi. Even if she hasn't abandoned the sex trade altogether, at least now she's insisting her clients use condoms. Most of our patients do."

"Yes, but since she's already HIV-positive, what difference does it make for her?" I asked.

"That's one of the other areas of our research," he said. "We think the rapid progression of the disease from HIV infection to full-blown AIDS in Africa may be closely related to the rate of exposure to other sexually transmitted diseases. That's also why most of the HIV transmission is Africa seems to be heterosexual. So, by reducing the exposure to infections through the use of condoms, it seems that the progression to AIDS is slowed down. Of course," he added, "as fast as our patients are trained in methods of safe sex or set up in other kinds of business, there are new malaya. Especially during droughts, when crops fail in rural areas, we get a lot of new patients. Often girls, sometimes as young as thirteen, who come to the city looking for a way to get money to pay their own school fees. We have some women patients who have been able to send their children to university on what they made here. One of those is in law school in Dar es Salaam. Anyway, there's a lot of opportunity here to find out why people get AIDS, find out what the immune system is doing."

As we climbed back into the Nissan, I glanced around once more at the dank alleys and the cornucopia of colours, smells and sounds in Pumwani. I was perplexed that a Nairobi slum could seem so much richer in life and humanity than the posh, lush neighbourhoods that expatriates and well-heeled Kenyans tended to inhabit. Neighbourhoods like my own, for example, which was no neighbourhood at all. Not in the true sense of the word.

"It's pretty exciting," said Frank in that deadpan way he had of downplaying the importance of this work. We were driving towards town and Kenyatta Hospital where the project had its laboratories and headquarters. The midday traffic was heavy, suffocating actually, and we were driving through clouds of choking black fumes from ailing diesel engines. I asked him to elaborate a little on what, in particular, he thought was "pretty exciting." I thought it was more than that, but I didn't want to sound too much like the gushy novice.

"Well," he said, "for a long time we thought that everyone could get HIV and that once you got it, it was forever and you died from it. The paradigm on AIDS is shifting and this work in Kenya is helping to shift it, showing us that not everyone is susceptible to HIV. Once we understand why that is, we should be able to come up with something to treat or prevent AIDS — absolutely."

In the back of that same notebook, I found a piece of paper Frank had given me shortly after our outing to Pumwani. It was the eulogy he had delivered in December 1996, at the funeral of five of his closest Kenyan colleagues, who were killed in a car accident while returning to Nairobi from an international AIDS conference in Uganda. I'm grateful to him for allowing me to print it here. It speaks for itself.

> My name is Frank Plummer. I am here to speak on behalf of the Canadian component of our project. Before telling you something about those we are here to honour, I would first like to express something about the closeness of our project and how deeply the loss of these fine people hurts us.
>
> Our project is now sixteen years old. From very modest beginnings and through more than a

194

little adversity, it has been built into a world-renowned enterprise where leading research, prevention of disease and development of people go hand in hand. People from many countries, of all races, have created a small world where there is no room for racism, sexism or tribalism, where people bound together by ideals, friendship, loyalty and love work side by side to make the world a better place. Together we have created new knowledge, cured and prevented disease and taught others to do the same. In doing so, we have touched the lives of millions and in a real way, we have changed the world. Twenty-six of us went to Kampala to tell the world about our work. Five of us did not come back, leaving a terrible hole in our midst. The five who were torn from us so tragically and senselessly last Thursday will be long remembered for their role in our enterprise. Their families, our project, this country, and the world are poorer in their absence, but we should take comfort in knowing that they were each an important part of a great thing.

I folded the piece of paper back up and placed it back into the notebook, then closed the notebook and put it back in the file marked "Frank Plummer." For a while I stared into the fire, then looked around me at the home we would be leaving behind. I was ashamed of all the complaining I'd been doing, without any inkling of what "hardship" really meant. It was time to try to dispel the gloom I'd been carrying around with me for weeks. Kenya had been wonderful to us but it was time to head west, to Mali. Once I was on the outside again, I would be free to write about anything and everything. I began to look forward to the trips I would take to whatever places the stories would lead me. Strangely enough, the first stop for stories would be not Mali, but Cameroon.

Cameroon

Chapter 16

The Lord's number one office

Everybody big in this country steals. When I see how well the big thieves live and how honest people live in misery, I decide that I want to become a thief.
— A street boy in Yaoundé, Cameroon, 1999

Cameroon

I asked him — nervously — if I might be permitted to take his photograph. His eyes were hidden by the broad brim of a straw hat more reminiscent of a shady place in Panama than of anything specific to Cameroon, but his wide smile suggested I had nothing to fear.

Then he said: "It is not for me to give you permission to snap photographs. This is a decision for the Lord. If the Lord doesn't approve, that is to say if your intentions are not honourable, your camera will be destroyed."

I stepped over the low wall to enter his realm and began to shoot photographs of this man who was said to be crazy, a *"fou."* I told myself that my intentions were honourable, if rank curiosity can ever be deemed entirely honourable. My BBC colleague, Salifu, was already closing in with his microphone. The taxi-man, I noticed, had taken a position well out of range of the man's tongue or an exploding camera and was cowering behind his battered yellow car.

"My name is Gabriel," said the crazy man into the microphone. "You can ask your questions and I will be obliged to speak openly to you because we are standing here in a heavenly place. The whole world around us is a mess. But this place, all that I do here, is coordinated from on high. I make it beautiful. This is the Lord's Number One Office."

His smile was dazzling. I was sure if I could just see his eyes I would know whether I was looking at a sane man pretending to be crazy, or the reverse. I dropped to my knees and aimed my lens upwards. But his eyes were still hidden by the brim of his hat and I was blinded by the equatorial sun.

It was a sweltering afternoon in Yaoundé, the cluttered and chaotic capital of Cameroon. The heavy layer of grey clouds that had brought downpours earlier in the morning had finally broken up. Strands of misty clouds were still draped over the remnant patches of forest on the seven hills that encircle the city. But in the city centre, the sun was now a relentless glare that made my head ache. Car fumes interwoven with humidity formed a thick, hot blanket that made breathing bad for the health.

We'd been turning in circles all morning, trying to find officials to talk to us about corruption or about the destruction of Cameroonian rainforests by foreign logging companies. There was no shortage of willing commentators on the streets ready to give us their take on corruption. Just a couple of months earlier, the international watchdog group Transparency International had pronounced Cameroon the most corrupt country in the world. The reaction on the streets of Yaoundé? "They made a mistake. We are not champions of the world in corruption. We're champions of the universe." "It's shameful. We must pray for redemption. But with this government, there can be none." "First prize? They made a mistake. We should have got Super First Prize, no government can be more corrupt than this one."

On the subject of disappearing forests, we also had lots of tape. We had stood on the roadside outside the capital city and counted for ourselves the logging trucks roaring past, loaded with those choice logs on their way to the coast for export to Europe and Asia. We'd learned from lowly forest officers and conservationists about the windfall profits accrued by the logging companies, mostly European and Asian, and the hefty bribes received by the Cameroonian officials who dispensed the timber concessions. In the markets, women had moaned into the microphone about the rising prices and increasing shortages of all their staple vegetables, spices and medicines coming from the rainforest.

"You know, so much of what we eat comes from the rainforest. So this logging is really killing our food products," said one woman. "Soon it will also kill us."

But Salifu and I still didn't have the official voices giving their side of the story, despite all our time squandered and sweat expended. No one in high office was exactly leaping at the chance to defend their government's integrity or justify the plunder of Cameroon's forests.

The ministers were all "unavailable for interviews," the most common excuses being that they were abroad or were attending (a) a seminar, (b) a conference, (c) a workshop, (d) a colloquium, or (e) a meeting somewhere. Others, mere directors or forestry officials who actually were in their offices, said they could not speak to us without obtaining permission from their ministers or superiors, who were of course unavailable for the above reasons.

Next we'd tried to track down some of the kingpins in the logging companies. They were very elusive. They simply made themselves invisible when we called, turned off their cellular telephones when they heard who was on the line. I suppose they didn't have much to gain from talking to the media. This was not a country where top officials or foreign business had any need to account to the public or to the media. The Cameroonian public had no clout whatsoever and the international community didn't seem to be watching or listening, which was just how the government and the resource-seekers from abroad wanted to keep it.

I was losing heart. Round and round we went. I was sure we'd made the downtown circuit at least a half dozen times. Each time we did, we'd passed the city hall, or the *mairie* in French.

It was one of the few landmarks I still recognized. The Cameroonian capital had billowed and bulged like a mushroom cloud since the last time I'd been there in 1985. I had strong memories of Yaoundé because this was where I spent my very first day in Cameroon in April 1984, which happened to be the same day that a bloody coup attempt started.

The coup-makers were not successful. After three days of violent fighting in the capital, from his hiding place — perhaps the bomb shelter deep underneath his glorious palace — President Paul Biya had convinced the airforce to fly in from the west of the country and save his presidential neck. They did this by retaking the airport and radio station from the rebellious presidential guard that had held them for seventy-two hours. But the end didn't come before a lot of blood had been shed and buildings destroyed in the capital, much of which I'd observed from the balcony of a third-floor apartment overlooking this self-same *mairie*. At some point during those crazy days of fighting, a passing military plane had bombed a hole right through its tin roof.

It was encouraging to see that in the intervening fifteen years, the municipal authorities had managed to patch the hole. Apart from that, however, there was no other sign that a working hand had been laid on the place since 1984, or perhaps when it had been constructed in colonial days. The exterior seemed to be covered with mildew. All the metal bars over the windows were corroded, broken or rusted. The premises were sorely in need of a spruce-up.

The only sign of any industry around the *mairie* was on the island of red earth that fronts the building and borders on one of the city's main thoroughfares. One end of the mud island was under intensive construction.

A lone man, his back bare and gleaming with sweat, was on his hands and knees slaving away, sculpting clay urns along the front of a mud wall, which enclosed various other works of art. These included: some barbed wire festooned with coloured bits of plastic; a bell that was mounted on shards of scrap metal; and a blackboard with very neat script in French, the meaning of which I could not decipher although it alluded to God, the police and water. I had no real sense that this masterpiece held together as a work of art, but then I could say the same of many public monuments I've seen in other public places in the world. In another city, say Ottawa or Berlin, this intriguing work in progress might have cost the taxpayers a considerable sum, have a very meaningful name and bear the prestigious (costly) name of a renowned sculptor that no taxpayer had ever actually heard of. But this was Cameroon, and Gabriel didn't cost the city a single franc.

Each time we had passed the town hall that morning, our taxi-driver had chuckled and shaken his head. He said the man working like an ant day and night on that small private project of beautification was a "fou," a "crazy man." Using a pick and shovel, he had dug up and smoothed out the entire meridian, then walled it in and decorated the wall with inscriptions addressed to the Lord. "But just when the place starts to look fine and people start saying how hard this man works," said the taxi-man, "along come the municipal authorities and bulldoze it down. And the man he just go on and start over. Truly, he must be crazy."

In Cameroon, as elsewhere in West Africa, insanity (if that's what it was) was rarely handled by mental health experts in any kind of health institution. Psychiatrists were few and far between, as were mental institutions. Most people whose minds were not in "normal" working order were allowed to roam free, rant at the heavens, traipse the byways in bare feet, remain nude if they liked or dress themselves up in rags, adorn themselves in anything that took their fancy — bits of plastic or bone or even spare parts from automobiles. These accessories they strung like crown jewels from their matted hair, or around their necks or waists or ankles.

Most of these "market lunatics" as they were called in Ghana, for example, had a strong sense of aesthetics, and their costumes were put together with obvious attention to detail, from whatever could be found in the heaps of garbage that were consuming African cities. And they could do as they liked as long as they threatened no one. In all my years in Africa, I never heard of a case where they did.

But in Yaoundé, it seemed that this particular fou was beginning to seriously disturb some highly placed people. Single-handedly, without salary or construction equipment or donor grant or loan from the World Bank, he was busy doing public works that made the government's efforts at urban upkeep look slovenly, inefficient and uncaring.

"Look how neat he makes this place," said our taxi-man-cum-guide. "He builds and he builds and he digs and he digs. Twenty years the mayor's office couldn't even keep the place swept clean. But this man he puts in trenches, smoothens it all out. Builds a wall, paints it. What does our government do? Thank him? No. Town hall sends out its men on the Caterpillars to break down the whole thing."

"Do they really do that?" I asked.

"Yes, many times already. The mayor's office say it have no machinery to fix roads or do public works, but they find the Caterpillar they need when they want to break down this crazy man's monument."

We had driven past the crazy man one more time, been turned away at yet another government ministry, and were just passing city hall yet again when Salifu and I exchanged glances. Salifu asked the taxi-man to stop. I don't know what we thought we might get from chatting with him; it was unlikely we would be able to put his voice in any broadcasts on the BBC. We were not even sure he would react well to our interest. The taxi-driver had indicated he thought we might be as loony as the crazy man.

But the reality of what we had been seeing in Cameroon, where it seemed that an entire nation was being pillaged by a very few powerful individuals at the top while the whole world averted its eyes, had begun to take its toll on any absolutes. Who but a Greater Being could say what was normal, and who was sane and who was not? Every evening in my hotel I watched Cameroonian state television, and learned more about the great works of the president and his government that flew in the face of everything I had seen and heard out there in reality-land all day. Why shouldn't we ask this man about his great works too? Surely he had things to tell the world too? And even if it weren't suitable for broadcast, let me admit it, I was also curious. Insanely so.

So now here we were — Salifu armed with the microphone, I with my camera, hoping God's wrath was not going to blow it to smithereens in my hands. And Salifu was asking Gabriel if he wasn't afraid of the authorities who kept coming to destroy his work.

"Yes, the municipal authorities want to make me quit this place. But I don't fear the authorities. Why would I when I do not fear even death? When you are working for the Lord, you don't tremble before the government, even if they come with a hammer to beat you."

We asked him if he viewed himself as a Christian, a Muslim, or just a believer. He said that he knew God personally — he'd been lucky to cross Her path on high and to have a child with Her. He went on to say that God was in fact a woman, albeit a woman with both sexes. She was the one coordinating his work on that small patch of ground, work that was going to help change the world.

He said he was surrounded by "invisible ones," who were his bodyguards and who protected him when the authorities came to raze his work of art to the earth and chase him away. I smiled when he said that, but only for a fleeting second. It dawned on me how many invisible forces — radio waves, telephone conversations or even e-mail messages — were floating around us at that second, on frequencies which we with our limited five senses were unable to pick up. Visible didn't mean much without eyes tuned to see; tangible was meaningless without the sensory tools to feel.

Salifu asked him how he felt about being called "fou" by those who drove or walked past him every day.

"Me, I don't know this thing they call crazy. Only the Lord can define it, no one else. I have dignity and that is important. My work here," he said, spreading his arms to take in his walled-in small park of wonders, "is known far and wide. It is known by heads of state. Bill Clinton, he knows the work of the Lord. I burn here in the hot sun each day so that the world will not suffer. My work says what people are afraid to say on the radio or television. I bring out words and thoughts that are hidden. If they come and kill me, I do not mind. God will take me in peace. Crazy? Say so, it doesn't matter. I don't listen to the words of man, I listen to God."

By now, the traffic was building around us as motorists slowed to get a look at the fou giving an interview to a couple of journalists. Then a yellow Caterpillar grader pulled up, its driver shouting at other motorists to move on and clear the way. When they did, he ground to a stop beside us.

It was a rare apparition, that still-functioning Caterpillar just metres from us. In most places I've lived in Africa, it was almost impossible to get a stretch of road graded by any public works department because there was no grader available, usually because (a) there was no money left for fuel, (b) there was no budget for a spare part it needed, or (c) a highly placed Somebody had put it to work on some private construction project somewhere, which would in turn lead back to (a) and (b).

But that afternoon, lo and behold, just when no one was in need of or requesting the services of a Caterpillar, there it was, idling away and deafening us just as we were trying to get Gabriel's prophecies on tape.

The driver stood in his seat and began to shake his fist. "What is the meaning of this? Who are you and why are you talking to that lunatic?"

We ignored him.

He went on. "Gabriel, you may think you're some kind of angel and important because they're talking to you but don't think that's going to stop us. We're going to destroy anything you build there. No matter who you think you are, we know that you're just a fou."

Salifu packed up his microphone and beckoned to me to put away the camera and get out of there; if we continued to draw attention to the crazy man, we might bring down the government's wrath on Gabriel sooner, rather than the usual later. We thanked Gabriel and made a speedy exit from the Lord's Number One Office, heading off into the traffic to continue our search for official voices from officials who run the show in Cameroon.

Later, still driving round and round the city, still searching in vain for at least one government official who would talk to us, I asked Salifu if he thought Gabriel was really crazy.

He laughed. "I don't know," he said. "In this country, crazy doesn't mean anything any more."

Salifu, a Cameroonian journalist who was back home for the first time in eight years, was deeply depressed by the changes in his country. He'd been going on and on about the despair that was new to Cameroon and mounting steadily. He blamed this on a disreputable regime that didn't care about the people and that was also, he said, blatantly supported by French President Jacques Chirac — a big obstacle to any political change from within the country.

Salifu also attributed the malaise to the economic crisis, brought on by devaluation of the CFA franc in 1994 and structural reform programs that seemed to be making a privileged few even richer while the rest of the country grew poorer by the day. Salifu reminded me about something a sociologist had said to us the previous day.

"In this country," said the professor, "with the corruption being what it is and the economic crisis, it is impossible to earn money honestly through hard work."

So what could people do to keep the despair at bay, to make ends meet?

"Some are turning to crime," he said. "But most are turning to religion. They either go along with the system or they look beyond it, find sustenance in their faith. Those are their choices if they want to stay sane."

Sane. Four little letters that the dictionary said denoted "soundness of mind." Soundness of mind? What did that mean?

For years now, I had spent my days reporting on a part of the world where big white lies not only prevailed but were evident enough that they might just as well have been written right across the sky in puffy clouds for the wry amusement of people on the ground. These were African countries that international lending agencies, Western donor countries and the international community said were "developing." For proof, the lending agencies conjured up a few figures on paper about gross national product and used these to justify more loans that would add to the debt load that every single African man, woman and child was bequeathing to their descendants. And they extolled the benefits of a globalization in which a few multinational corporations were gaining more and more control of more and more of Africa's resources and markets — while most Africans grew poorer and received nothing but the crumbs. There was hardly a country on the continent where the annual average income had gone up and where living standards were higher than they had been at independence.

While in Cameroon, I watched an announcement on state television in which a visiting delegation from the International Monetary Fund heartily patted the Cameroonian government on the back for its "sound progress" in economic reform. The very same week, the World Bank announced that the average annual income of Cameroonians had dropped by half in the previous ten years.

So who was nuts? The lending agencies that claimed they were helping Africa? The donor countries that were running projects to develop Africa, while their own corporations pillaged her resources and their own nationals sold arms? The Africans for going along with it all? Or me for worrying about any of it?

Gabriel had it just about right. God alone knew what crazy meant.

Chapter 17

Expensive voices

The Environmental Management Plan states that "A population of Pygmies exists in the Kribi area forests at a distance from the Cameroon Transportation System's land/system easement" . . . What does it mean that Pygmies exist at a distance? Again, there is no indication of how the Pygmies are likely to be affected by the project . . . In a Wall Street Journal article of October 14, 1997, the chairman of Exxon states that developing countries ought to avoid environmental controls because otherwise they risk losing foreign investment. There appears to be little recognition that most people in Africa depend directly on land, forests and on the water in streams to meet their needs. Africa has witnessed a long history of extraction of its natural resources, which has contributed little to improving the quality of life of ordinary citizens throughout the continent. We call on the World Bank to use its skills and resources to find alternatives to the presently risky Chad/Cameroon Oil and Pipeline project. — Open letter from eighty-six non-government organizations to World Bank president, James D. Wolfensohn, July 1998

I sat down on the wooden bench they had conjured out of nowhere for their unexpected visitors — one of them this Nova Scotian who had somehow been beamed in from another world. I was happy to fold myself down onto the bench. Sitting, I could almost convince myself that I wasn't all that conspicuous. I was, of course. In this "Pygmy settlement," even to myself I seemed too tall, very white and very much like another nosy intruder — all of which I was.

I pulled out my notebook and pen, the primitive tools I use to orient myself on my travels. When I was scribbling, I could almost forget all the curious stares directed my way by the multitudes of children who had come to giggle and gape. I set about taking down all the coordinates I'd need later to recall where I had been, what had been said — and what I had been doing there in the first place.

I knew roughly where we were. We were somewhere in Cameroon's southern province, a few kilometres north of the splendid beaches of Kribi, a resort town on the Atlantic coast and future outlet for a proposed and very controversial oil pipeline. Continuing north from here, we would need a couple of hours to reach the country's economic capital and port city of Douala. Or else we could head inland for three hours to reach the capital, Yaoundé.

Vague coordinates weren't good enough. I needed details — hard facts — that might help me believe I had things more or less figured out and under control. A ridiculous illusion or delusion in the wild and woolly world of reality.

François Bivina had brought us here to talk to the Pygmies, so I turned to him for help with those facts. He came from a village down the road a piece, and a different ethnic group altogether. We'd visited him there, and he had told us he ekes out a meagre living as a small-scale farmer, moonlighting as a poorly paid local prospector for the international logging and pharmaceutical companies at work in the region, hauling out Cameroon's forest wealth. Unlike the Pygmies, who have been pretty well excluded from the few positive developments in Cameroon in the past few decades, François had attended school and learned to read and write, so he was able to help me get the orthography straight. He told me the name of this Pygmy settlement was "Nkngmdzp," a mouthful of consonants that I had no hope of ever pronouncing correctly. I asked him to spell it for me. Slowly. He did: N-k-o-n-g-m-e-d-z-a-p.

On the national map, this village, like most Pygmy settlements, doesn't exist. In fact, most of Cameroon's southern province is still identified as uninterrupted coastal rainforest. Here on the ground, things were different. There were lots of villages and there sure wasn't much forest. Looking up and beyond the circle of excited villagers who had swarmed in to see what all the excitement was about, all I could identify in the way of forest was a few incongruous trees reaching skyward, left behind like monuments to a forest that once was. These orphaned giants were surrounded by a sea of low green scrub, which is what remains after the loggers have done with another patch of rainforest.

N-k-o-n-g-m-e-d-z-a-p was just another Pygmy village that had been left exposed to the world when its forest cover vanished. No, "vanished" isn't the right word. It didn't disappear overnight and it wasn't any magical disappearing act. It had taken a few years, plus a lot of machines and permits from high-level Cameroonian officials for the loggers (French, Dutch, Italian, Malaysian, Indonesian, Lebanese, German, Cameroonian too, you name it) to dispense with forest that took centuries to grow. And when the forest went, so did Cameroon's main supply of food, oils, spices, resins, twine, wood, bush meat . . . and medicines.

It was the medicines that had brought me there, to Nkong-medzap, to make a nuisance of myself. One of the more wonderful aspects of my work with that research institute in Nairobi had been that I did occasionally get away from the office, and when I did, researchers out in the various regions had opened my eyes to the magic of tropical trees.

These experts might disapprove of my calling it magic. They used science to capture some of the best traits of some of the most valuable trees in simple horticultural operations that will eventually make it possible to save, and even promote, some of the riches of the rainforests by transferring the trees to farms. But for me it was magical, the potential of those trees. I was now following a tangent the researchers had set me out on two years earlier, and had landed in Nkongmedzap to try to find out more about some of the medicinal species that grew in what was left of the forests.

I was particularly curious about a tree called johimbe, which produces in its bark a powerful male aphrodisiac that Pygmies have known about and been using effectively for centuries. A cure for male impotence that doctors around the world have been prescribing for years — long before the male potency drug Viagra appeared on the scene.

With the help of François and Marie-Laure, a young Cameroonian scientist who was working on saving some of the valuable forest trees, I'd finally wound up in this Pygmy settlement with a Pygmy traditional healer, from whom I hoped to hear more.

The healer was leaning back on a rickety wooden chair, calm as could be despite the furore caused by our arrival. He was dressed in tattered second-hand clothing from another continent: white shorts and a beige muscle shirt. He sported a bushy moustache, which made him seem large and imposing and impressed me.

Even before I took out my tape recorder, he was already eyeing me warily or with amusement — I couldn't read the look around his eyes. Then again, I felt stymied by much in that village. There was something that didn't feel right, but it wasn't anything I could put my finger on or define with words on paper. I think it had to do with the fact that our unannounced visit hadn't interrupted anything — except idleness.

I had never seen any village in Cameroon — or in any of a dozen other African countries in which I'd lived or travelled — where people were idle. Of course in any rural community there are times of the day when people rest, seeking shade under trees to sleep or to talk. But not at that hour of the morning, and never everyone in the village.

Villages in Africa are studies in human industry and industriousness. Although people will always put down what they are doing to welcome visitors — even unexpected and inconvenient ones — it is extremely rare to wash up somewhere where everyone is not hard at work. People are always busy. They're in their fields or their gardens around the household; they're busy spreading out grains or fruit to dry; they're busy processing this oil or that flour to store for periods of shortage. Women are collecting water or firewood, or preparing meals or mending or weaving, on their way to or from the market. When the girls aren't helping out with these, it means they must be in school with the boys. If there's a village school, that's where the little boys will be. If not, they'll be helping in the fields, or herding goats or sheep, or playing with toys they've made themselves from bits of wood or old tires or old tin cans. Men are busy trading or moulding blocks for house construction or farming or making tools they need to farm, or discussing politics.

In Nkongmedzap there was none of that. It was just past nine a.m. and already most of the men were red-eyed — as though they'd been up since before dawn drinking palm wine or even more powerful spirits than that. The children were mostly empty-handed and their rags so frayed and full of holes that they might as well have been naked. They had swollen bellies that suggested serious parasite problems; their runny noses attracted flies.

There wasn't a school for miles, unusual in Cameroon where education seems to be a parental obsession. I don't think I was imagining the malaise in the tiny settlement, which was an L-shaped collection of small huts fashioned from mud and sticks, set unpleasantly close to a new super-highway that had paved the way for even faster destruction of the rainforest. Nor did I see any of the things that in villages in other parts of Cameroon and Africa hint at human endeavour, ambition and even relative prosperity — things such as small radios, bicycles, neatly swept compounds, nicely tended gardens, small village schools. I saw only a collection of huts and no forest left to sustain the people who lived in them.

The traditional healer was still eyeing me, but giving no sign he was prepared to talk, even though we'd long since exchanged greetings, been introduced and been given that bench to sit on. Marie-Laure whispered to me that he wasn't going to talk unless I put up some beer money to "loosen his voice." I pulled out a few thousand CFA francs and slipped them to Marie-Laure, who passed them surreptitiously to François, who headed off to one of the mud huts in the encampment where warm beer was sold. He came back dragging a red plastic case of twelve large brown bottles of "33."

The healer placed the case of beer next to his feet, passed a few bottles to some of the men who were jockeying for position right behind him, and advised François that I could begin to ask my questions. I produced my microphone and tape recorder. The excited noise around us increased. The healer spoke his own language and Ewondo, so François, who spoke Ewondo and French, would do the translation. Before I'd even come out with the first question, the healer had popped open a beer and begun speaking very loudly into the microphone.

"My name is Benoit Bitanga and I look after the men and women and children here. This is the work my father gave me and his father gave it to him. My job isn't talking, talking, like this. I'm here to treat people who are ill. I am known all over Cameroon. People are coming from very far from all over for treatment. People come from Gabon and Nigeria to see me."

I asked him where he found his medicines. He tossed out the local names of a dozen varieties of lianas and trees that produced in their leaves or bark the medicine he used to treat everything from worms to menstrual problems. He said he knew the forest because it was his home. "I have been brought up here, now I'm old and I will die here and leave my children here. I'm not a healer for nothing. As my father and grandfather gave this practice to me, I will give it to my sons."

I asked him if it had become more difficult to find the medicines with the forest receding as it was, if those forest medicines would still be there for his sons, if things had changed for him.

He looked at me hard for a moment. "The only change that matters is death," he said, enigmatically. And no, he had nothing to add on that subject. He had a hard gaze that deflected even my dogged persistence.

I decided to leap right into the subject that had led me there — the original male potency drug, johimbe. "And what about johimbe?" I asked. "Do you know this tree?"

"Of course I know johimbe," he said. "The bark is a strong drug for men. We have other medicines from other trees and these do the same thing, of course. And we also use the fruit and the seeds from johimbe trees to treat stomach and breathing problems. We don't use johimbe ourselves. Other people come to us to get it. The bark is used to make men strong. Johimbe is very potent."

This I already knew. I'd been following the story of johimbe for about two years. A year earlier I had come to Cameroon and travelled to the south with researchers who were trying to assess the damage that thirty years of exploitation of the bark had wrought on the population of johimbe trees.

On that trip in 1997 I'd managed to wheedle a few chunks of the bark from a friendly young botanist in the employ of the French pharmaceutical company that has the monopoly on its export from Cameroon. He'd explained to me there were in fact two species of trees that produced the aphrodisiac, but one of them was "false johimbe" or "four o'clock." The one he was giving me was the real johimbe, called "five o'clock" because it was reputed to keep a man going that extra hour into the wee hours of the morning. He also said that sometimes the false johimbe got mixed up with the real johimbe in the bundles for export, which might well produce inconsistencies in the drug sold around the world, and account for some inconsistencies in the Western medical views on the drug's effectiveness.

A bashful Cameroonian forester, who had originally told me about this natural aphrodisiac from the rainforest two years earlier, had illustrated his account with a tale about a "friend" of his who had taken excessive amounts of the bark. This friend had ignored the advice of traditional healers who counselled that no more than a tablespoon of the bark be ground up and placed in water or red wine, and then drunk. The friend had foolishly ignored the wisdom of the elders and their traditional recipe and just chewed up hefty chunks of the bark. He'd "suffered the consequences."

"What consequences?" I asked.

He lowered his eyes and fiddled with the reading glasses dangling around his neck. "Things . . . well . . . he had to go to the hospital . . . because . . . well . . . things can rupture. Look, do you need to know all the details? In Africa we don't talk about things like this in public. It's not correct."

That African correctness and modesty on public discussion of matters sexual meant I still felt I didn't have all the evidence I needed on johimbe and its potency. I had wanted to get that five o'clock bark home and try it out — on someone else of course. At the airport in Douala, the customs man rifling through my suitcase wanted to know why I didn't have a certificate for exporting a tree bark and what kind of medicinal properties did this one have anyway?

I leaned over and whispered to him what it was and what it could do for a man, and asked him if he wanted a small piece himself. He laughed and said no, he didn't need it. Not yet anyway, but maybe he would when he was older. He laughed, then he glanced at my colleague, Tony, who was heading the research work meant to save some endangered species of medicinal trees. In French, the customs man whispered to me, "Your husband, there? Young like that and he needs this?"

I glanced at Tony, whose good humour and knowledge of tropical trees were almost limitless, but whose French was not. He looked terribly concerned that Cameroonian customs might seize my — and his — supply of johimbe. To the customs man I said, in French, "Indeed, he does needs it. Desperately."

He shot Tony a look full of pity, closed my suitcase, gave it his chalked mark of endorsement and waved us through. "Well, in that case, you should have taken even more of it. I hope he has some in his suitcase too."

"Oh, he does," I said. "Enough for a year."

As we stood in line for check-in, Tony asked me how I'd managed to convince the customs man to let us through with the johimbe, without the mandatory certificate that was required for any plant products taken out of the country. "I suppose you told him your husband needed it?" he said, laughing.

'Yes," I said, smiling. "How did you guess?"

I didn't offer the bark to my husband, because I saw no need to perform my informal and non-scientific experiments that close to home. I offered it instead to some of his male friends. Without exception, they insisted they had no need of it, but it might be interesting to try it out anyway. After their valiant experiments, those male volunteers spoke of johimbe with reverence and respect. Some even asked if they might not try it a second time, not that they needed it of course.

A Malian woman who agreed to prepare some of the bark for her husband came back to me the next day looking like death was nibbling at her toes. She said she wanted some more, but this time for herself and her husband. "I got no sleep at all," she said. "And my husband got all the satisfaction. This time I'm taking it too."

Even before I returned to Cameroon in 1998 to try to track down a traditional healer who could attest to the potency of johimbe, I had collected a fair bit of information about its powers. But there had still been the riddle of how this traditional knowledge — and medicine — that really belonged to the Pygmies of Africa's coastal forests had been usurped by European pharmaceutical companies. I also needed to see for myself how the bark got from the rainforests of Central Africa to the shelves of pharmacies around the world.

That history I obtained on a trip to Germany, to a pharmaceutical company that got its supplies of johimbe from the French company that exports the bark from Cameroon. The German pharmaceutical researchers told me that more than a century earlier, German missionaries in Cameroon, which was then a German colony, had "discovered" the Pygmy secret and begun sending the bark home to test its powers. Those powers were recognized officially in European medical journals at the beginning of the twentieth century, when researchers wrote that the alkaloid, yohimbene, the active ingredient in the bark, was a powerful male stimulant that "dilated blood vessels" and "increased blood flow to the extremities" while "enhancing pelvic reflexes."

After that, it was just a matter of time before big business got in on the act. Aphrodisiacs that had never worked — such as powdered horns of the unfortunate rhino — were a huge money-making venture for unscrupulous poachers and international dealers. Or they had been until they just about wiped out the world's remaining population of rhinos. It stood to reason that trade in a proven cure for impotence would be too lucrative to leave to the Pygmies and other Cameroonian healers who took only small pieces of the bark, who had done a superb job of managing their forests for centuries and who were not in business to make profits to please shareholders.

It also stood to reason that international pharmaceutical companies would not hesitate to take full advantage of the situation in Cameroon. The corruption at high levels in Cameroon and the desperate dislocation and poverty of people in forest areas added up to almost unlimited opportunities for windfall profits from forest products — be they timber or plant medicines.

There was more than johimbe in the Central African forests. A vine found only in the Korrup National Park in Cameroon was being tested as a cure for AIDS. There were some 13,000 species of plants in the country, many of which had yet to be classified. One can only imagine what medicines and other biological treasures were disappearing with the forests.

There was also the bark of the pygeum tree, which provides the world with one of the major medicines used to treat ailments of the prostate gland, which affect more than half the world's males over the age of fifty-five. Like johimbe, pygeum was another invaluable tree for ageing men around the world. And also like johimbe, it had been hacked almost into extinction. Pygeum was already officially classified as an endangered species by the Convention on International Trade in Endangered Species, or CITES.

For the past three decades, a French conglomerate with its Cameroonian subsidiary, Plantecam, has been commissioning the collection of both of these tree barks for the world markets. The collectors of johimbe, many of them Pygmies, needed to get a lot of bark to make even a few dollars for their hard labour. Naturally, since no one was telling them not to, they obtained the bark the easiest way there was — they just chopped down the whole tree.

But there was not a word about that in all the hype on "yohimbe" (the commercial spelling) that I found on the Internet. Last time I looked, I found more than 4,000 references to yohimbe products that were available in virtual health, sports or sex shops. And there were a lot of lurid promises about what yohimbe could do for a man's — and a woman's — sexual prowess. It was also promoted as a stimulant that could enhance athletic performance, or just virility, vigour and vitality. As for how it got into cyberspace markets, not a word — just that it came from the "heart of Africa."

Of course the supplier in Cameroon, the French company, Plantecam, certainly didn't shed much light on how it got its johimbe or other forest medicines. Tony and I had visited the company the previous year, enduring a search of our bags, leaving our cameras at the door before we were permitted on the high-security premises of the pharmaceutical plant. Later that same day, the French director of the company wined and dined us in Douala's most expensive restaurants, and waltzed us about in some of the city's most racy and disreputable nightclubs.

All the while he lectured us on Plantecam's good intentions and his good relations with the Cameroonian government, forestry officials — and the president, whom he said he knew personally and dealt with occasionally when environmentalists or pesky forestry officials complained about Plantecam's harvesting techniques. Then he handed us glossy Plantecam brochures that claimed the company was actually in the business of nurturing Cameroon's forests that produced this wealth of pharmaceutical gold.

This second trip to Cameroon had pretty much shown those claims up for what they were — a pack of half-truths or outright lies. The researchers had already taken me deep into the forests to the south to talk to the men who supplied Plantecam with the bark; we'd done a good deal of traipsing about in the forests with Pygmies and local men who did the cutting for Plantecam. The paths we followed were littered with felled trunks, stripped clean — hundreds and hundreds of them. A johimbe tree took up to thirty years to mature and to produce quality bark. Given all the cutting, the future of this tree looked downright dismal and Plantecam had no program of replanting or cultivation.

The contractors who had official agreements with Plantecam sold the bark to the company for about forty cents per kilogram. The underlings, local men like François Bivina and the Pygmies who did the actual work of cutting the johimbe trees into extinction, got paid a few cents per kilogram. When johimbe sold on the international market, a couple of milligrams cost more than that. The mark-up was roughly 200,000 per cent.

There it was. The medicinal tree that the Pygmies discovered in their forests was now endangered because they let slip their secret to Europeans a hundred years ago.

Firmly back in the present, in the presence of Mr. Bitanga, I noticed things had got a bit out of hand in Nkongmedzap. The villagers had been steadily creeping closer to the scene of the interview, straining to get close enough to hear every word Bitanga uttered and every question I put to him. Either that, or those men who were pressing in on him from behind were trying to get at those remaining bottles of warm beer at the feet of their healer.

I cleared my throat meaningfully, placed my fingers on my lips and smiled at the assembled villagers to indicate that I'd like a bit of quiet for the interview. The children all started to mimic me and then to giggle. I practically shouted my next question, hoping to be heard over the ruckus that my plea for silence had evoked: "Do you know that johimbe is being used all over the world?"

He shouted back. "I'm very worried and disturbed about the fact that people are coming from everywhere to fell down the trees for the bark. I'm scared about this."

He turned around suddenly and bellowed for quiet. Several of the men were now angrily yelling at each other, and Bitanga was gesticulating and shouting for their silence. At first I thought perhaps they were annoyed their healer might be telling me secrets that should not be divulged to strangers. But that was either wishful thinking or my own Western guilt speaking. The problem, as Marie-Laure whispered to me, was that they were demanding more beer, beer for the whole village.

Bitanga turned to François and spoke to him at length. François translated it this way: "Mr. Bitanga says he's very pleased to tell you all you need to know about johimbe and any other medicines from the forest, but he wants to say that it is not just beer that will loosen his tongue and make him talk. As you can see, the beer is already gone and the village is asking for more. And he says his voice is very expensive and if you wish to calm him and get him to reveal more of his secrets, then you should give him 15,000 francs."

"But I don't have 15,000 francs here," I lied. I waited for this to be translated.

Bitanga let loose quite a stream of words in response, which François reduced to this: "Then he says he can't tell you any more secrets."

"I understand, and please tell him I thank him profusely for all he has said already," I said. And then because I was feeling that I owed him something, even if it wasn't 15,000 francs (about $40 Cdn.). I passed the headphones to Bitanga so that he could listen to his expensive voice for a few minutes from the tape.

The men behind him were becoming more belligerent by the second. Bitanga had already passed out the rest of the beer, but there hadn't been nearly enough to go around and I suspected we could empty the settlement's one tiny beer shop and there still wouldn't be. The angry shouting made me want to get out of there as fast as possible, which was exactly the advice Marie-Laure was giving me. She followed a little behind, talking to one of the women who was asking her why we had come and "laid fire" to the village this way. Couldn't we see that the men were going to start to fight now that some of them had had beer and others hadn't? Marie-Laure and François apologized at length, saying to the woman that more beer would not "put out the fire," but would just fan it into a huge blaze.

The woman agreed, saying we should not have given them beer in the first place. "It's not good, all this drinking," she said, delivering another of those remarkable African understated punch-lines, which say more than an entire anthropological tome on the problem of dislocated people who are being swept into historical dustbins by a commercial world in which they have no place and no voice.

Off we drove, returning the forlorn waves from the women and children who had spilled onto the road to say goodbye. We found we didn't have much to say as we sped away from Nkongmedzap, passing a few more desolate Pygmy settlements on either side of the road, more scrubby bush, and occasional bits of what was once rich and magnificent forest.

After that came mile after mile of oil palm plantations. A billboard proudly announced these were "Swiss Farms," called Golden Palm. I mused on how much money might have gone into Swiss bank accounts to obtain such large stretches of choice real estate in southern Cameroon. Never mind that by right — tradition — it was land that belonged to the local people. By law, made in the capital by all-powerful men whose main concern was not the welfare of their people, that land now belonged to foreigners. They had burned down the forest to plant endless hectares of palms that produced oil for the inglorious products I grew up using a world away — margarine, mild dish detergents that were good for the hands, soaps. The television advertisements with Madge and her gentle detergents of palm oil certainly never told us a word about where the oil palms grew, or what had been destroyed to make way for them.

While my mind was off doing its usual loop-the-loops, Marie-Laure was preoccupied with more immediate and productive matters. She had opened one of the huge white plastic bags at her feet and was busy spraying the contents with a fine mist of water. Inside were "wildings," or seedlings of johimbe trees that she'd collected in the forest, seedlings that she was taking back to her nursery in the capital. There, she was cultivating johimbe, using tiny shoots she cut from the stumps of felled trees or seedlings she found in the forest.

The fastest-growing individuals, with the most potent bark — "superior" johimbe trees — were then being "selected" and multiplied using very basic horticultural techniques. Marie-Laure was part of a dedicated and enthusiastic research team that was producing a small population explosion of this endangered tree in their nursery. They intended to distribute these as planting material to people in southern Cameroon, who could grow them in their fields or around their villages along with other trees that provided nourishment and health.

It was a novel approach to saving trees threatened by over-exploitation or deforestation. By bringing them out of the forest and onto farmland, the trees could become a cash crop for impoverished farmers — maybe even for forest-less Pygmies.

When Marie-Laure finally closed up the bag and saw that I'd been watching her, she grinned. "These are my children," she said, patting the plastic bag. "This is the first time that these forest trees have ever been brought out of the forest for cultivation. The very first time."

"I don't know why no one ever thought to do that before with all the valuable trees here," I said.

She said it had to do with outsiders not knowing enough about the food and medicinal value of the local trees. So it would take Cameroonians — or foreign researchers who knew how to listen to Cameroonians — to see the enormous value of these trees and to try to save them before they and all the forests completely disappeared.

We were moving inland now, upland towards the capital. I had begun counting the logging trucks zooming past on the way to the coast, each loaded with logs big as small jetliners. I lost track after I counted fifty such trucks in just one hundred kilometres. I was recalling the words of a man at the World Wide Fund for Nature, who had told me a few days earlier that much of Canada's "development assistance" to Cameroon over the years had been in the form of logging equipment.

"There goes our forest," said Marie-Laure, before turning her attention back to her "children" in those white plastic sacks.

As we neared the capital, she and the driver start recalling the events in the village, and they chuckled about Bitanga and his "expensive voice," worth more than a case of beer.

I didn't say anything because I'd been mulling it over and had decided Bitanga was absolutely right. Unfortunately it was a bit late — a century or so — for traditional healers in Cameroon to be finding their voices and realizing the value of their knowledge and their forests. If they'd only known how valuable their secrets were way back when, when the first colonists and missionaries came in, or even more recently, when bio-prospectors came looking for more of the hidden riches in the forests, the Pygmies of southern Cameroon might still have their healthy populations of medicinal trees, their forests — and their dignity.

It could have all been too depressing for words, the rape of the forests by foreigners and that pillage of Cameroon's heritage. It was depressing, but there were always small glimmers of hope and lots of humour. Along the way in Cameroon I had met many people like Marie-Laure and her Cameroonian colleagues on that research team, who were trying in their own small, heroic and underfunded way, to do something to reverse the ways of their world. All they needed was for the world to lend them an ear.

Chapter 18

Destiny is fatal

The regime of President Paul Biya, in power since 1982, became increasingly unpopular. But his party stayed on through successive elections — the most recent in 1997 — criticized as unfair by opposition and human rights groups. Cameroon's leading journalist, Pius Njawe, spent most of 1998 in prison under charges of "spreading false news." — Africa's Debt, Background Paper 12, December 1998, Africa Policy Information Center, Washington, DC

The roads were even redder and more rutted than I remembered. The hills were drier, the houses and public buildings more dilapidated. The roadsides were more crammed with vendors, their kiosks more filled with imported plastic trinkets and cheap electronics than ever before. The countryside was accordingly strewn with yet more non-biodegradable litter. But what hit me was that the people seemed poorer — in all respects.

Our battered taxi careened along a stretch of grey pavement, past volcanic hills on a stretch of Cameroon's highland plateau, heading from the sprawling city of Bafoussam through villages and markets, towards the town of Foumban. This was *Pays Bamoun* — the traditional territory of the Bamoun kingdom and people.

Nothing in the landscape looked as idyllic as I had had it stored in my rosy memories. Our time in Foumban — as newlyweds —

seemed several lifetimes ago. In some ways I suppose it was. Since then, we'd had the two children and lived in four more countries in Africa. A sympathetic Cameroonian friend had once told me it was natural to feel so bleak each time we had to up and leave a place that felt like home. He said that moving and leaving friends and a life behind was a "small death." He was right.

Apart from the reporting I had come to Cameroon to do, for me this trip back to Western Province was supposed to be a sort of *un*-dying, an emotional resurrection and a trip back in time. It did look as though time had been moving backwards since we'd left fourteen years earlier. The change might also have had to do with a new perspective. On this return trip to Foumban, where I'd lived for two years, I had the advantage — or disadvantage, because it meant an inside and sometimes depressing view — of seeing it all from over the shoulder of a Cameroonian, Salifu, my colleague and friend. For him, this was a very emotional return because he had not set foot in his fatherland for eight years. As we drove into his home territory, Salifu didn't cease to recall — loudly and bitterly — much greener and better times in his country.

Typically, I was preoccupied with my very own little self, musing on how much baggage I'd lost over the years and along the way, since I'd first set foot in Africa. Some of what I'd lost was greatly missed, starting with the feeling that I belonged somewhere, that I still had a culture to call my own.

But other bits of my original self, bits I should have ditched but hadn't, were still right there, weighing heavy. Some of the vague but pointless guilt that came with being a "have" from the developed world was still there. So was my penchant for worrying. The latter I had tried to suppress or at least conceal from African friends because they had gone to great lengths to teach me their secret of managing stress. In their view, any problem that wasn't actually life threatening should be viewed as a "mere inconvenience" and thus should not be worried about. Furthermore, they said, it was just as pointless to worry about a "real problem," one that posed a real and immediate threat to life or limb, because that was in the hands of God or Allah or Jah, or whoever was hearing their prayers.

There was a wonderful irony in Africans preaching Christian or Muslim doctrine back to people who hail from the nations that exported these faiths to Africa, and not always in a very Christian, Muslim or even humane way. This at the same time when many of my friends back home in Canada were turning to more "traditional" or exotic (to them) faiths that found their roots in Africa or Asia in search of spirituality.

Typically, Africans usually cajoled me into accepting God (by whatever name) in a gentler and more enticing way than any particular faith or religion had been introduced to or hammered into them. African friends, Muslims and Christians, told me they included my family and me in their prayers. The preaching from Africans on matters of faith was another of those things I'd at first merely tolerated and later greatly appreciated.

Try as I might, intellectually I still couldn't leave my life entirely in the hands of God-by-whatever-name, and Stop Worrying. This was one impossible mental leap. Ask anyone who had to suffer through a voyage with me. I worried all the time. And I especially worried on the roads, which African friends tended to view as a necessary risk best handled with a calm acceptance — destiny was irrevocable. Or, as I saw written on the back of a minivan crammed to high heaven with passengers more courageous than I, and moving at a speed sure to kill soon or sooner: Destiny is Fatal.

I argued hotly, insisting that this approach to life and mostly death on the roads was irresponsible and the worst form of fatalism. With that attitude, I said, nothing would ever improve. God helped those who helped themselves, I insisted, and God surely approved of defensive driving and seatbelts. On and on I prattled . . . life was risky enough without defying gravity and physical laws. It was sheer stupidity to travel at ridiculous speed on bad roads, on bad tires, surrounded by bad drivers, many of whom had no driving permits.

I sanctimoniously pointed out that 110 kilometres an hour had been deemed an appropriate speed limit for safety-inspected vehicles moving on the wide, smooth and straight double-lane highways in Nova Scotia. What in heaven's name possessed drivers in Cameroon (and many other African countries) to press the accelerators to the floor and move at speeds of 140, 150 or 160 kilometres an hour on those treacherous roads?

No matter what I said, friends would always counter that I could do a lot for my health and sanity if I could just learn to enjoy the ride of life — and the speeds on the roads.

"Joan, at the end of the day . . . ," they'd say with that patient tone that made me instantly impatient, "it's this way. When you're born, there's a number stamped on your forehead. If today is your day, there's not a thing you can do to change it. Look, maybe you go a little more slowly, okay? And because you're trying to stall your own fate by driving slowly, you are coming around the narrow bend up ahead at the same moment that the oncoming logging truck is overtaking a bush taxi and so there is a collision. You and the logging truck. You can't second-guess fate. You can't undo what has been decided for you."

On the other hand, these same friends — Ghanaian, Burkinabe, Kenyan, Cameroonian, Malian — often went to great pains to counsel me on the foolish risk I took by working as a journalist in Africa. They told me I was "flirting with dangers of the worst kind" or "begging for trouble" when I broadcast irreverent and critical reports on African leaders who had the will, and also the means, to have annoying critics silenced. Now this, they said, was life threatening and a big problem. But it was not something to *worry* about — it was something I should *change*. Criticizing Big Men was a foolish and *unnecessary* risk. Not, they said, like going from one place to another on the roads; that was something one had to do.

No amount of their patient lecturing worked with me. I'd get defensive and start listing all the things I claimed I had adjusted to in Africa. I'd learned to eat boiling hot cereal dishes and sauces with my hands, developing the necessary calluses to enjoy a meal eaten that way. I'd figured out a few of the ins and outs and turns and twists of African politics and philosophies, and come to grips with the humiliating reality that I would never understand more than a smattering of customs and how things really worked. I'd learned to listen — sometimes even managing to keep my mouth closed and my ears open — to heated condemnations of feminism, homosexuality and other "imported Western ills" (as many people in Africa saw them) that were blamed on "us."

Although I steadfastly maintained the right to disagree and sometimes did — loudly — I could now at least see why some Africans reacted so strongly when outsiders preached to the continent on sensitive and private social issues such as female circumcision, polygamy and marriage customs. Many Africans described the Western world as a society in decay, particularly the US that made such an easy target and advertised its own social ills in Technicolor around the world. They merely repeated what they heard on the news from America: horror stories of children going on killing sprees, and of the proliferation of drugs and weapons in schools in a country where child pornography was a multimillion dollar commercial enterprise.

They generalized terribly, took incidents out of context and greatly exaggerated them as representations of everyday life in the West. But then that is exactly what "we" did all the time about Africa.

Africans offered me numerous insights into what they saw as blatant Western hypocrisy on issues of morality and social values. Take the touchy issue of polygamy, a criminal offence in the West and the norm in many parts of Africa. Africans liked to point out to me that with our elevated divorce rate, and the number of men or women in Western society who were already on their third, fourth or even fifth spouse, it wasn't exactly obvious that monogamy worked all that well.

They asked me tough questions, challenging me to prove there was anything inherently superior about a so-called monogamous system in which a man could simply ditch a first wife and a first batch of children to take up with another to produce more children (and so on). They pointed out that in a society where polygamy is the norm and quite legal, a man with several wives was obliged by taboos and customs to look out for all of them and their children.

I argued and said this was a nice theory, reminding them we had laws to ensure alimony was paid to abandoned wives (or husbands), noting that I'd met many women in polygamous marriages who received virtually nothing from their husband for themselves or their children's upkeep. They might admit that there were men who did this, then leap to the next question, asking me if men didn't beat their wives in North America. And I realized we were treading thin air, that everyone had right and wrong on their side.

There were several Western cultural practices that people in Africa said they viewed as barbaric — starting with how elderly people could be put into those "homes" rather than taken into the homes of their grown-up and often affluent offspring. Equally incomprehensible was how people could isolate themselves from their own family, not leap in to help out a brother or cousin or distant relative in need. That there were homeless people living on the streets in the cold North American cities in the richest countries in the world, and that cats and dogs might be fed diet lines of special pet foods or be taken to have their fur done in special beauty salons for pedigrees, were simply beyond most Africans' comprehension.

Many Africans I knew found it downright "shameless" that Western women wore such skimpy shorts that showed off not just their knees but their thighs and sometimes even bits of their buttocks in public. In much of Africa those bits of the body were to be kept hidden at all times, even though in many areas it was quite permissible for a woman to bare her torso because that region of the female anatomy was not thought to be sexually provocative.

And while the rest of the world tended to regard Africa as a hotbed of promiscuity and lax attitudes towards sex, my experience had proven it to be somewhat prudish and almost puritanical on the subject, in public that is. Open affection between a man and a woman on the street was unacceptable, something to be excused only in lovesick teenagers, and then only if they were no one you knew. Sex itself was something to be enjoyed in private and not talked about in public, at least not in mixed company.

But for every rule there was an exception, in Africa just as elsewhere. And Africa is infinitely more complex than, say, North America, in its diversity of cultures, languages and norms. Cameroon, for example, had two official languages, just like Canada, but on top of that it had to deal with more than 250 different ethnic groups, each with its own separate language.

All this made it impossible for me to generalize without being castigated, or cast any value judgements on social and cultural issues and differences. So much was just the thorny matter of perspective. I'd studied about cultural relativity and cultural blinkers in books, at university, in dreary social anthropology classes that went on forever. But in that campus context, and mostly at an age when I was more interested in the parties coming up on the weekend, I had understood absolutely nothing about what all that anthropological jargon was really trying to tell me.

In Africa, just about all the "truths" I'd grown up believing had been challenged time and time again, and with them my confidence in my own reason and sometimes my own sanity. Universals had dropped by the wayside a long time ago. What was right in Africa and for Africans was not necessarily right for, say North America, and vice versa. It sounds so obvious that it makes me sigh as I write those words, but it took me years and years — far too long — to really believe the truth they contain.

Then Africans started to push my "truths" even further into the ether by insisting that what we thought was right in North America wasn't always even right for North America either, because in their view it wasn't right for the world. North America, the land of plenty and more, didn't exist in isolation nor did it get rich and stay that way without a little plundering and bullying abroad.

Africa welcomed trespassers, many of whom came to change the continent in one way or another. And yet so far, Africa had left the rest of the world alone and done little to sell itself either at home or abroad. Africa certainly hadn't sent out battalions of missionaries to convert people's faith or impose their beliefs on us.

Nor did African experts dictate social policies, imposing cuts in public spending on health and education in London, Bonn, Washington or Ottawa. It was only because I lived in Africa that over time, African points of view had slowly rubbed off on me. My own version of how things worked was challenged so much that I was no longer sure I had a version.

But having said all that, nothing — absolutely nothing — would change my attitude to road safety. If anything, I had become yet more extreme because I had seen so many lives zapped in an instant on African roads, so many accidents caused by speed on bad roads in sorry vehicles. At that moment, heading through Pays Bamoun, we were in a well-aged Toyota Tercel, hurtling at 145 kilometres an hour along a narrow, winding stretch of pavement towards oncoming trucks loaded to kingdom come with logs.

I had asked the taxi-man repeatedly to slow down a little, but he assured me I should not worry because he was an excellent and God-fearing driver. Salifu was otherwise preoccupied, still offering a running checklist of every kind of decay he was witnessing in his country — social, economic and moral. And I was (typically) busy worrying about my own confused life and its imminent end. I recalled with remorse that fourteen years earlier I had sworn to all the gods by all their names that I would *never ever* again set foot in a taxi or bush taxi on the roads of Cameroon. But there I was; "never ever" was now.

I leaned back with a fatalistic shrug, covered my eyes and prayed, which is the best — only — thing a passenger can do on Cameroon's roads. If I had had enough cash, I would have reduced the risk by renting a newer vehicle with built-in safety features — seatbelts, headrests, perhaps an armoured bumper — and hired an experienced driver to whom I could dictate speed and refuse his drinking and driving. But I didn't have the cash; I had seriously under-budgeted for this trip to Cameroon to report on the forests.

Although I tried not to, I was just then longing desperately for the comforts and safety of home. These included: credit cards; reliable and respectable car rental operations that accept those cards; automated teller machines; government legislation on safety features in cars; well-paid and thus honest policemen who enforce speed limits and safety features; phones that work (in the case of an accident); hospitals with the supplies and medical staff to cope with accident victims; ambulances to get them there.

Much as I'd like to pretend I didn't, on much of that voyage in Cameroon I sorely missed the props of the privileged expatriate life that we had just begun again in a new home in Mali. There I had my own car, my own house and garden with a gate, a walled-in refuge from the sheer volume of openly expressed need that is always knocking at the door in Africa. I had made a mistake. I'd left home with a credit card (useless outside the Hiltons and Sheratons in many African capitals) and without the cash I'd need to insulate myself from reality, including life-threatening situations.

That is perhaps one of the fundamental marks distinguishing a "developed" country from one that is, in euphemistic terminology, a "developing" country. In a developing country the difference between being a "have" (cash in your pocket, something in the bank) and a "have-not" (almost no cash at all and certainly not enough to open a bank account) is often a matter of life and death.

"Having" in Africa means possessing the status and influence and money to afford (a) your own vehicle and to keep it in safe working order, (b) medical treatment for a life-threatening injury or illness, (c) a private school education for your children to ensure the "having" continues into the next generation, (d) "gifts" to the right authorities to ensure respect and fair treatment at the hands of the police, government officials or the justice system.

Have-nots comprise the vast majority and what they have not is, well, all of the above. Even if they do have a source of income, it is generally paltry. The average annual income in most of the countries I've lived in hovers around $300 Cdn. and this must be shared among so many have-even-less members of the family that materially, they are just able to survive. How they do survive is still one of those small miracles I have never been able to fathom or explain.

In Ghana, a journalist friend had laughed when I expressed my amazement aloud to her that she could always look so well turned out, support her ageing mother, and pay the rent on a small room in a shambly shack with her salary that was the equivalent of about $100 a month. Then she said with her usual equanimity, "Actually, I think we Ghanaians are magicians when it comes to money."

No wonder Africans put their lives in the hands of God. Certainly, neither their governments nor their police forces appear to have their welfare or safety at heart. Why would they? Despite all that has been done in the name of democracy, those people at the top or in positions of authority generally still account to no one except themselves (and to international lending agencies), while the have-nots learn to perform magical tricks to make a few coins stretch into a week's supply of food.

In western Cameroon in early 1999, I tagged along with Salifu, his family and his friends, and this meant a lot of walking and death-defying trips in taxis and in bush taxis that travelled at breakneck speeds on breakneck roads. We ate large amounts of extremely cheap food in roadside eateries that didn't charge for decor, hygiene or seclusion because there wasn't any. We also ate large amounts of wonderful local dishes — maize porridge they call *couscous,* delectable sauces, chicken or fish spiced to perfection with nuts, barks and leaves collected from the forests, the delicious stew of bitter leaves called *ndole* and served with boiled plantains. And we did this feasting in the homes of Salifu's family and friends, who really couldn't afford to feed us.

In that setting, from that perspective, it was impossible not to notice the poverty or the dust or to hear the bitter complaints about what seventeen years of governance under the same president had done to Cameroon's prosperity. "Buried it under a stinking mountain of lies," was one version. And they used the verbs "chopped" or "eaten" to describe what the Big Men had done with the country's wealth.

"So what did they do with it once they ate it?" I asked.

"They built palaces. They bought Mercedes and BMWs and Mitsubishi Pajeros and Gallopers. They used it to keep girlfriends dressed in fine Paris fashions and gold," they replied. "But mostly, you'll find it in your banks. That's where it lands, in your banks."

"My banks?" I said.

"You know, your banks. Switzerland, France, America. All your banks. That's where our money has gone."

I didn't bother pointing out that I wasn't Swiss or French or American. Anyway, I had no grounds on which to argue. Was I sure that no Canadian banks kept large amounts of crooked capital from crooked leaders in developing countries? And they were right that in Cameroon itself there was no sign of the vast revenues accruing from the exploitation of the country's offshore oil, forests, mineral resources, or huge plantations of bananas, tea, oil palm, rubber. It certainly hadn't been pumped into the roads, public buildings, hospitals, schools or anything that would have been for the public good. And their suspicions echoed a lot of my own, which was quite natural seeing as mine had been built up slowly and painfully over my years in Africa.

Quite apart from the overall, but still unfounded, impression I had that things were deteriorating rapidly in Cameroon, on ground level there in Bamoun country there were some tangible changes that I could see and confirm for myself. After asking around for news of our former landlord, the infamous Alhadji who had headed the coffee cooperative where Karl had worked, I finally found someone willing to speak his name. I learned that after our departure he had spent a couple of years in prison. On his exit from the cell, he had been poisoned. Word had it he had made himself "Too Big, Too Fast" and stolen more money than even his bosses, which contravenes all the unwritten rules on corruption in Cameroon.

The only other tangible change, this one a real improvement, that I saw on the return to Bamoun country was the new bridge over the River Noun. The old one, vintage 1938, had collapsed when we were there in 1985, leaving a gaping hole in the country's main north-south axis just at the time when emergency food provisions were desperately needed to ease the famine in the north of the country. When we left Cameroon, many months after that poor old bridge had crumbled into the River Noun, officials were still bickering over who was going to finance a replacement. It had finally been built, but almost a year after our departure. I pointed this out to Salifu, saying this was worth at least a bit of applause.

He made one of those sucking noises in the back of his throat that indicated my comment wasn't worth the air used to utter it. For him, the shock was in seeing what had happened not just in Foumban but in the whole country in the eight years he'd been away. In the intervening years Cameroon had undergone what was officially known as democratic and economic reform.

In Cameroon, the opposition had garnered popular support in 1990 and '91, in the lead-up to the first multiparty presidential election of 1992. They had openly called for an end to the heavy-handed and corrupt rule of the president, and declared "dead city" days of protest against the man who was preparing to turn himself into a democratically elected president of the people.

In Foumban, the rampaging mobs burned down the *Palais de la Justice* and a few people were shot in the mayhem. But the opposition and popular uprising had led to naught. The president went on to organize, allegedly rig, and win the presidential election in 1992, and the subsequent one in 1997.

The gutted Palace of Justice in Foumban was left as it had been after those days of heady optimism that blew through Africa with the first wave of multiparty elections in the early '90s. A monument to the small flicker of hope in the country, which had gone up in smoke and blood and, by all the accounts I heard in 1999, had left the people even worse off than they had been before.

After seven years of "democracy," in Cameroon, it seemed that people had become equally disillusioned by the opposition, which they saw as little alternative. I was told many of the opposition leaders had been forced into exile, discredited by smear campaigns spearheaded by state media or the secret service, or else "bought" by the ruling party. It seemed that it was this lack of an alternative that led to the loss of hope that led to the new cynicism and even despair that I sensed in Cameroon, revisited.

While still standing, the coffee cooperative where my husband had worked in 1985 now looked deserted and much worse for wear or for no work at all. It had obviously not had a coat of paint since our time there, when Karl had organized a general clean-up one day and had the whole place whitewashed. It was sad to see the legacy of his enthusiasm — walls now faded and brown with age. It made me feel just as faded and old, and it made me feel his time there had been wasted. It probably had. The coffee cooperative was, people said, still as corrupt as it had been when Karl worked there and when the late Al-Hadj Ismael ran it like his own personal credit institution. Farmers were receiving even less for their coffee now than they had then. That seemed to be the effect of the "liberalization" demanded by the lending agencies, at least that was what the coffee growers told me.

Certainly, despite my searching there was no sign of progress in the country, if progress could be measured by improved hygiene, amenities, living standards. I think, though, that the physical deterioration was not as disturbing as the malaise and fallen morale I encountered on the return to Foumban. Everyone went on relentlessly about what the government had obliquely decided to call the "economic crisis." There had been the devaluation of the CFA franc in 1994. Literally overnight, that devaluation had sliced francophone

West Africa's fortunes in half next to the French franc (to which the CFA franc was pegged), and thus to other "hard" currencies.

The former president, Amadou Ahidjo, had allegedly left about $6 billion dollars of oil revenue in a special account when he left power in 1982, stipulating that it was a kind of national insurance policy for any period of economic hardship in Cameroon. That money had disappeared without a trace, despite years of economic reform that international lending institutions claimed was cleaning things up.

Despite the economic crisis and the hints that Cameroonians viewed their plight as hopeless, good humour and what Nova Scotians would call down-home hospitality prevailed, as they almost always do in Africa among "the people." Everyone shouted and danced, hugged or whispered thanks to Allah or to Dieu (his family was split between Islam and Christianity) when they laid eyes on Salifu, their long-lost son/brother/nephew/friend.

I was still reeling after that long, fast cross-country ride. I pestered him constantly because he seemed intent on introducing me to the entire population of Bamoun country and I wanted some solitude and rest.

"Don't be silly, you're not meeting everyone," he said to me at the end of the first day, during which I swear I shook the hands of a thousand people. "That's just my family."

Chapter 19

Humouring the darkness

NAIROBI, 26 March 1999 (IRIN) A UN report has highlighted the "worsening activities" of mercenaries, especially in Africa, which it says is affecting the continent's political stability. The report, by Enrique Bernales Ballesteros, the Human Rights Commission's Special Rapporteur on mercenaries, also notes the expanding activity of private security firms and warns of a "dangerous trend against the free determination of peoples and human rights in general." "The activities of mercenaries have affected deeply the political stability of Africa," Bernales Ballesteros told a press briefing on Thursday. "The situation is very bad in Angola, the two Congos and Sierra Leone." He dwelt in particular on Sierra Leone, where the humanitarian disaster was due in part to mercenary activity. All sides in the conflict — rebel factions as well as the government and the West African intervention force ECOMOG — had reportedly resorted to the use of mercenaries which had led to talk of "good and bad" mercenaries. Former Israeli colonel Yair Klein had recruited many mercenaries, paid them vast amounts of money and put them at the disposal of Revolutionary United Front (RUF) rebels, he said. Bernales Ballesteros also said private security firms were "becoming private armies." He warned that their activities affected the sovereignty of states and contributed to state "impunity and irresponsibility." — This item is delivered in the English service of the UN's IRIN humanitarian information unit, but may not necessarily reflect the views of the United Nations.

It was our second evening in Foumban. We were sitting in yet another house that belonged to yet another member of Salifu's extended family. Salifu said the elderly man was his "uncle," married to the woman who was his "aunt." But it wasn't clear whether he was using the strict Western terminology for my benefit (meaning she was a sister to either his father or his mother) or the looser African terminology, which meant she could be just about any relation to him — aunt, great aunt, related by marriage to one of these — or she might be no blood relation at all. An aunt or uncle could also be someone related to the family by affection only. She told me that she had helped bring Salifu into this world. He said she had helped raise him, been like a mother to him.

I was reluctant to hound him more for genealogical details and earn myself another of those bemused or exasperated looks I got whenever I let slip another of the questions not even a child would ask — or need to ask. Salifu had already spent most of the day trying to explain to me who was who in that never-ending family of his, whispering asides to me as I shook the enthusiastically extended hands of his extended family, or submitted to an embrace that squeezed the breath right out of me.

"Okay, Salifu, let me get this straight, which uncle or brother is this . . . " I'd mutter in the seconds preceding another of those hearty sessions of greeting.

"But I already told you," he'd say. "This is the son of my real uncle, the elder brother of my father, same mother same father, who directly precedes my father. But his father, my uncle, is dead and this is my 'brother' who inherited his estate so you could say he's like my uncle and brother at the same time."

"Your cousin, then?" I'd say after a very long pause.

"No, I told you, he's my brother."

I had grown up believing that there were brothers and sisters and then there were cousins and that was where the family stopped. I was simply not equipped to fathom the incredibly complex network of family relations in any African family, particularly a polygamous one where there were even more complex relationships — half-brothers and half-sisters and a multitude of "mothers" who were a father's co-wives.

And there were added complications in his family — weren't there always? His mother had borne him in her early teens. This hadn't been well received by her father, Salifu's maternal grandfather. So his actual father had not stuck around to raise his son and Salifu had been raised by his maternal grandparents. Until he was eleven,

233

he was told that his grandparents were his parents and he believed that his real mother was his elder sister. And even then, his grandmother continued to be, in his mind and in reality, his mother.

His father had then married a woman who had already had four children and would bear another six for him. I figured that at least those six should be called his half-brothers and half-sisters. He insisted there was no such thing. A brother was a brother and a sister was a sister.

"We don't put up all those picket fences around ourselves," he said, laughing. "You whites. Here, you could say that all the men in Bamoun country are my brothers. In Mali, any Cameroonian would be my brother or sister. And in Europe, any other African would be my brother or sister. *Tu vois?*" No, I didn't actually see, but I resolved to keep on trying.

That evening I was sitting in the small and tidy living room, next to the woman he called his aunt, in a plush and padded sofa that was designed, I'd decided, to make quick escape impossible. Crocheted doilies had been spread lovingly over the backs of the sofa and armchairs and there was a larger one to match on the coffee table, which was adorned with a plastic vase sprouting a bouquet of plastic flowers.

I supposed this was a normal human quirk, this desire for artificial flowers in a country where poinsettias and roses grew wild and huge as trees. In northern climes, where plastic flowers were dirt cheap and real flowers were expensive and rare most of the year, we went to great effort and expense to decorate our interiors with real flowers. Here, the bounty of nature and year-round warmth were available to all, so people took efforts to adorn their homes with whatever they could find that came from elsewhere, that smacked of the exotic and the modern world — plastic, for example.

On the walls were faded black and white portraits of long-ago weddings and of this or that deceased family member. Interspersed with these photographs was some authentic Bamoun paraphernalia — hunting bows, wooden carvings of the two-headed snake that was the totem of the Bamoun people. The concrete floor was neatly swept and smooth; the walls had been painted deep shades of green and blue. It was tidy and comfortable, evoking the same feeling of warmth and homey pride that had filled my grandparents' farmhouse in River Philip, Nova Scotia.

This was family, in the broadest and best sense of that word. And in Africa, the family is still a sacred responsibility. Family members had to share what they had — and anyone who tags in on the heels of a family member is treated like family. No questions asked. No limits.

The family was the only welfare net there was. Unfortunately, as poverty grew and fewer and fewer family members had any source of regular — or even irregular — income, the pressing needs and demands of a never-ending family could nearly kill the one or two family members who did have "some small money and means."

This family pressure made many young people flee the country — work abroad and accumulate a little material well-being, far away from the watchful and often envious eyes of the family. Most continued to send money back, but when they were out of range of constant haranguing and begging and the oppressive need around them, they were better able to choose the amount and keep at least a little something for themselves.

As the sun set that evening, the blood-red light filtering through the thick foliage of the mango trees just beyond the front veranda of the small house, I was awash in conflicting emotions. On one hand, I was dismayed by the unexpected poverty that prevailed in that formerly rich (relatively speaking) coffee-growing region. At the same time I was thrilled to be back.

I was also worn out from the immersion course in social structure I'd had for two days. And I was incredulous at the unlikely chain of events and people that had landed me here, fourteen years later, as the guest of a colleague I'd met in Mali, only to find that his "aunt" (the woman in whose house we were sitting) lived footsteps away from the house we'd inhabited for two years.

Like the rest of the town, our former house had also suffered the effects of time and weather since we had left it. Someone had chopped down the huge avocado tree inside the compound; the gate was rusted and falling off its hinges, and the only sign that it had once been my home, the only indication of our passing, were the large cacti we had planted along the wall. Had we left no real mark at all?

Everyone agreed that they did recall, vaguely, that at one time "some Germans" had lived in the neighbourhood. But it was distressing to realize just how isolated we had been, how removed we'd been from all that was going on around us. How much we had missed by not getting to know the people around us, these warm and giving people who were welcoming me into their homes now.

I rationalized that it had partly to do with the timing of our stay in Foumban, which began a few days after the failed coup d'état in

1984 and lasted through a year of heavy political tension and repression that had made people afraid to speak openly, particularly to strangers. It also had something to do with our not having any children at the time. Women without children were simply incomprehensible, and children were like passports to entry in an African neighbourhood — striking up friendships almost instantly with every passer-by, or vice versa.

They assured me that I shouldn't worry that we had left no trace of our passing. God had surely brought me back this time so I could get to know the people and see what I had missed first time around.

"What changes do you see here?" Stephan, a distant "brother" to Salifu, asked me. I'd been listening to his caustic wit for the past hour, and to the chorus of laughter it invoked. I'd been happy to listen only. I had no urge to offer any of my own views. But now Stephan was not only asking me a question, he was giving me a penetrating look that made me unsure just how much I was expected to say — or to know.

I hesitated.

He persisted. "Have you not noticed all the progress we have made under our democratic government?" he asked, involuntarily smiling when he uttered the word "democratic," enclosing it in audible quotation marks.

I was searching for the right words to make it at least sound like a right answer, the right answer being defined as the one he wanted to hear. This was something that I had found Africans excelled at — telling strangers not what they really thought but what would be sure to please them, perhaps echo their own views. And even though I wasn't particularly good at that kind of diplomacy, I certainly didn't intend to blurt out what I was really thinking — that the town looked as though it had gone to the dogs. It was one thing for Cameroonians to criticize their own country, which they did all the time and without mercy. It was quite another thing for a foreign visitor to do so.

"Well," I began, "that's a tricky question. Hard to say, really. I can say that the roads haven't changed much."

Everyone in the room exploded in laughter and Salifu pounded my back in what I interpreted as resounding (if a little painful) approval. I sat back and tried to fade into the background, never an easy thing to do when you're a pale interloper in Africa.

Nightfall had brought more visitors. The room, good and full already (by my definition), was still filling up. There was always more room, enough to go around even if it defied all the physical laws that I had grown up believing and respecting. It seemed the whole neighbourhood had to come to greet their long-lost Salifu. More and more chairs and floor space had to be found, and so of course they were.

Stephan was off and running again. "Really, I don't know why we in Cameroon are so ungrateful for all the blessings we have. We are number one in the world when it comes to corruption. That's no small feat, especially when you consider that Nigeria is in the running for that title. But no, we are the champions now. Such victories are not to be sneered at."

When the laughter faded, there was silence for a few minutes and Salifu's aunt whispered to me that a silence like that, in a room full of people, signalled the quick passage of the Devil through our midst. The sounds of the night outside — chirping insects, chickens clucking, the breeze rustling in the fronds of the palm trees — suddenly seemed muted. Those melodic echoes from the blackness outside seemed to encircle the house, closing us in. I had the unsettling impression that the world had suddenly been compressed to fit inside this single room, that it was no bigger than the circles of light shed by two dim lamps mounted on opposite walls, which cast the wood-carving of the two-headed Bamoun snake into sharp relief.

I was also suddenly aware of the absence of sounds from this century — not a car engine or car horn within earshot. The men in the room had come on foot. None seemed to have a full-time job or any obvious source of income, but all were well-educated and eager for work. Of course they all made do somehow, with a bit of farming here, labouring there or trading anywhere. But there was no money for such luxuries as private vehicles. And despite their discussion about the political and economic injustices in their country — problems that to my Canadian sense of right and wrong were so horrific that I thought they should evoke tears or at least outbursts of loud indignation and cries for rebellion or revolution — the room was filled with laughter.

Maybe they were trying to humour the Devil — humour the darkness that surrounded us and filled a country that was no longer as jubilant and joyful as I recalled it.

"And furthermore," Stephan was saying, "I don't know what's wrong with us in this country. We don't even see all we have. Why, there are wonders here you can't see anywhere else in the world. It takes a European to see all the attractions we have in this country. I mean, just look. It's not in Europe that you can see a dog die in the middle of the road, and then watch the corpse rot day after day. People come from Europe to see these things in Africa. They don't have these things there. We're so lucky, and we don't even know it."

I laughed, along with everyone else. Even though I wasn't sure whom he was making fun of — Cameroonians who admittedly did let dead dogs lie, or Europeans who came and took notes on such things, even photographed them and presented them as representative images of Africa. Thinking back on it now, by the clear light of day, I suspect he was actually taking us all, Cameroonians and Europeans, for a ride on the double-edged blade of his wit.

"And look at the wreck of civilization we keep in front of our homes," he said. "Those dusty and rusty and broken carcasses of our cars that break down and stay that way." He waved his hand in the direction of that darkest of nights outside, where we were all summoning images of the paths that were littered with car bodies he had so accurately described. "Just as we bury our dead in our compounds to keep their spirits close to us, we like to keep our broken-down vehicles there too. Europeans, they put their dead in cemeteries and they crush up their old cars to make new ones. We keep our junk around us so we can remember the good old days when we could once afford a car that worked, even if we can't have one now in this thing the rest of the world and our government tell us is a democratic and developing country. We're so ungrateful. You wait and see. One day Europeans will come and see all our junk, our antiques, recognize them as the *objets d'art* that they are and buy them all back from us. Then we'll be rich again."

The laughter reverberated in that room, even as the talk grew bleaker, homing in on the rampant crime and brutality they said had become epidemic in the country. The night out there was too dark; I missed my city lights. My skin had begun to crawl, so much that I'd begun to feel itchy all over, and it wasn't just because of the mosquitoes feasting on my ankles and arms. There had been no mosquitoes in Foumban when we'd lived there. Nor had there been any talk of armed bandits who terrorized people by day and by night on the paths and roads of this town. Something ominous was afoot in that town, the whole country.

My own experience with criminals in Cameroon back in 1984 had been limited to a few brushes with tricksters who flattened tires and then grabbed handbags, or men brandishing machetes with no obvious intentions of putting them to use. The idea of men wearing head masks and touting machine guns was something new, something I associated with war zones in Africa or my worst nightmares back in Nairobi. I had left Nairobi and had always made a point of avoiding war zones. Aloud, I asked how it was that there were suddenly so many armed bandits in the country. A simple question that, as usual in Africa, earned a very long answer.

They said the arms had flowed into the country at the same time as "democracy" arrived with multiparty elections in 1992. At the time, it had become clear to many people that it would take a strong and determined alliance of opposition to fight against the incumbent president, who had had total control of the country since 1982 and who clearly had the backing of the French, their former colonial masters.

Indeed, it was "common knowledge" in Cameroon that the former ruler, Amadou Ahidjo, had been tricked into handing over power to his successor in 1981. The story was that French politicians had conspired with French physicians, who then convinced the Cameroonian president that he had a terminal disease. It turned out that once he got to France, after handing over power to his successor, the former president had no such thing. But by then it was too late and the French had managed to get the man they wanted in power. And Cameroonians were adamant that even in 1999, France still kept Cameroon on a short leash — or chain.

Before the elections, when there were glimmers of hope that this was Africa's moment for taking control of its own destiny, it was clear to all in Cameroon that regardless of how unfair the elections might be, if major ethnic and linguistic groups united in opposition to the all-powerful ruling party, they could at least make themselves heard. In this way, the SDF political party formed, bringing together the country's main opposition groups as well as the anglophone minority and the Bamileke chiefdoms, which formed the economic powerhouse in the country.

Perhaps as a sort of kamikaze insurance policy — if I can't be president of this country I'll make sure it vaporizes — the president allegedly orchestrated the distribution of small arms to all his supporters, primarily in the southeast corner of the country from which he hailed. He ostensibly warned his supporters that if the SDF, with its powerful Bamileke component, won the elections their only recourse was to use these weapons against the victors.

I had a friend who belonged to one of the many chiefdoms that made up the Bamileke. He told me that before the elections he had been working away one day, minding his own political business in his office in the forestry department. His work colleague, from the president's ethnic group, who had been his "brother" since they'd gone through secondary school together, pulled a pistol out of his desk drawer and showed it to him.

"What's that for?" said the Bamileke man to his friend.

"It's to protect myself from the Bamileke. The president wants us to protect ourselves against the SDF. If they win the elections, we're going to kill them."

My friend said that he was quiet for a time, waiting for some words to come to him. Then he said, "But, my brother . . . I'm a Bamileke. Are you saying that even though I'm an old friend, you would kill me because the president's party says to kill Bamileke?"

The other man realized his gaff and hastily reassured his Bamileke colleague and long-standing friend that of course, no, he would never have shot him. But he insisted that the president was right in arming the people against the possibility of an SDF victory. He had been firmly convinced by the government propaganda that said if the Bamileke controlled the reigns of power in the country, they would "take over everything." Indeed they already controlled a good deal of the economy, at least that proportion not controlled by Lebanese and Greek merchants or French corporate interests. That, apparently, was democracy as the ruling party viewed it, or at least promoted it using unofficial rumour mills operated by secret service agents or by the official dispensers of half-truths that doubled as the state media.

Throughout my return visit to Cameroon in 1999, and no matter where I went, people told me they put up with the lies, the corruption and the injustices for one reason only. They were watching carefully events in Sierra Leone, Angola and their neighbours, Congo (capital Brazzaville) and the Democratic Republic of Congo (capital Kinshasa). In all of those countries, people had given in to ethnic, political and economic rivalries and headed out on the dead-end road of violence and warfare. In some cases the fighting was aided and abetted by foreign concerns that hired mercenaries or private armies to help out whichever "side" they thought would best serve their interests. And their interests were not hard to identify; all four countries were rich mining grounds for diamonds or oil or a host of other precious minerals. But that still didn't exonerate the Africans who so willingly joined in. It was the scenario of violence with no end that Cameroonians told me was the key to their patience and tolerance.

"That's why we stay quiet and keep taking what this man dishes out, the injustice and the lies and the stealing of all our resources," said Stephan that night. "Being poor isn't as bad as being at war. We all know how to start the violence, start a civil war, especially after the hatred this man has seeded between ethnic groups. But none of us here on this earth knows how it can end. Once it starts, it might never stop. So we pray to God to give us patience to wait peacefully until this man leaves office, or dies. There are too many arms in this country. We cannot risk sparking off a war."

So the ammunition for a war was already there, literally. And the supporters of the ruling party hadn't had to use the arms because they had won the elections easily despite muted cries of foul from international observers and loud outcries from international human rights groups. Today, now that the elections were over and "democracy" was in place, many of those weapons had made their way into the hands of criminals on the streets, for use against the common men and women of the country.

Cameroonians told me there had never been doubt in anyone's mind that the president would win, given the way the elections were held. So they could not understand why he even bothered to prepare himself for possible defeat. Indeed the president probably still regarded himself as universally revered, except by those "few radicals" who dared to criticize him publicly, and had the stature and voice to do so.

One of the paradoxes of dictatorship is that after a few years of suppressing opposition and critics and handsomely rewarding sycophants, dictators begin to believe their own propaganda. They tumble headfirst into their own traps. They start to delude themselves that those mobs of schoolchildren and women who gather to dance and shout praises of The President at any given public appearance are there out of pure adulation. They seem to forget, or lose sight of the fact, that their very own President's Men have generally arranged for the crowds to be bussed in or even paid for their presence. They forget that it is the very fear they have instilled into the populace that silences their would-be critics. They forget who they are. They forget they are mere mortals, and fail to notice when they become universally unpopular. However, that doesn't stop them, when they're putting on democratic clothing at the behest of the donor countries and international lending institutions, from ensuring that elections are rigged in their favour, just in case.

I recall an interview done with the former Zaire's late president, Mobutu Sese Seko, about a year before he fled his country and died in disgrace, friendless in his final weeks as even his former "friends" in Paris and Washington abandoned him. In that interview, Mobutu said it was obvious that the people of his country still adored him — didn't they all line the streets to salute him every time he passed? Hadn't he, time and time again, won the elections with 99.999 per cent of the votes cast? Never mind that he was the only candidate. That didn't seem to register with him.

I wished someone had had a chance to interview him when he was fleeing his country in 1997, being turned away by his old "friends" when he sought refuge in their countries. I wish I had been able to speak to him before he died and hear what he had to say about "international diplomacy" and his friends who had first hoisted him to power and created with flattery and money a caricature, then suddenly disowned him for being what they had once needed and needed no longer. Mobutu was not the only one who fell into this category. The same had been true of former Ugandan president Idi Amin, whose vicious antics had at first inspired amusement among the British who branded him a harmless "clown," before he went on to have hundreds of thousands of people killed. Another foreign creation had been the president of the Central African Republic, Jean-Bedel Bokassa, who had been for years a good hunting buddy of and giver-of-diamonds to French president Giscard d'Estaing. Eventually Bokassa became an embarrassment for even the French, although not until after they funded his coronation as Emperor in 1977 to the tune of about $20 million US. They finally noticed that the power seemed to have gone to his head; rumours abounded that he had a developed a cannibalistic bent. Their former "friend" had to be deposed, and so the French made sure that he was.

At death's door, Mobutu's confessions might have been of interest to the world and fingered a great many Western dignitaries and secret services. Alas, no one got near him. He died quietly of prostate cancer in Morocco. But sometimes I wonder if it wasn't the truth of his own unpopularity that killed him even before he left his country, disgraced and humiliated.

But as they reminded me that evening in Foumban, not all the "Mobutus" in Africa were gone. That night, I listened to the room full of men making light (or dark?) of their own president's ego and hubris. They laughed themselves to tears recalling the year their head of state had held the post as head of the Organization of African Unity and yet failed to show up for the OAU meeting over which he should have been presiding.

"Why do you criticize him for that?" said Stephan. "He probably had important engagements in France. On the golf course."

They were unanimous that their leader was loathed by just about everyone who did not hail from his ethnic group or who was not in his inner circle with their hands on the spoils of the country's wealth. And yet, two sets of elections later, there he still was. International observers from donor countries had endorsed neither election as free and fair, but those same donor countries were still offering development assistance to the "elected" government and helping themselves in return to oil, timber, plantation crops and mineral resources. The contradictions were enough to boggle bigger minds than mine.

It was that old tricky thing called perspective again. There is gross national product, which can be calculated based on the value of raw materials flooding out of the country, which in Cameroon was rising. There is also gross lack of distribution, which can be easily missed on a bank ledger. It all depends what you're looking at, how much of it you are seeing, who's saying it to you, and whether you're seeing it in an air-conditioned office with the prospect of an evening dinner at the Hilton before you, or from a more typical setting — hot, dirty, crowded, empty-handed and hungry.

A charming and affable man in a Cameroonian ministry found a simpler phrase to capture the sense of futility that prevailed in the country in 1999. It was my third visit to his office in as many days. And as on the two previous visits, I had come to collect my press accreditation. Was it done, I asked him hopefully. No it wasn't. I asked him if he had any idea what was holding it up. He said that the people who had to move my application from his office to another office for subsequent movement upstairs to the minister's office for a signature had not shown up. I asked him why.

He laughed. "It's like this," he said. "Here in this country it's all pretence. They make a pretence of paying us. So we make a pretence of working."

It was close to midnight when the welcome party for Salifu began to break up. After all the terrifying tales of armed bandits and violent crime, I was vastly relieved when the men announced they would escort Salifu and me to the hotel, which was a few kilometres outside of town in a desolate area of grassland. The night before, a gang of heavily armed men had hijacked a vehicle on that road, just in front of the police station.

We headed out into the night, strolling past the carcasses of broken down and abandoned cars, picked clean of all that wasn't the original metal frame, and parked for eternity in front of mud homes.

"You see?" said Stephan. "See those *objets d'art*? I'm sure you don't have those in Europe."

I cleared my throat, said I wasn't from Europe and that, if truth be told, my brother, who lived in rural Nova Scotia, had several *objets d'art* just like that parked behind a shed on his farm. They were unanimous in their disbelief that rural Nova Scotia was adorned with such wrecks. Certainly this was not an image that would make it often onto African television screens, which tended to feature US- or Brazilian-made soap operas in which everyone was rich, lived in a palace and had a vineyard in which to hide to commit adultery. Just as our television screens were filled with selected and extreme glimpses of Africa — either horrific scenes of famine and warfare or else marvellous dreamlike safaris among the lions and elephants — the images of the developed world that made it onto African television were equally skewed.

We strolled along, my seven self-appointed bodyguards and I, talking about the rich comedy of misconceptions piled on top of mis-understandings. We'd gone about two hundred metres in the dark-ness before we came to a house where one of the men knew someone who had a car that was still in working order. It was a neat little Peu-geot, not quite big enough for eight adults, but never mind, one of the men would stay here. It was okay to be a bit squeezed for the few minutes to the hotel, if it meant deterring any would-be militias from hijacking us at gunpoint. I was strategically placed right in the mid-dle of the back seat, protected, they said, from any bandits who might ambush the car. I think they believed I found this reassuring.

As we turned off the main road, almost safely at the hotel and past the favourite hijacking zone, a rear tire on the Peugeot exploded. They said it was too dangerous to stop and change it there. And so we drove the next two hundred metres over sorry ruts pretending to be a road in someone's precious car, destroying the wheel rim, until we were safely inside the walls of the hotel compound and they felt they had delivered us "home" safely.

Even there, behind bolted doors in my room, I tossed and turned the whole night, wondering why on earth I had left my family behind in Mali. I had had enough travelling and kicking around. It was time to go "home" — or at least to Mali.

Mali

Chapter 20

Browner pastures

I drive a mini-cab all the nights and some days too. Me, I'm not the only Ghana boy driving mini-cab. One of my brothers in this mini-cab company was Ghanaian ambassador here in Britain. He say he make more money driving cabs than that. You make more money cleaning toilets here than medical doctor make back there in Ghana. That's the only reason why we come. It's just for money, so we get something small to help our family back home. You think we like it here? We come for the hi-life? (laughs) — Anonymous taxi driver in London, 1995

Mali

Kofi was a man of all trades on a continent where none of them was very lucrative, particularly none that involved honest and hard work. Our paths crossed in 1997 in Nyala, a small village claiming municipality status in the far north of Mali. He was earning about a dollar a day making and selling what he called "meat pies." In fact, these were tarts filled mostly with air and a meagre spoon of sardine mashed together with hot pepper.

On Mondays — market day in Nyala — the population shot from about 15,000 to 30,000 and Kofi could double his daily take. In a good month he could earn enough to pay the rent on his tiny room in a large compound of mud dwellings. In bad months he would try to plead his case with the owner of the compound, and when that failed, find a cheaper place. He was already on this third room. It was hardly big enough to turn around in; there was no running water, no power and no toilet facilities. As in most rural areas in Mali, latrines were rare in Nyala and the most common toilet facility was the great hot and dusty outdoors.

The municipality was really just a collection of mud dwellings plonked down on the very edge of the sands of time, which didn't seem to be moving at any breakneck speeds on the southern flank of the Sahara Desert, a stone's throw from Mali's northern border with Mauritania.

Kofi spent most of his time with his fellow Ghanaians, the odd development worker or the occasional European tourist who passed through town after crossing the Sahara and tracking down a cool drink in the little bar known affectionately as the Ghanaian Embassy. It wasn't really an embassy of course. Ghana no longer had one in Mali, not even in the capital, Bamako, four hundred kilometres to the south.

This embassy was just a bar. It was owned and run by members of the small Ghanaian community, people who had washed up for one reason or another in Nyala, a couple of thousand kilometres from their own Gold Coast. There at the edge of the desert there was lots of sand; what was missing in Nyala was water.

Granted, in the mid-'90s a new town water supply had gone in thanks to German financing. There were now a few public faucets in town where clean, clear water could be had. The German consultants who did the work said the water came from a non-renewable fossil source a couple of hundred metres below the surface and about thirty kilometres away — they hadn't been able to locate a closer or renewable source. They predicted it would run out in the middle of the next century.

Few people in Nyala were looking that far ahead. Most people were preoccupied with the problems of the day. These included overwhelming poverty, failed rains and hunger, disputes between the Fulani herders and sedentary Sarakoli farmers over grazing rights, and making ends meet — mostly through funds sent back to the area by relatives who had left for other parts in West Africa or Europe or America.

A bar like the Ghanaian Embassy was just the ticket after a day of sucking up sand and dust that permeated the air, ears, eyes, nose and lungs. Those who were smart quickly adopted the local dress —

long robes and turbans that left only the eyes exposed. The Embassy was the only place in town where you could get a cold — okay, cool-*ish* — drink. A coolish drink was a very big deal in Nyala, where during the hot season (which lasted about ten months of the year) night-time temperatures might just plummet to below forty degrees Celsius.

The Ghanaian couple who ran the bar had a functioning kerosene refrigerator where they kept the standard supply of Coke, Fanta, Sprite, beer (if the weekly beer truck had not had another accident on its way north from Bamako), and the odd flask of sweet red wine brewed out of God-knows-what chemicals or alchemy. Unlike the local population in Nyala, the Ghanaians were Christian with no aversion at all to alcohol.

The Embassy was smack dab in the middle of the town that didn't look like a town — a few steps away from the sand-swept collection of rickety stalls that comprised the market, and across from a plucky little stationery shop. There was no signboard in front to distinguish this crumbling mud establishment from any of the others in Nyala. But one wall did bear a large loopy scrawl, which said, "Schultz was here." A brash German traveller who had passed through town a couple of years earlier had used a can of black spray paint to splash his name across the side of the bar. For this reason, many people in Nyala now referred to the place as "Chez Schultz," just as they did a string of bars on the long, washboard track that led from Nyala south towards Bamako.

Schultz was long gone and I thought he'd seriously overstepped the limits of hospitality by writing his name on walls on his way through Africa, so I stubbornly clung to the original name for the bar and called it the Ghanaian Embassy. In the evening it was a good place to sit a spell with Ghanaians, who were almost as foreign in this desert outpost as I was. Some Malians also frequented the place, but far less conspicuously. They would slip in after dark — there was no town power in Nyala — and order a couple of bottles of beer or gin or a flask of that sweet potent red "wine" — and slip out again with their bottles tucked inside the folds of their robes.

It was a lovely little oasis in that dusty and windy northern outpost. The walls were kept fresh with whitewash. A single solar panel provided energy to keep a couple of fluorescent violet lights humming in the evenings. The ebullient and bright-eyed children of the proprietor were always on hand to bring drinks, and then to stick around to talk and ask questions, even draw a picture or two if someone offered them a pen and a scrap of paper. There was also a lame blaster mounted in one corner, with a steady supply of Ghanaian music — not always playing up to tempo because of ailing batteries or the simple fatigue of its inner workings. Somehow that seemed like just about the right speed for Nyala. Any little bit of technology, no matter what age or condition, seemed like a great treat in the Nyala context.

But best of all, the Embassy was a great place to collect stories. It was a meeting place for people passing through town in their search for greener pastures, and for people who had somehow got stuck in the brown sands of Nyala — and then gone about making the best of it.

There was Kouame, who ran his photography service right in front of the Ghanaian Embassy on the sand path that doubled as Main Street. His camera was homemade, an art he'd picked up from his father. It was a wooden box, painted bright blue with white trim and lettering "Photo Nyala 1997, Kouame." You sat on a stool with your back against the warm mud of the Embassy wall, while Kouame bent over and stuck his head more or less inside the box, covering it with a black shroud attached to the end of the camera. I've seen pictures of Ansel Adams using similar antique apparatus to photograph American landscapes, but I wonder if he made his own out of scraps the way Kouame did.

Mostly, Kouame photographed people in town. His muffled voice would warn you he was ready to "snap" and then he would reach around the box with his right hand, remove the beer cap that was his lens cap, count the seconds out loud and replace the cap. Then you would sit there on the stool and wait, exchanging pleasantries with the hundreds of children who had gathered to take in this exciting event in their town. After that, using a mirror to re-shoot and re-reverse the original negative, Kouame would miraculously conjure four small passport-size prints out of that magic blue box.

My children found all of this just as intriguing as a good game of *Myst* on the computer. With their photographs in hand, off they set on their own, hailing their own taxi — a wagon pulled by a donkey. As they headed off, perched on the hot tin surface of the wagon, the whole image faded rapidly into the squirming heat waves and blowing sand. I stood there breathing dust and shading my eyes, illogically content. I think it had to do with the realization that hit me at split seconds like that, that we were enormously privileged to land in a spot like Nyala.

It was late 1997. Even in comfortable and cosy Nova Scotia, in the country that boasted the highest living standard in the world, my parents had in recent years suffered all manner of nasty little crimes in their neighbourhood. Friends in Canada with daughters spoke to me of their fears every time their teenage or pre-teen girls ventured out onto city streets alone. In Nyala, we were hounded by ever-growing mobs of curious children, yes — but we were safe. My ten-year-old daughter, were she part of the local Moor society, was actually just getting on to prime marrying age. But she was not part of their world and was thus ineligible for male advances, which in any case would have been very strict, in accordance with the unwritten but strict laws on courtship in that highly traditional society.

This was the first time the children and I had come to Nyala. Karl had been working there for almost a year, while I finished up my contract in Kenya, and he had settled in quite well. That is, he had finally got a project office open and functioning, found a house to rent and located the Ghanaian Embassy to cool him down on those hot Nyala evenings.

We rounded off our first day of exploring Nyala with an evening in the Embassy. I found myself sitting at a table beside Kofi, who had sold enough of his meat pies that day to afford a glass of the dubious red wine. It had been a delightful surprise to find a small community of Ghanaians in town — it was four years since we'd left Ghana and we had never stopped missing the country and its people. I just couldn't understand what on earth all these people who had grown up on the Gold Coast were doing way up here, so far from the humid ocean breezes on the vibrant West African coast. Brash and insensitive as ever, I set about trying to find out. Kofi introduced me to some of the Ghanaians present.

Victoria, a laughing woman swathed all in pink and wearing a coppery wig, seemed to be what my friends in Ghana would have referred to as "the town helper." She stood around the table for a while, cracking jokes with her countrymen, bouncing someone's child in her arms. She was jovial and bright, just doing what a woman on her own far from home could do to make a bit of money. After she had left, her laughter still ringing in my ears, Kofi told me Victoria had come with a husband but that he had simply left one day, crossed the border and trekked north across the desert towards Europe. No one knew what had become of him. In any case, Kofi assured me that the Ghanaian community in Nyala "took good care" of Victoria.

Then there was Kwesi, decked out in full Rasta regalia as though he'd just stepped off the boat from Jamaica, who was working as a photographer in Mauritania. I wanted to know if it wasn't a little difficult as a black African to work in Mauritania, a country that has the dubious distinction of being the very last in the world to practise slavery — which it did legally up to 1981 and has done illegally since then. Slavery of black Mauritanians by their whiter Moor brothers was still common practice even in 1997. Indeed there had just been a spate of arrests in the capital, Nouakchott, when anti-slavery groups took to the streets to demonstrate against ongoing slavery. Even the journalists who covered the demonstration had been taken into custody.

But Kwesi assured me he was doing well in Mauritania, even if he did admit that it hadn't been easy at first. He said you had to "know the Moors" to live there, and since he'd been there for some years, he figured he did know them. In the town where he lived, out in the middle of the desert, people came from far and wide to seek his photography services for arranged marriages of pre-teen brides and middle-aged or elderly bridegrooms. Then, perhaps to prove to me how well he was doing in Mauritania, Kwesi led me around the corner to show me a brand new bicycle he had just bought in Bamako. He was just stopping overnight in Nyala. Tomorrow he would continue back up into the desert, with his bicycle.

"But wouldn't it be easier to work in Ghana?" I said.

"Not at all. No. In Ghana, you see, my people are not easy," he said, giving his woollen Rasta cap — crocheted in red, green and yellow — a little tug. "You cannot be able to take up just any profession. You have to be born with the right to do that thing. Your birthright tells you what you can be able to do in your life. At the end of the day, people in my village would never accept me as a photographer because I come from a farm family and they wouldn't let me rise up and do something better. They are difficult, my people at home. In Mauritania no one knows the place I was born, or how I came by my talents as photographer. So there I am free. You see."

Did I see? Not really, maybe a little bit. From what I had gathered over the years about social mobility in Africa, it still seemed to be one of those advantages of life in the developed world that was lacking in most rural traditional societies. For a while after independence in a few countries — Ghana, Kenya and Cameroon spring to mind — the new leaders made every effort to make education a right for all and not a privilege for a few. But nowadays, decent education in Africa is once again becoming a privilege for the rich, who can afford private schools, or for the very few fortunate enough to have a job with an organization that helps pay hefty fees for private schools.

There are, of course, other avenues for upward social and economic mobility, including churches and the army. But these are not for the majority. So many Africans opt to leave home, leave the country, and take their chances just about anywhere, or somewhere where anonymity is an asset. Kwesi said he was making enough money to live on and, as I could see for myself, he was doing even better than his Ghanaian brothers who had settled there in Nyala, none of whom had so much as a bicycle to their names. And he was able to send money back to his family in Kumasi as well, an obligation respected by nearly everyone in the African Diaspora when they head away from home in search of a "living."

Kofi, however, had a different story to tell. In fact, he had such a story to tell that he agreed to drop by the house the next afternoon to tell it into a microphone — that way I could tape for him a few of the songs he said he had written.

The sun was beginning its final descent into the scrubby acacia trees on the Nyala horizon when Kofi struck up his tale. We were well into the dry season, which meant the wind that eternally lambasted this desert town was dry in addition to being hot. Sand and plastic refuse from the market tumbled down the wide sandy avenue that bisected the town. Nyala houses four distinct ethnic groups in four distinct neighbourhoods, discernible by different costumes and customs and laid out by intersecting sandy roads — one north-south, the other east-west. It was a gentle and informal social segregation that involved customs and tradition rather than laws, walls without any kind of brutality.

Most of the rubbish came in the form of paper-thin pink and blue plastic bags, and their proliferation was taken locally as a sign of progress and development. The ones that didn't get pinioned on a tree just blew up and down the street depending on the direction of the wind. Many of them came to rest in the thorns of the scraggy acacia trees or small shrubs hearty enough to poke their stems up through the deep sand, turning these trees and bushes into haunting and noisy things that rattled in the wind.

Kofi took a chair inside the compound and began to talk, serenaded by the brittle sound of plastic in the breeze. He directed his words alternately to the eastern horizon (brown with blowing dust) and to his feet (in oversized running shoes). He was neither whining nor complaining, although I thought he had plenty to whine and complain about. He was just telling me his story because I asked him to; he seemed surprised that I would be interested. It's not the kind of thing anyone but a stranger would request. After all, Kofi's moving story was anything but unique. It was just a series of adventures (not for thrills but for survival) of an engaging and God-fearing young man stuck unwillingly in a rather typical plot on the continent. Here was just another young African man confronting the ludicrous odds that had been stacked against him at birth. Here he was trying to "make it" on a continent where getting ahead was highly improbable, if you were not born into the family of a Big Man or willing to sell your integrity and allegiance to the Powers That Be.

I asked him how he had wound his way north to Nyala from the splendid coastal town in Ghana where he had grown up.

"I started my journey right down from Nigeria — that was 1982. I spent nine months there before the mass repatriation came." He said he'd had a good job then, working for a kind "patron" who even allowed him to get a driver's license and drive a Volkswagen around Lagos doing errands for him. But then in 1983, Nigeria decided to expel its huge population of African expatriates, including three million Ghanaians, including Kofi.

He said when he returned to Ghana he went to the state-owned cotton plant where he had worked before, but they refused to take him back. So Kofi, undaunted, decided to take his chances with him and head back to Nigeria.

"I was still thinking to find greener grass," he said. "And when I go there to Nigeria, things move smoothly at first, but later it changed entirely. So I made up my mind to make a route to Libya. That was '89."

I wanted to know what would draw a Ghanaian to Libya. He said many Ghanaians worked there. The pay was good and there were labourers' jobs to be had.

"At first I got stranded in Niger. That is because at the border, when we were leaving Nigeria I mean, the authorities there removed all our money from our pockets. We were three boys in number, namely Adu, Adams and myself, Kofi."

They had sold all their worldly belongings so that they would be heading to Niger with some money in their pockets to set up some kind of small business — trading or sewing or manual labour.

But thanks to the ruthless officials at the Nigerian border, they were, as Kofi put it, "unlucky to enter Niger without money." They then moved from one village to another, looking for some way to earn honest income.

"So in Niger we first started carrying bread, selling up and down. Later we decided, no, this is not a good job for us so we changed to tailoring. In fact, we bought a second-hand sewing machine and we started our adventure. We stay there for almost two years before we get some small money. I said to myself, no, Kofi, this small money cannot cope with the conditions I'm going to face when I go home some day to Ghana. You know, we sons are responsible for helping the family, especially our mothers and younger brothers and sisters in the whole extended families, and if we can't send or bring money, they will suffer. If they suffer, then we too suffer."

"So I decide then that I cannot stop there in Niger. I still have to continue my journey to Libya. I walked north of Niger border, that is to Tamanrasset in Algeria but I couldn't make it. I came back to Niger again. Then I started right down from Gaya, trekking with sewing machine up and down, till I reach Tahoua — that's one of their cities. There, too, I stay for some time." He sat quietly for a bit, his hands on his lap, immersed in his memories.

Since we had left Niger in 1983, the rebellion of the Tuareg nomads, who inhabit the desert from Chad right across the Sahel to Mali, had broken out in full force. Spurred on for years by pirate radio emanating from Libya in their Tamarsheq language, the Tuaregs had decided to take up arms to end what they saw as administrative domination by black African governments in Sahelian capitals, domination by people they had traditionally regarded as their inferiors, even slaves.

In the late '80s and on into the '90s, the Tuaregs had taken control of the desert again, making it unsafe — impossible — to travel in regions they claimed as theirs in northern Niger and Mali. They were undoubtedly supported in large part by Libya, but they were also able to build up their own strength by helping themselves to hundreds of vehicles belonging to development agencies and to the United Nations High Commission for Refugees (which had moved into the area to help refugees).

By 1996, Mali had brokered a peace agreement with the Tuaregs, and held a much-publicized ceremony in Timbuktu at which arms were stacked up and burned before international television cameras. But shortly thereafter, aided in large part by massive influxes of development money into northeast Mali — money meant to pacify the Tuaregs — the noble nomads had begun to re-arm themselves, perhaps preparing for the day when all that development assistance would dry up and spur them back into armed action. In both Mali and Niger, Tuareg bandits and remnant gangs of the rebellion, who weren't big on recognizing or respecting borders, continued to hijack vehicles — making for insecurity that wouldn't go away. Nyala was exempt from that only because there were no Tuaregs living there. Another reason people like Kofi had made it this far, and then stayed on.

Said Kofi, "Tuareg rebel activities were there in this town, Tahoua, there in Niger. So I decided to quit from that place, because I couldn't just lose my life like that in the hands of rebels. So I quitted from that place then decided to go down to Ghana." He paused, held up his palms, as though in supplication to the forces that had been buffeting him about like so much litter in the wind.

"But how to go to Ghana? Where is the means? Then a friend of mine who just came from Mauritania told me, he say 'Kofi, try Mauritania, if you really want to make it over to Europe then you better go to Mauritania and pass to Europe over the desert.' So I try to come to Mali here but I get only as far as Burkina Faso. In Burkina Faso I learn from one Ghanaian woman, my girlfriend there, how to create glass objects like Christmas flowers and so on. But in fact, things were difficult, harder than before. I say, eh, why? Then later I gathered a little amount and made it down to Mali. On getting to Bamako, I said, no, I have to go to the last checking point. And I made the journey to Nyala, which is almost the last border town to Mauritania. So here as I'm speaking to you, I'm staying in Nyala doing my normal business. Anyway, Nyala is a small village, but still, I'm struggling harder. These days now, going to Europe or going to anywhere in the world is out of my mind. Now I'm trying harder to go back to Ghana to see my parents before they depart this world."

I didn't say anything for a few minutes, just listened to those plastic bags gasping in dry breaths of the fading day that cast its own shadows on his face. There was no resignation there. He hadn't seen his parents for fourteen years he said, unthinkable in Africa where parents — and age — are revered.

I sighed on his behalf and asked him if he felt the search for green pastures had been worth it, if he had found some kind of life after all his travels.

He shook his head. "I have no means to marry. I'm thirty-seven years old but I cannot bring children into this world if I do not have the means to look out for them, I cannot do what others do and bring children into this world to run up and down, up and down, no food, no school."

Afterwards I asked him about the other Ghanaians in Nyala, wanting to know whether they had landed there with hopes that this desert outpost would be their stepping stone, their starting point to get across that desert and on to Europe. Europe was where so many Africans longed to go, not because the bright lights and fast pace attracted them (it usually did the opposite) but because they all had relations or friends who had gone there, worked hard and made a little money. Got ahead. Come back as "beentos" (*been to* Europe, been to America), handing out their hard-got money to family and friends like candies. Few ever told the tale of how hard they had worked for the money, where they had worked, how they had been treated, what demeaning experiences their small savings had cost them.

Kofi said he couldn't speak for the other Ghanaians in Nyala. He himself had come here with dreams of crossing the desert, making his way over two thousand kilometres of sand to Mauritania's coastal capital, Nouakchott, and from there perhaps getting on a boat to Europe or finding his way to Gibraltar. Yes, he had once considered that path. But no longer.

"You can't cross this desert," he said. Then, with that enchanting understated turn of phrase that is an art form in Africa, he added, "Crossing this desert is just too tedious."

Did he know of people who had tried? He did. He had watched them go, said goodbye to them — his friends, his brothers from Ghana — and never heard from them again. His guess was that they had perished in the desert because if they had made it to Europe they would have written to him and told him their news as they promised to do. Others had set out in the other direction, east across the desert, for Libya. "People have lost their lives. Crossing to Libya it's not a joke. People normally lose their lives. Vehicles broke down on the road. You walk. But that means you're waiting for your death."

"People would have to be pretty desperate to start out on a two thousand kilometre journey to cross the desert on foot," I said. "What's driving them . . . ?"

"Money, that is the evil. It is money that makes people cross across this serious desert, this dangerous desert. So it is the money. The old enemy, the money."

"Money, okay," I said. "But is there no chance for young West Africans to make money in their own countries? Wouldn't you be better off in Ghana?"

It would have been, once, he said. No African had ever gladly left his or her family and taken off in search of money, not until recently with all the "economic reforms" sweeping the continent. "Traditionally, you see, you would never leave your mother and your father because it is particularly difficult for one person to rise up without the support of the whole big African family. But it is not that way now. Our governments, you see, they are changing everything. Now even our mothers and fathers and our uncles no longer have the means to help us rise up and then we cannot have the means to help support them later."

I waited a second, then asked him if it didn't get to be too much sometimes.

"Sometimes, I do lose faith," he said. "Sometimes too, I have to encourage myself. Since if I do not go contrary to what is written in the Bible, I believe God will actually one day answer my prayers. As long as I don't go stealing, I don't go contrary to God, that means if life is long for me, actually I may make it in future."

"And for you, what does 'make it' mean?"

"Actually, this is a big question but I have to answer. I believe in God almighty because He's the one who created me to the earth. And if He is actually seeing me, then He will not let me depart this world before I can make children of my own, because if that were so, there would be no means for my spirit to come back to the world in my children's children." He offered me a smile.

"Really, if my dreams came true," he said, "I would establish small-scale industry in my town or within my community. Okay, that is my first priority. And again, that is to make sure that I cater for my parents, especially my mother before she dies, and also my younger brother and sister."

He paused. Venus had now appeared in the indigo vacuum of the desert sky. "Really," he began, "if my mother dies, that will mean that I have been the cause of her death. Because as a mother she'll be worried, she will say, 'Where is my son? People are making good, people have gone to Europe, they come back with this and that and still my son is not arriving. What is happening?' I don't want to write to her because I have nothing to send. I know my mother may be crying over my whereabouts and this will eventually lead to her death. These days I write songs," he said. "In my songs I am talking about the hardships we are encountering every day, the jobless men in the town, food especially, shelter at the same time, many more deaths than births, and prostitution and political crisis, especially in Africa here."

He began to sing, using his feet and occasionally clicking his tongue to drum out the rhythm, nodding his head as he sang in a gentle and melodic voice:

> In my day, I get no job to do
> In my day, I get no food to eat
> In my days, prostitution rising so high
> In my days, AIDS do killing us apart.
> Oh la, I come back, save this situation.
> Oh la lee, I come back, save this situation
> Oh na na, I come back say this once again . . .

When he finished, he looked up and said, "I also wrote one song for my mother . . . my family is poor, so because I am the son, I have to find a way to cater for them and for my mother before she dies. So I travelled out to do that but things are so hard. And because I cannot be able to send money to them, I cannot even send a letter to my mother. So I just want to tell my mother, in this song, it's a kind of pleading. It isn't my fault, it's because of money and hardship I'm encountering, that's why I haven't been sending her money."

So then he sang the song he had composed for his mother. Only the wind and I were there to hear it.

The next day I set off with the children to try to find pencils and paper to buy. After a long string of false starts, we'd been guided at last to the town's one claim to a stationery shop. It was a tiny, hot shop with a few dusty shelves with some sparse stationery supplies. There were slates for the few children in Nyala who attended primary school in town, one of two such schools in a radius of a hundred kilometres. There were envelopes, writing paper, pencils made in China.

We wanted to buy some paper and something to write with for Abena, the daughter of the proprietor of the Ghanaian Embassy. After three years in the local school in Nyala, she still could not print the entire alphabet, at least not in small letters although she was pretty neat and precise with the capitals right up to M. It was not that she wasn't smart — she was bright and quick, precocious and bashful at the same time, and prone to burst into laughter when my children tried to talk to her in a language she might recognize a little. They settled on pidgin French. Abena, at the age of seven, spoke Twi (her mother tongue), Bamanankan (the most widely spoken indigenous language in Mali but used only as a lingua franca in Nyala), a smattering of the three other languages used in town, and a bit of French she had picked up in the school.

The problem, as elsewhere in Africa, was not any lack of enthusiasm or aptitude on the part of the children. The problem was the school — there were no benches, no books or notebooks, no utensils for writing, and classes that held over a hundred children. It amazed me that Abena had even learned the alphabet. But she had. Just that no one had ever asked her to use her imagination and creativity to draw something. I had offered her the use of my notebook and pen the previous day when we had gone to the Ghanaian Embassy for a plate of yams, and she had not stopped drawing pictures — her house, the bar, my children.

Today we wanted to get some writing materials that she and her brother could call their own. My two children were undecided over whether the slate and chalk would be the best bet, or the pencils and the paper. We were mulling this over, not paying much attention to the gathering of young men inside the stationery shop when someone asked us, "Hi, where you from?"

I glanced around me, startled by the strong American accent. Nyala was off just about all maps, except those of the desert-crossers and Maghreb traders. It was an obscure place to have been invaded by American tourists. Still, there might have been a Peace Corps or two around. They were usually posted to out-of-the-way places like this.

"Sorry?" I said, searching among the friendly faces for a plausible candidate.

"I wondered where you come from," said a young man seated on a three-legged metal chair at the doorway. "You speak English. You must be Americans?" Huge smile.

"No, not exactly," I said, laughing. "Anyway, I think I should be the one asking you where you're from with that accent and English of yours."

He shrugged. "Oh, I come from Nyala here," he said.

"Here?" I said, voice squeaky with surprise. "Where did you learn to speak English like a, well, a New Yorker?"

"Manhattan," he said.

"Manhattan," I said. "How on earth . . . ?"

He laughed. "Now that is a long story.'

"I have time," I said, truthfully.

"You see, it's this way. I got myself to Abidjan and then I head to Paris. Then I go to Montreal and made my way down to New York. Two good years I was a cabby in Manhattan," he said.

"But Manhattan? It's, well . . . " What could be said of Manhattan, especially juxtaposed with a town like Nyala, with its donkey carts doubling as public transport? There were, as far as I knew, only a handful of people who owned cars and the sounds in town were mostly animal — goats and sheep bleating, horses neighing, camels snorting, and always donkeys braying. The donkeys, attached to small-wheeled carts, known as tro-tros, were the town's taxis that my children so enjoyed. Manhattan and Nyala: reconciling the two extremes was beyond me, all right. But not at all beyond him.

"Oh it was fine. I make money there. Yeah, money."

"But isn't it dangerous in New York? I mean, it certainly isn't like Nyala where people don't have locks on their doors, and in many cases don't even have doors."

He laughed, spread his arms. "It was not easy. I didn't tell my people here about the danger. Twice thieves steal my cab and two times they rob me with their guns. But I make money. You can make money in Manhattan when you work hard. We work hard there."

"So what are you doing back here?"

"I came home because I like being home here in Mali. I have my small money now and I want to start a business here."

"A business here? In Nyala?"

He laughed. "No, not here. There's no money in Nyala. In Bamako. Car business. Bringing second-hand cars up from Togo and selling them in Bamako."

"You think it will work?"

"Oh that, I don't know. Allah knows. If it does, that is fine. If not . . . well." He shrugged and grinned.

"If not, then what?"

"Then what?" He shrugged again and gave me a huge and disarming smile. "I don't know. Maybe I make my way back to Manhattan and make more small money. I can always try something else." He lifted his arms, showing me his palms, shrugged a third time. "Inshallah," he added. It was all in the hands of the Almighty.

Chapter 21

Go ask God

"A total of only 385 billionaires are worth more than half the world's riches. And while the rich are getting richer, the poor are getting poorer." — UN Human Development Report, 1996

First came a couple of his more modest jetliners, a Fokker and a Boeing, screaming in for touchdown on the overheated runway. Then, from out of the wild blue yonder — or to be precise, the brown dusty haze — came that monstrous, white 747 barrelling in to land. The hot blasts of wind threatened to remove my skirt and blow it all the way to Timbuktu. I put my notebook away with a sigh, clutched at my skirt to keep myself decent, and moseyed along after the throng already off and running towards the jumbo jet that had brought their prodigal son back home.

Here was the person I'll call "Baba," a mystery man who had left Mali penniless a decade earlier, now arriving direct from Miami with his own fleet of planes from his own personal airline, which was named after his native village. He had just been released from prison in Florida, where he'd done time, charged with attempting to bribe American customs officials to expedite the export of two military helicopters to Africa. Ex-con, yes, but also a hero. He'd made headlines in the US by handing out whacking sums of money to charities or anyone that took his fancy — school marching bands or disadvantaged children or just women he met on the street or in expensive jewellery boutiques in Miami or New York. And now he was coming home, bringing with him — so they said — billions of dollars.

It was Friday morning, November 21, 1997. Word had it there would be another jumbo landing on Sunday. That one would be bringing Baba's luggage — luxury cars, construction equipment and lavish gifts that he was going to give away to his own people.

As had been the case for about seventeen years in Africa, I was juggling with a whole heap of diverse facts and figures and places that just didn't fit. All this talk of billions of dollars was going on in Bamako, capital of Mali. Mali was officially the third poorest country in the world, with nothing to boast about in the way of education, health facilities, toilets, public sanitation, or any of the most basic amenities that I'd grown up mistakenly believing were God-given. For the vast majority of Malians, literacy was a luxury, life was tougher than nails and living standards were right off the lower end of any comfort scale in the West. Yes, the country was rich in history and culture, but there was precious little material wealth the average person could actually put their hands on.

It was hot. It was dusty. Half the country was already buried under the sands of the Sahara Desert, and that morning I had the impression there was enough of that sand blowing in the wind to bury the other half — perhaps by nightfall. And for heaven's sake, this was Bamako International Airport, with no claim to fame at all. Just a single overheated runway, a windsock that was being blown to bits and a low-slung, ramshackle and inglorious terminal building, all surrounded by dry, scrubby grassland.

The farthest cry from Miami and an incongruous setting for those airliners, gleaming in the sun like swollen gems from heaven, which was perhaps how many Malians probably imagined Florida anyway. Thousands of people had already broken through the arms of the policemen, who had tried in vain to form a human barricade by stringing themselves out across the blazing tarmac. That excited human scramble had caught me up and was now moving me at a run across the sun-softened black pavement.

Some of the people there were his family. Some were his friends. But the majority were just Malians hoping to be there when Baba arrived in a blaze of sun and glory, lured to the spectacle by big dreams of a little wealth — which they hoped Baba would toss their way. A very few of us, of course, were just on the trail of a story.

I have to admit that the whole thing — Baba himself — took me completely by surprise. I had thought — big mistake — that at my age and after all these years of kicking about in Africa, nothing could surprise me any more. I thought — silly me — that this would be just another little Friday story, a ninety-second report for BBC on an intriguing man. Lend him my ears, eyes and microphone for a few minutes, write up a colourful little tale, file it and be done with it.

I had headed out to the airport in the morning, doubting that he would even show. He had been the talk of the country for weeks; there was no one indifferent to the local boy who'd made good — or at least rich. On every street corner where people gathered each day to discuss life in their habitual chat groups, in every market stall, in every household, his name alone sparked off heated debate that could last for hours or days. One school of thought said he obviously worked for the Devil who paid him handsomely for evil deeds — how else could he have grown so rich so fast? Another view, prevalent among those who planned to camp out in front of his house until they received cash from him, was that his money was clean. They maintained that he worked with God, who paid him handsomely for good deeds.

Still the question begged: what deeds? The local radio stations filled hours and hours with speculative debate that turned in circles and made me dizzy. Everyone was fascinated by Baba's rags-to-riches tale; he was living proof that even the wildest of human dreams could come true.

But there was a powerful moralistic and religious bent in Mali that shaped public views on issues of right and wrong. By no means was everyone driven by money and even fewer people approved of ill-got wealth — if that's what Baba's was. Which meant the discussion always returned to that basic and worrisome point — where did his money come from? If it came from outsmarting other shady billionaires or African heads of state who had themselves stolen it from the people, then Baba could, by some turns and twists of the imagination, be seen as a latter-day Robin Hood. By this reasoning, it was only right that the money he had hoodwinked out of the biggest crooks in the world should be dished back out to its rightful owners — the people. It looked like he might have outsmarted rich white men in America and rich Arabs in the Middle East and that greatly tickled many Malians. This would be a novel turning of tables, reversing the usual direction of the money flow.

On the whole, though, most people were waiting anxiously for his return to see whether he was really going to do anything useful with his money, create local industries and jobs, for example, to develop the country — which no jumbo jets full of Rolex watches or Mercedes were going to do.

For weeks, the local papers (mostly four- or six-page tabloids) had been announcing in red banner headlines that today was the day Baba would arrive. For weeks he hadn't shown up. And all the while, his legend was growing by leaps and bounds. Rumours flew and quickly transformed themselves into fact. In Miami, it was said, he had rented the entire Intercontinental Hotel for a whole year to accommodate his ever-growing entourage. He'd had his entire fleet of aircraft (fourteen in all) flown to Miami to ferry him and his wealth back home to Mali, and then been delayed for a full week — wasting $9 million of non-accrued income from those planes. He was said to have dealt gold and gems for the late President Mobutu of former Zaire. So it stood to "common reason" it had been his planes that had flown much of that gold out of the country in the final days of Mobutu's regime, when they were supposed to have been on "goodwill missions" to rescue Malians and other West Africans from the turmoil in Kinshasa.

Then there was his legendary largesse. There were numerous stories about how he'd once given a passing stranger in Miami a Rolls Royce, on a whim. One tale had him handing over his Jaguar or Rolls or Mercedes to a woman he met in a jewel shop in Miami. Fanciful stories. I was too "old and wise" to fall for all that stuff. I remained sceptical. But then, I hadn't seen anything — not yet. I hadn't been to the airport and I hadn't seen the crowds. And I had yet to lay eyes on this man they called Baba.

By ten in the morning that Friday, there were already hundreds and hundreds of cars at the airport. Even the roads leading to the airport were filling up with hopeful onlookers. The parking lot behind the VIP lounge looked like a dealership for luxury cars — Mercedes, BMWs, Cadillacs. These were all gifts that relatives and friends had received over the years from Baba. There were also a few armoured jeeps — roguish-looking black things with smoky windows that smacked of organized crime and Mafia-Made-in-Hollywood. Those, said Baba's main legal man in Mali, Mamadou, were for transporting the vast sums of money Baba was bringing with him.

Mamadou didn't mind talking about his "billionaire" client, but warned me right at the start that the man was too big to fit neatly into anything but a very long book. He confirmed that Baba might indeed be a billionaire, in dollars, but that it would be hard to prove or disprove because he had no office and no formal records anywhere. He said his client kept all his records in his own head. Baba hadn't had a day of formal education in his life and could not read a word.

"What he can read is the zeroes on cheques," said the lawyer.

Baba, fifty-six years old, hailed from a village in western Mali, the son of an impoverished family in an impoverished village. He was a member of a "caste," which put him in a social class of griots. In Mali, where long-ago yesterdays are still inseparable from today, griots have a very special and particular role in safeguarding tradition and history. Ironic as it seems to me, it is the griots that prolong and protect a highly stratified society, in which they fall well below "nobles," although well above former "slaves." The griots' role has always been to sing praises of the "nobles," recount history and the magnificent accomplishments of their noble ancestors in their society and in return the nobles were responsible for their well-being.

For many of us strangers living in Mali, and that included friends from other African countries, this complex caste system was difficult to understand, if not incomprehensible, given the notions of human equality that prevail in the late twentieth century, at least on paper in high places. People of caste were still not permitted to marry nobles and noblesse was decided by your family name and the family into which you were born. In Bamaman society, Keita, Touré and Traore, were the most obvious noble names; among the Fulani the nobles usually bore names such as Ba, Ly and Diallo.

Non-noble Malians, or those who were said to be "of caste" underneath the nobles, defended this system. They assured me this built-in social segregation was neither offensive nor unjust, as judgmental foreigners tended to believe. They said the roles played by each social group were complementary and there was no real prejudice against — looking down at — people of "caste." Those at the bottom had more freedom and were looked after by those on top. Those on top were obliged to behave and comport themselves in "noble" fashion, which included making sure that their social "inferiors" never went hungry.

That's what I was told. I certainly didn't argue, but I did a lot of contemplating on the subject and talking to Malians of all walks of life. Mali did not exist in isolation. And human nature is human nature. Rare is the human being who really doesn't mind being considered or treated as an inferior by another. And in Mali, I knew of several people who had been born with a caste name but who had gone through all sorts of contortions of their own family history to concoct for themselves a new set of origins that offered them noble rather than caste status. It was widely agreed that Mali was not ready — and wouldn't be for a long, long time to come — for a non-noble or even a noble woman as president.

And then there was the case of Baba, who had sought out great riches that would give him powers and status that his griot origins could never afford him. Some people speculated that Baba had been driven to seek his wealth by the inferiority complexes that came with his caste. His wealth made him a Somebody he was not entitled to be, not by birthright. Malian nobles, by the year 2000, were not necessarily rich people. Half of the watchmen and rubbish collectors on our street in Bamako bore noble names, "Keita" or "Traoré," and were quite happy to prostrate themselves fully on the ground if that's what it would take to get a wad of money from Baba. They might still consider themselves his superior socially, but heck, money was money. *Noblesse,* I noticed, didn't always *oblige.*

I knew that if I were Baba, I would have derived enormous satisfaction from throwing around a bit of economic weight, especially in the face of the complacent and superior attitude of a few of those nobles. And the power that came with money must have been even more satisfying because it was not his birthright.

Baba did nothing to try to hide his modest origins. In fact, he almost revelled in publicizing them. He had named his airline after his village. He was building a five-star hotel on the banks of the Niger River in Bamako, to be named after his mother.

In the folklore that had grown up around him, it was said he began his "career" as a "houseboy" in Senegal. There, tired of sleeping on a straw mat on a hard mud floor, he had one day sneaked a lie-down on his master's soft bed. Apparently he found it to his liking and he set out on his adventures that would enable him to afford a bed like that. He moved from one country to another, at first in West Africa, and then far beyond.

One fable had him appearing for some years in a circus in China, where he was kept as a human curiosity in a cage to amuse circus-goers who had perhaps never seen an African before. Another had him passing through India and into the Middle East, where he allegedly worked his way into the good graces of sultans and sheikhs, by showing off his healing skills and powers as a Muslim mystic, or marabout.

People told me yarn after fuzzy yarn, many of them supposedly spun by Baba himself. None did a thing to solve any of the mystery that shrouded the man's recent history and wealth.

This wasn't his first splashy arrival on home turf. Ten years earlier, he had taken the people of Mali by storm when suddenly he appeared in his home village and told everyone there to lay down their hoes because he was going to build them villas, give them Mercedes and riches and look after them forever. Work had actually begun to transform a dusty village of mud huts into an American-style suburb of villas and paved roads, when Baba found himself in trouble — both legal and financial.

He had been embroiled in a court case, in which German contractors working on a mega-hydro dam at Manantali in Mali accused him of making off with vast amounts of construction material and equipment for his town improvement project in his native village. But that wasn't the worst of it. When he took on the construction of a Las Vegas-style city in the African hinterland, he had underestimated the tidal wave of need in the country. The population in the village suddenly exploded as people got wind of Baba's project, and sometime in 1987, according to his lawyer, the money ran out and Baba did his first disappearing act.

"In fact, he didn't disappear, he went to Kinshasa," said his Malian lawyer. "He had about $100 in his pocket. The rest of his wealth was gone. But he booked himself into the most expensive hotel in town, not even knowing how he would pay for it. Then a gem dealer came to his door with a huge emerald he wanted Baba to help him sell." And that is how, according to Mamadou, the Malian wheeler-dealer got back into business again. He reportedly sold the gem for three times its actual value, pocketed the profit and off he went. Touching down in capitals throughout Africa and the Middle East — oil deals here, gems, arms or gold there, a couple of five-star hotels here and there, an airline that spanned West Africa. He himself was quoted as saying the only things he wouldn't deal were drugs.

The presidents of The Gambia, Gabon, and Togo were said to be his personal friends. He was said to know just about every head of state on the continent, and many off it. He apparently rubbed shoulders with individuals who ruled the globe from up there in the murky echelons of the super-rich, where the definition of "clean money" can get so blurry. And on this basis, Malians defended him, their self-made man. They maintained the only reason Baba was nabbed by the law or derided was that he was African and because he didn't hide his wealth — he gave it away.

Mamadou insisted that even though Baba had done time in prison, he'd not been guilty of attempting to corrupt American customs officials to export those military helicopters, not according to the rules that were generally applied — or not applied — to international military hardware deals at that level. The lawyer maintained Baba hadn't even been in Florida when the offence occurred; he'd been in Geneva. In Mamadou's view, the whole thing had to do with a "misunderstanding" between Baba's French agent, who was handling the helicopter deal, and the customs officials.

When the customs officials found fault with the documentation for the helicopters, the French man acting for Baba had done what came naturally to him and to anyone who dealt in Africa. He offered them a small sum to make it worth their while to overlook all the red tape. According to Mamadou, the customs men looked aghast at the offer. The agent interpreted the looks as dismay because the offer was too small. In front of the closed circuit televisions, he then rang Baba in Geneva on his cellular telephone and asked if he could up the offer. Mamadou said that Baba believed he was behaving like a true gentleman when he said to go ahead and give the customs officials what was needed. Next thing he knew, Baba was being extradited to the US to face trial and a possible sentence of forty-five years for the offence. He was found guilty and sent to prison in Florida.

But strangely enough, Baba was released after only four months. It was said that an "understanding" had been reached between the American authorities and the Malian government or The Gambian government (Baba carried both passports), that he would serve the rest of his sentence in Mali or The Gambia.

Now this was plainly ludicrous. If the Malian authorities tried to lock up their prodigal son, who was bringing his wealth back home to divvy up with his countrymen and women, they would be committing political suicide. Instead, they gave him a hero's welcome. It looked as though Mali's entire police force was on the streets that Friday to escort him safely through town, past hysterical crowds that lined the roads leading to one of his villas in a posh part of town.

At the airport, even Mali's finest in their great numbers could do little to keep back the chaos, or the seething mass of humanity desperate to get within arm's reach of Baba as he came out of his jumbo jet. I had sauntered up behind the expectant multitudes, hoping there might be a chance to stick a microphone up there somewhere to catch a few words from The Man himself as he descended onto the blazing tarmac of his homeland after an absence of almost a decade.

No chance. And the problem wasn't the crowd on the ground. It was those burly men who spewed out of the jet, muttering threats in *Miami Vice* accents, who began manhandling us all. Some had their grey hair pulled back in ponytails. Others wore crew cuts typical of bodyguards straight off the silver screen. There were so many of them I wondered if Baba hadn't brought with him Florida's entire population of mafiosos. Then came a long string of immaculately dressed young women, each worthy of a magazine cover all to herself, stepping daintily down the metal stairway from heaven while a television crew from Florida caught their every step on video.

They were followed by a lot of human odds and ends — such as the young man carrying the guitar case, who looked about as much like a musician as I looked like Celine Dion. I chased after him and asked him in French if he were here for a concert. "I don't speak no French," he said. I asked him again, in English this time, if he were a musician here to perform in Mali.

"I don't give no interviews neither."

"What do you have in the guitar case? It looks . . . "

"Look lady, I'm not here to do no fuckin talkin, you unnerstand?"

Our pleasant little exchange was cut short when we had to leap out of the way of a convoy of black Mercedes that screamed to a halt at the base of the stairway. At that moment, Baba himself, dressed nattily in a navy suit that looked custom tailored to fit his slim frame, appeared at the top of the stairway. For a few seconds, he stood there smiling and waving like a royal while the crowd went berserk, chanting his name. But then more of those bodyguards quickly swooped in and blocked him from our view as he made his way down the stairway, straight into a black Mercedes — bullet proofed — that sped across the tarmac as though the devil himself were on its tail, rather than just a very crestfallen and disappointed crowd of well-wishers.

In Bamanankan and in French, the family and friends in the crowd berated the army of Florida bodyguards that had kept them from so much as delivering a greeting to their man. But the bodyguards were either deaf or, more likely, didn't understand a word of either language. I took that opportunity to sneak away, along with my BBC colleague, to find Mamadou, who was waiting to lead us through the angry mob and into the VIP lounge for a quick interview with "the richest man in Mali."

Baba was seated calmly on a plush leather armchair, and he eyed us coolly as we moved in with our microphones.

"Are you planning to make Mali your home?" I asked.

"Mali is my home," he said, evenly.

"Yes, but this time are you planning to stay?" I persisted, feeling myself shrinking under that appraising and not at all complimentary stare. It was his eyes — glittery and unnerving as a predator's that has decided the prey isn't even worth stalking.

"Only God makes plans for men," he said. "That is a question you had better ask of God."

Well, God wasn't around just then, as far as I could tell, and I had a report to file, so I headed home, ploughing my way slowly through the massive chaos of streets. Kilometre after kilometre, the roads into town were lined ten deep with people hoping to catch a glimpse of the man — and just possibly to catch a dollar bill or two. Word had already reached people in the centre of town, some twenty kilometres away, that each policeman on duty at the airport had been given a crisp new hundred-dollar bill from Baba.

The nation-wide hysteria didn't let up for weeks. Mobs took up permanent residence on the mud road in front of Baba's villa and he continued to make headlines long after his arrival. At first they were all praise and flattery, full of not very subtle suggestions about what he could do with his money to make Mali a better place — sink it into industry and local processing that might kick-start a weak, resource-based economy that relied almost entirely on exporting raw cotton and gold.

Baba, however, didn't seem to have a head for such long-term and tedious investments. He preferred outrageous gestures that made instant headlines and magnified the Baba mythology. He handed out a quarter of a million dollars to the Malian soccer team after their victory over Senegal, and then sent his jumbo jet to Dakar to ferry the team back home. Women griots, who sang his praises for hours on end on local radio, received many hundreds of thousands of dollars from Baba. Certain private newspapers, those six-page tabloids with tiny budgets and running-on-empty coffers, took up his cause from time to time. They usually did this just when Baba felt it time to help out on the empty coffer front and "encourage" the journalists to remind Malians that he was a true patriot, and that all allegations about criminal activities were made by mean-spirited people jealous of his fame and fortune.

His five-star hotel on the edge of the Niger River in Bamako did start to take shape, and in another quarter of town suddenly there arose out of the dust a massive new enterprise called "Great West African Works." Inside those high walls — blinding white — dozens and dozens of dump trucks and earthmovers, still bearing Florida license plates, came to rest. All this fuelled great expectations of the great works that Baba was going to undertake. All the great works that had for so long been neglected in Mali — roads, buildings, just about all the infrastructure in the world that was so sorely lacking in that Sahelian land.

But nothing happened. Doubts set in. Attitudes changed. People were angered by those unpleasant bullying bodyguards who moved everywhere with Baba. And there was no sign of any work by the Great West African Works. The construction equipment parked there started to disappear under layers of dust and blown sand. The original concerns about the origins of his wealth resurfaced. In response, Baba broke his silence and appeared on state television late one Sunday night. The journalists immediately asked the question the whole country had been asking for years — how did he get so rich? He retorted that he saw no need for them to ask such a question. Had they ever asked a poor man how he became so poor?

I got perverse satisfaction in noting that Malian journalists didn't have any more luck prying information out of him than I had had, when he advised me to point my microphone skywards and ask God what plans He had for Baba.

In the end, it turned out that Interpol, and not God, would decide whether Baba would stay put in Mali. Less than a year after his homecoming, word sped through the town that an international warrant had been issued for his arrest.

Immediately, two of the private newspapers that always sang the praises of their benefactor hotly denied the existence of such an arrest warrant. Their line of argument was that Baba had committed no crime, except being a good businessman whose success had evoked jealousy in America and in Arab countries where he had operated.

But the rumours persisted and other newspapers published photocopies of the arrest warrant. Thanks to those kind editors, I was eventually able to track down a Malian businessman who did millions of dollars of trade each year with Dubai and was close to the authorities there. He had been chosen as the interlocutor between Dubai and Mali.

He showed me the arrest warrant addressed to Interpol worldwide, which said: "We, Jasim Mohammed Baqer acting Chief of the Public Prosecution, do hereby order to arrest and apprehend Mr X X," (the man I'm calling Baba) "who is charged of committing the crimes of fraud and magic practice . . . we request you to arrest, apprehend and chase him internationally."

In a letter addressed to the Malian minister of justice, the attorney general of Dubai described how Baba had used " black magic" to "brainwash" the director of the Islamic Bank of Dubai. "To perform his act, he took the bank director into an isolated place with flashing lights, and he spoke to him in a guttural voice. The bank director was afraid and asked to be taken back to his house. But Baba told him the voice he was hearing was the voice of the King of Devils. The director then heard the Devil's voice instruct him to give to Baba all that he asked for. After this brainwashing, Baba and his accomplices received money from the bank director in the form of cash and bank transfers to their personal accounts abroad and by using a credit card issued by the bank."

I was also shown photographs sent by Dubai to the Malian authorities of the odd fetishes made up of shells and hair and skin, with which Baba allegedly cast his spell on the director of the Islamic Bank of Dubai.

I sat musing over all these documents, wondering who was telling the truth . . . what was authentic and real in this story. The whole thing — all those documents — looked too real to be fake. But in my mind, it was all too fantastic not to be a work of fiction. But then life in Africa had proven to be the best work of fiction I knew.

There were photocopies of money transfers made in Baba's name with the Visa card given him by the Dubai bank. The detailed list for expenditures on the credit card read like a wild spending spree tour down luxury lane, which is exactly what it must have been. At Mayor's Jewelers in Miami, for example, between September 13 and 18, 1997, those records showed that Baba's Visa card drew a total of $200,000 US out of Dubai's bank, and in January 1998, more than a quarter of a million dollars. All this on an account that was backed up by nothing more substantial than the "trust" that Baba had created between himself and the bank manager, allegedly using the voice of the Devil. The balance column on those credit card records was blank.

In all, the authorities of Dubai were contending that Baba swindled the bank director out of a quarter of a billion dollars. Baba could not set foot outside the country without fear of being picked up by Interpol. Then word came that the Swiss and even the Americans were also after him for fraud. In Senegal, three top-level businessmen with links to Baba were arrested on behest of the Swiss. This was followed by news reports that most of his aircraft, which were parked at home base in Banjul, The Gambia, had been seized for non-payment of staff salaries and bills. Reports reached Bamako that the US Committee on Standards of Official Conduct was investigating a Florida senator who had lobbied Baba's case with a range of top US officials, right up to the American attorney general herself. In exchange for these "favours," said the reports, the senator was alleged to have received from Baba a Lexus and a condominium in Florida.

Work slowed on that glorious hotel-to-be in Bamako and in 1999 came to a complete stop. The formerly white walls of the Great West African Works had been dusted a browner shade of pallid by the weather and by time. Rumours flew that the president of The Gambia had confiscated Baba's six-star hotel in the capital, Banjul, and that the Malian "billionaire" was also being sought by a bank in Togo.

And Baba's reputation, just like his empire, began to crumble. It was said in some disillusioned quarters he was nothing more than a confidence trickster, of the genre developed and perfected by Cameroonians known as "fe-men." "Fe" (pronounced fay) is the name of the sophisticated psychological games used to persuade a chosen victim into handing over any amount of money, often hundreds of thousands or even millions of dollars at a time. The father of "fe" was a man from Cameroon whom I'll call Donatello. Donatello was said to have taught Baba everything he knew. But the infamous Cameroonian had gone missing in recent years, and many people in West Africa believed he was dead, until news reports emerged from Yemen in 1998 that he was in prison there.

But back in Bamako, Baba was still free, although he was keeping a very low profile. It was impossible to find out from the Malian attorney general whether or not they intended to arrest him — his secretary seemed to have had lessons from some of Baba's musclemen and refused to let meddlesome journalists near his door. The minister of justice admitted that the Interpol warrant for Baba's arrest was being "processed" but wouldn't breathe a word more than that, at least not to me.

The Malian authorities were in a difficult position. They were under no legal obligation to arrest Baba on Malian territory and they had no extradition treaty with Dubai. But Mali could ill afford not to comply with demands from Dubai, a major trading partner and an economic colossus next to Mali. On the other hand, if the Malian authorities did appease their friends abroad by arresting Baba, there were fears of a serious public outcry — and of even more serious embarrassment.

Mali's president, Alpha Oumar Konaré, and his Prime Minister had publicly refused the luxury vehicles that Baba had publicly offered them. But the private press (the newspapers that kept their distance from Baba and relied strictly on sales to replenish empty coffers) alleged that nine government ministers had not turned down huge cash gifts from the man. There was apparently some fear that if Baba were arrested, he might just sing like a bird and bring down some political heavyweights. He was, after all, a griot whose birthright was song. He had also managed to get himself elected as mayor of his village, and his visits to the capital became few and far between.

And so it rested. I wouldn't have been any the wiser about where Baba was, or what he was up to, had it not been for . . . fate. Fate being the marvellous and mischievous thing it is, Baba had acquired a small house almost directly across the street from us, ostensibly for one of his wives. It wasn't clear exactly how many wives he actually had around the world, or which of them were official — but it was generally thought that he was legally wedded to four.

Whether the lovely woman who moved in across the street from us one sunny day was included in that official list didn't matter. She and her children quickly endeared themselves to the entire neighbourhood, and while she knew that we all knew who she was, she never referred to Baba by name or let on that she knew we knew. She called him only "*mon mari*" (my husband).

At first, he came to visit her a couple of times a week, arriving after midnight and leaving again by four in the morning. She showed up for little informal neighbourhood get-togethers sporting some of the most magnificent jewels — diamond and sapphire earrings with ring and bracelets to match — that I, for one, had ever seen close-up. Mayor's Jewelers in Miami, perhaps?

I was frankly delighted she'd moved in because she was wonderful company and so were her children. I stopped complaining about the furore that the arrival of her husband created on our narrow little mud alley — when hundreds of people came on the run each time his convoy of Cadillacs or Mercedes (no license plates) and those dreaded thugs, who tagged along in overland vehicles, pulled up late at night.

But it was her seven-year-old son who managed to work his way deepest into my affections. Amin was constantly in our house, tagging along behind me and asking me point-blank how much our piano cost, or if it was true that the American school cost more than a million francs (CFA) a year, and did I know that he himself had billions — whether this was in dollars or CFA francs was not clear.

He was a lonely kid whom the rest of the children in the neighbourhood tended to shun or tease mercilessly. He was bossy, demanding, far too old for his years, bragged incessantly about how rich his father was — even when it seemed that his father's fortune had not just eroded, but imploded and the man was unable to leave his country without being arrested. And yet that small boy knew exactly how to get around me and get what he wanted.

He came almost every day to borrow a bicycle, to ride up and down the road. But twice he had come back muddied and bleeding when he fell, and twice he had got lost. After that, I told him he was to drive the bicycle around the compound, but not to go on the street. And to spare his pride, I was being protective because I didn't want any big boys to attack him or steal the bicycle from him. He looked aghast.

"Auntie," he said, giving me a tough he-man look from his diminutive height, "don't you worry about thieves. I know how to protect myself and I will also protect you. You come with me and you'll see how I do it. You see how I do this with my eyes?" he said, squinting and giving me a reptilian glance I'd seen once before, at Bamako airport when I dared to put a question to Baba.

"You see this?" said Amin, pointing now to the narrowed slits of his eyes. "I make my eyes like this, see, and everyone will run. I can tell you one thing, Auntie," he said, now pounding his little ribcage. "Me, Amin, standing here before you, I'm the most dangerous man in this Mali here."

I started to laugh, then stopped. Once upon a time a year earlier, when people told me the story of Baba and how he connived with God or the Devil to make his money, I had also laughed. And that had most definitely been premature. So I stood there on the roadside and regarded this boy — a fascinating kid with the make-believe demeanour of an international tycoon-gangster five times his age — and smiled.

"I believe you, Amin," I said. "But you're still not taking that bicycle on the street. And furthermore, you forgot to say please when you asked for it."

Suddenly the slit eyes were gone and he was grinning. "Please, can I take the bicycle on the street," he said.

"No," I said. "Even if you are the most dangerous man in this Mali here."

I wondered then, and I wonder now, what kind of man was this Baba. Somehow, I couldn't drum up much sympathy either for him as his legendary empire collapsed, or for any of his alleged victims, the rich men who operated in that clubby ether of international high finance, whom he may or may not have swindled.

I could, however, drum up a lot of sympathy for his son. Baba was an international show-off, a man who would squander millions of dollars at a go, buy himself a fleet of airplanes, buy praise time for himself on the radio and in newspapers, give away a Jaguar to a stranger for the sake of seeing his name in banner headlines in Florida.

He was also a man who didn't get around to noticing that his country needed investment and local industry, not more imported luxuries. Nor did he apparently notice the needs of his children, at least not the ones who lived across the street from me. I guessed those children would probably have appreciated a bit more time with their father more than they did those plastic pistols and dolls they showed up with after each of his very rare, late-night visits to their house.

There isn't much about Baba that I do or ever can understand. I expect I'm doomed to keep on pondering his puzzle forever. And I'm no closer to putting the pieces together now than I was the day that fleet of jetliners landed in Bamako.

But I suppose there is always the off chance that one day I might be able to do as Baba instructed me, and get a chance to put some of my questions to God.

Epilogue

A serious pair of shoes

The elderly man who tended the lush gardens of the posh hotel in Harare, Zimbabwe, was a true gent. He never failed to greet the two visiting scientists from Nairobi and never failed to admire the solidly respectable shoes worn by the lanky British man when he strolled through the hotel garden. The scientists were puzzled by the gardener's fascination with those shoes, which were by no means new and despite all the careful polishing they'd been given, still showing the wizening effects of many years of wear. Besides, there was no shortage of footwear to be had in Africa. Yes, the traditional arts of African cobblers, no slouches when it came to fashioning fine hand-made leather boots and shoes, were dying out, killed by imports. Across the continent, marketplaces were flooded with second-hand shoes from North America and Europe, with cheap plastic footwear made in China. So why was the gardener so fixed on having this particular pair of shoes from the British scientist? What was it, they asked, that so appealed to him about this pair? "I can see that those shoes have travelled many places, covered many miles and seen many things," said the elderly gardener. "Sir, that is a Serious Pair of Shoes."

Bamako, circa 2000

The beggars are mostly barefoot; I'm wearing quality German sandals with cushioned soles and sitting comfy in a Turbo Jeep. But, I console myself, at least I'm down here in the river valley where the people live and experience the city close up, every day. I'm not perched on a lofty cliff in a white presidential palace, surrounded by immaculate gardens, breathing in rarefied air and soaking up sycophants' praise. From up there, or from behind the tinted windows of one of those spanking new Mercedes or Peugeots in the presidential fleet, it must be difficult to remember this is one of the world's least developed countries with all those dreadful statistics on childhood morbidity and malnutrition to prove it.

I decide that it's not my imagination. The beggars have indeed proliferated in the past few months. They are certainly out in force today, congregating at major intersections. The bottlenecks at intersections make motorists easy targets, immobilizing them so they are unable to accelerate away from all the need.

As usual, it's not red lights keeping us idling away in the heat and exhaust fumes and chaos of downtown because, as usual, the traffic lights are not working. This time, though, it's not because of an ongoing electricity crisis. The rains have already come and gone, replenishing the rivers enough to keep us in hydropower until the peak of the dry season that looms ahead. Now those traffic lights, which should be telling us to stop or to go in an orderly fashion, are not working for the simple reason that many of them have been battered to smithereens. From the looks of the ruins on those poles, it appears as if someone must have gone at them with sledgehammers. The traffic lights, that were all new and bright and officious on gleaming new aluminium poles just three years ago, are now dangling from wires, broken and forlorn. Breezes buffet them about, ringing the chimes of destruction.

This is the work of angry vendors whose daily income, measured in cents, comes from selling and trading this and that on the roadsides. In recent weeks, City Hall, headed by a major figure in the Ruling Party, has decided to begin restoring order to the city. Predictably, they didn't start at the top, or impose any regulations on certain Party Barons whose shady and lucrative dealings are always tax-free and often at the expense of the people, law and order, and the city coffers. Instead, City Hall decided to raze thousands of kiosks belonging to the "little people" who struggle every day to survive by trading or selling some of the cheap, second-hand or illegally imported goods being dumped into this country. This flooding of the markets with second-hand and third-rate consumer goods is the most visible sign here of that wondrous phenomenon called globalization.

I don't know quite where City Hall expects the vendors to go to earn some kind of living. There is no central marketplace for them in Bamako. The government hasn't got around to building one that would serve the city's needs. An African city without a market is like an ocean without a shoreline.

Obviously the vendors don't know, any more than I do, where it is that City Hall wants them to go. Each dawn that follows another night of razing and burning kiosks brings those persistent and desperate vendors back to their habitual place of business. Each day they try to reconstruct their kiosks out of rags and scrap metal and plastic sheets emblazoned with the name of the United Nations High Commission for Refugees. And each day the Ninjas are there to stop them. "Ninjas" is the name the people have given to the tough militia of riot police the government uses whenever any segment of the population gets a little out of hand, that is, decides to stand up for its rights. When the pesky vendors reappear on the scene to try to resurrect their livelihood from the ruins, those Ninjas are always there to beat or gas them senseless. And since the men who run City Hall are not within bludgeoning reach, the vendors take their frustration to the streets — or more precisely, to the traffic lights.

I'm not sure why the mayor, in his enthusiasm for order in the city, doesn't remove those shards of traffic lights from their poles. Then again, there are many things I don't understand about what City Hall does and mostly doesn't do in this capital. I am constantly dumbfounded by the erection of pretentious monuments commemorating this and that, which are taking shape, and consuming precious money, on the sorry roads that hardly warrant being called roads. And I might have thought the clogged and reeking open sewers might have been a priority for the mayor's campaign for a city clean up. Apparently not. Those have been left as they are to spread disease and stench throughout the capital.

In any case, functioning traffic lights are now another of those little glimmers of hope that led a few people to believe what the government was telling them when I landed here three years ago: that Bamako was transforming itself into a clean, modern and orderly city.

Now that the authorities have attacked the vendors, I wonder when they will have a go at the beggars who make these intersections their homes. At the last non-functioning red light, I counted the number of blind, the disabled or big-eyed kids who stood there with their plastic bowls or hands or stumps outstretched. They numbered twenty-two. I gave to the man with the bulging eyes and leprous limbs, and to the girl leading about her elderly father or grandfather whose eyes have gone completely white from the ravaging effects of river blindness. After that I shrugged, showed the rest of the throng my own palms, and told them I didn't have enough coins for all of them. They didn't complain. They simply moved away to try their luck elsewhere.

At the next intersection, it's a Ghanaian man who approaches me. He's selling dishcloths, at least that's what I think they are. I ask him what he's doing here in Bamako and he says he was hoping to make his way to Europe, but when he got to Mali he was robbed. So he's had to start saving again for bush taxi fare or a fake passport and visa, and whatever else he needs to fulfil his dreams of making it to Europe. I pass him the two coins I still have in my pocket, worth about twenty-five Canadian cents, apologizing that they won't get him very far. He showers me thanks, saying "God bless you" over and over again.

It's not just the beggars that have multiplied on the roadsides. Now that a whole section of town where they once had their kiosks has been "cleaned up," the vendors seem to be taking advantage of traffic jams to harass trapped motorists. In the past twenty minutes and five intersections this morning, I could have bought, from the comfort of the driver's seat of my car, any of the following items: Chinese alarm clocks that look great until you open them up and they start to come to pieces; packages of biscuits made in the Middle East; Marlboro cigarettes; polyester socks or cotton handkerchiefs made in China; odorizers done up in the stars and stripes to be dangled from car mirrors; banana-flavoured chewing gum from a northern part of the globe where bananas don't grow; Kleenex; tinny "Rolex" watches; faked "French" perfumes; faded Malian tourism posters showing glorious images of Timbuktu but printed in France.

I could also have bought copies of the *Herald Tribune* and *Newsweek* that came in on last night's Air France flight. I know that because there's a stamp at the top that says they are complimentary copies for Air France passengers and that they are "not for sale." That may be the case inside the Air France airbus, but it sure isn't once the Malian cleaners emerge from the plane with all that "garbage" that is quickly channelled into the local market.

There's not much here that is made in Mali, at least not in the marketplace. The cars and motorcycles are mostly second-hand, imported from Europe after they no longer met emission or safety standards there. The textiles, bedding, upholstery, and clothing are nearly all seconds or thirds from Europe or North America or firsts from China, which amount to about the same thing when it comes to quality.

Most of those imported textiles are cotton. Mali grows cotton and has done for centuries. But in the last hundred years or so, French concerns have had an unwritten monopoly on the cotton grown here. After harvesting, most of it goes straight to France, which then processes it there or in places like China, before selling it back as finished textiles to impoverished Africa.

A tiny percentage of Mali's cotton, somewhere between 1 and 5 per cent, stays in the country, where people spin and weave it on handlooms. These narrow woven strips are used to make traditional clothing and the marvellous bogolan, or "mud cloth." The bogolan is coloured with extracts from tree leaves and barks, and intricate designs are painted on using mud dyes from the Niger River. This traditional Malian cloth is being lapped up by the outside world. These days it has become *de rigueur* for musicians and artists around the world who want a look that says Made in Africa. Tourists love it. Visitors don't go home without it. But very few Malians wear it any more.

What a crazy, mixed-up, absurd world we live in.

This is what I'm thinking as I approach the French Cultural Centre, where this morning Mali's musicians will be taking to the streets, a demonstration I don't want to miss. A demonstration I've been waiting to see every day for the past three years.

Malian music is big the world over, but there's hardly an authentic Malian CD or cassette to be had in this country. The vendors who assault me at intersections with boxes of Malian music on CD and cassette are selling pirated copies only, produced mostly in Asia. All the Malian music I have, I've bought in Canada, where the musicians are protected by international copyright and where I am guaranteed original studio sound. Neither of those exists in Mali.

For many years, the Malian musicians put up with the injustice and their own poverty. Today they're making a break with their acquiescent past; they've planned a demonstration to protest.

As I pull in to the curb in front of the French Cultural Centre, I brake quickly to avoid striking a diminutive woman in overalls and crowned by a mane of flaming red hair. She's standing right in my way on the roadside with a video camera in hand. Turns out she's Bonnie Raitt and she agrees to be interviewed and unassumingly says she's here to learn more from Malian musicians. It's not unusual to see big-name North American musicians in Mali, here to discover more about the blues, right at the source. People such as Ry Cooder, Jackson Browne, Taj Majal, and Bruce Cockburn are no strangers to Mali. But this morning, Bonnie Raitt is the only foreign musician present. The rest are Malian.

Some are well known in World Music circles, Malians with international recording contracts — Oumou Sangaré, Habib Koite, Rokia Traoré. Their income comes from sales in the developed world so they don't really have to worry that there's not a franc to be made in their own country from their music. But they'd love to be able to stay home rather than go to Europe or North America to make their music, and they're also throwing the weight of their names behind their younger and less known musical colleagues. It is the latter who suffer most from the rampant and blatant piracy of Malian music. The minute their cassettes come out here, copies are sent by some unscrupulous Somebody in Mali to Thailand, where they are multiplied like fruit flies. The containers that come back filled with hundreds of thousands of pirated cassettes and CDs are somehow "allowed" to get through customs.

Even here at home, the music industry is worth many millions of dollars. The problem is that, typically in Africa, that money is not in the hands of those honest souls who have produced something original to sell. Ninety per cent of all cassettes sold each year in Mali, probably 7 or 8 million copies, are illegal. The copyright laws that exist have never been enforced and the musicians tell me that everyone knows who is behind the piracy. As usual, they appear to be too well connected to feel the full — or even partial — force of the law.

So, this morning, one hundred of Mali's best-loved singers and musicians are taking their frustration to the streets. It's a joyful noise indeed, as they sing, dance and chant their way along Independence Boulevard in the roaring heat of midday. They circle the roundabout with the imposing Independence Monument, stopping traffic and attracting fans and well-wishers as they go. The women singers, many of them griots, are decked out in satiny boubous in exuberant lime green or orange or yellow. Habib Koite, who is trying his best to keep the noisy throngs from causing a disturbance that would evoke the wrath of the authorities, is wearing bogolan, another of those under-valued riches made in Mali.

They don't stop until they reach the Prime Minister's office. He has little choice but to receive this pantheon of stars that, by any popularity poll, would leave him buried in the sand. He agrees to admit twelve of the top stars as spokespeople. He has a well-practised look of concern on his face as he listens to their long list of complaints. I've seen him don the same sanctimonious expression when he's talking publicly about the energy crisis (still unresolved), poverty (still growing) and Mali's model democracy (questionable, given the elections held here in 1997).

The musicians are really letting him have it. Not mincing any words as they inform him that musicians cannot even make a living in Mali, even though the rest of the world can't get enough of their music. They point out that the sixty-some radio stations in the country, including state radio and television, play Malian music round the clock but never pay the musicians a cent in royalties. They say they fear performing in public in their own city because their concerts are taped, duplicated and sold on the streets within hours of their performance. They say it's time Mali protected its own resources. If a Malian artist doesn't have an international recording contract and the copyright protection given by that, they are doomed, by their own uncaring government and population, to abject poverty.

The Prime Minister promises to do all he can. The musicians file out. They've made their voices heard. I head off too, back into the traffic, taking the long way home while I put together my radio report in my head, while musing on what I've just seen, in whose footsteps my shoes have trod in the wake of that lively demonstration. I'm deeply impressed that the musicians have discovered and decided to use their voices to urge reform. They've tackled their cause more positively and constructively than the vendors who unleashed their anger on traffic lights, but that's because the much-loved and famous musicians can't be silenced as easily as can, say, a hawker of bananas or peanuts. These shows of people power are, to me, a sign that despite all my complaints about the way democracy has been twisted and violated in Africa, times are changing.

But one change doesn't come without others. Malians say they're concerned about other trends, which they don't view as positive in the least. They point out that they have much to be proud of. Their society, poor as it is when the poverty is being measured in dollars, has an inherent order and balance that makes living here an immersion course in etiquette, good manners and "family values" in the genuine sense. Children respect elders, people of caste respect nobles, and nobles in turn are responsible for the welfare of people from castes, elderly people are venerated and the youth heed their advice, respecting wisdom that comes with age. Family members look out for each other as much as they look out for themselves, because no one can expect individual happiness if the whole family doesn't share it. This has made for a peaceful land, where people have managed to keep crime rates low and the devastating effects of famine and drought to a minimum. Tradition dictates that people look out for each other. At least that's how it's always been.

One member of parliament told me that her "heart fills with fear" when she sees Malian teenagers in baseball caps and baggy jeans, spouting obscenities they've picked up from American music videos and turning their back on their own past. "It's this thing called globalization," she said. "Homogenization that comes with all the television and videos." She's not the first Malian to complain about the effects of the foreign media that now bombard the country like guided missiles from outer space. But these complaints come mostly from those who have lived and studied abroad and have heard about the effects of uncensored and unlimited television on young people. For most Malians, a television set somewhere in the family compound or on the street is like a dream come true. So are the trashy programs that come on state television. Whether it's a Brazilian soap opera, or a horse race in France, or an American action movie that cost more to make than Mali spends on education and health in a year, the people lap it up and still want more. The irony of Malians gobbling up commercial pop culture from abroad, while the world outside soaks up their non-commercial culture would be less depressing if there were any economic give along with the all the taking from Mali.

The MP said it was hard to fight such influences. "The teenagers here are starting to think and behave like Western teenagers," she said. "That means they think of themselves first and not about the family. They reject their own culture and values. In Mali, if you reject your family, you reject yourself."

From out here in traffic, in the furore of downtown Bamako, in this urban wilderness that alternately thrills and amuses, then annoys and depresses me, the MP's studied and still life portrait of Malian tradition isn't immediately apparent. Or maybe this is exactly what she's talking about. This is the change she's talking about. This is the racket and confusion that results when an old established human order is struck by a different set of rules, by which money alone determines the pecking order. The senses are assaulted by the heat and noise and filth, the sheer mess that results when economics overrule culture, when everyone is trying to sell something — anything.

I am brought to a halt in the midday traffic near the Grand Mosque and my car is blocked by a mob of people gathered around an attraction that I can't yet see. When I finally do get a glimpse of what has drawn all the onlookers, I wish I hadn't. A fast-talking man is putting a deformed child through his circus paces. The boy looks to be about ten. He has no arms or legs, and is wearing a dog collar and a leash, which binds him to his master of an unsavoury ceremony. The boy is wearing oversize lime-green sunglasses and a small beanie. I turn away and am glad to see that several Malians share my revulsion. They are more vocal about it but it does nothing to deter the show-man who is calling for money, or the crowd.

I wonder if this is a sign of the new times in Mali, when anything — even birth defects — can be packaged up for their "entertainment value" and sold on the street. Or if this is just a sign of the growing need for cash in the new African society, for which those without money need not apply.

I edge my way past the crowd. The route back home takes me past the US embassy, located in the heart of the congested market area. After the Nairobi bombing in 1998, I had suggested one evening to an American diplomat in Bamako that the location of their embassy here was a nightmare waiting to happen — if a bomb went off in this busy place, hundreds of thousands would be killed. He replied they had beefed up security, ensuring the safety of their staff inside.

Although the Americans have been very tight-lipped about it, there have been bomb threats against American installations in Mali and several other West African countries. For security reasons, they have cordoned off several city blocks around their embassy in Bamako. This is inconvenient, to say the least, for the merchants whose stalls are on those streets now closed to vehicular traffic. It's also inconvenient for motorists; I have to take several detours down narrow muddy lanes to get out of the market area and back onto a main thoroughfare.

Except for one threatened sit-in by the merchants whose businesses were hurt so badly by the closed streets, and my own loud expletives each time I have to take detours around the US embassy or Peace Corps office, I've not heard a peep of complaint from anyone else, certainly not the Malians themselves. This is not atypical in Africa. Africans have always tended to forgive strangers their trespasses on their soil.

I sense this too may be changing. It is not just Western dress that so many African youth are adopting. They are also adopting more Western attitudes and behaviour. They don't seem as inclined to tolerate injustice as their parents did, at least not injustice that starts at home and not in a distant capital.

Those who have the power of their music take to the streets and make their plight known. Those who have lost their livelihoods in a city "clean-up" operation attack inanimate symbols of the powers of City Hall — the traffic lights. This kind of public revolt is relatively new, not just in Mali but across Africa.

It's still in its infancy, but I wonder how it will eventually manifest itself, especially among the youth of Africa. There are millions and millions of young people who have some education and no chance of any work that will ever bring in more than a couple of hundred dollars a year, which is what honest work generally earns in Africa. These days I'm hearing hints of resentment and despair that were barely audible when I first landed on the continent. Living standards are still dropping, and have been, almost steadily, since political "independence" brought a whole new kind of foreign domination to Africa, and with it more hardship and interference from outside.

It's not that Africans are helpless victims without their own home-grown evils, treachery and betrayals to deal with, without their own villains. There are crooks, big and small, horrendous ethnic rivalries and hatred, atrocities inflicted on Africans by Africans, corruption and greed — just as there are everywhere. But many of the ills that have marred Africa's first forty years of independence could not have taken place without the complicity and, all too often, the direct involvement of people from our own privileged and rich world.

Nevertheless, despite the hints of despair and anger I sense among the urban youth, most Africans remain true to their own values that stress patience, tolerance and forgiveness. Given the hardship, the fact that the entire continent is not embroiled in war is nothing short of miraculous. The prevailing peace in the majority of countries on the continent speaks volumes about the positive and peaceful side of Africa, which is so often eclipsed by news of war and ethnic hatred and disasters. That "other side of Africa" is a bright, lively, charming, warm, and intriguing place. It's full of small miracles and fascinating people facing odds — just to survive — that would deter even the most blindly optimistic lover of lotteries. Most

Africans I know draw on their deep faith in God or Allah to face life with optimism that is not blind, merely strong, stubborn and essential.

It's taken me a lot of years, and several pairs of what an elderly gardener in a hotel in Zimbabwe would call "serious shoes" with thick soles, to wade and blunder my way through the contradictions and confusion and complexities that Africa throws in the way of its visitors, often obscuring its own light and masking its own riches. I've also filled a lot of mental trash bins with the useless litter of pre-conceptions and cultural yardsticks by which I once judged — mis-judged and so misunderstood — Africa.

And even now I know I've barely scratched the surface and am hard pressed to explain or even to understand what makes Africa work, despite all the obstacles mounted against it by history and the world's superpowers. I do know that it does work in its own indomitable fashion, thanks to an undefinable but indefatigable spirit of sur-vival that starts and ends with human relations. That is what leads me to believe that one day, when our "civilization" has imploded and lies in ruin for whatever reasons — in whatever century or millennium that may be — Africans will still be there, working away at life with little in the way of creature comforts or any earthly security or sala-ries or pension plans, telling each other "Ça va aller."

"It'll go okay," they say. Over and over, when to my mind, "it" most certainly won't even "go," let alone go okay.

"How can you say that?" I retort, flustered and perplexed as al-ways. "People are suffering. People are poor. Nothing is getting any better or going anywhere. *Rien ne va nulle part!*"

"Ça va," comes the refrain. "God is great. Ça va aller."

And then, finally, I shut up and just listen. They're right. People in Africa seem able to make almost anything work, able to make the best of what I would call the worst. They can say things "are going" when my foreign reasoning says they're at a standstill or even moving backwards. And I'm absolutely sure that if times ever got so bad that even Africans could no longer tell themselves that things were "going to be okay," then elsewhere in the world the end would already have come.